PRESERVATION DIRECTORY

A Guide to Programs,
Organizations,
and Agencies in
New York State

Preservation League
of New York State

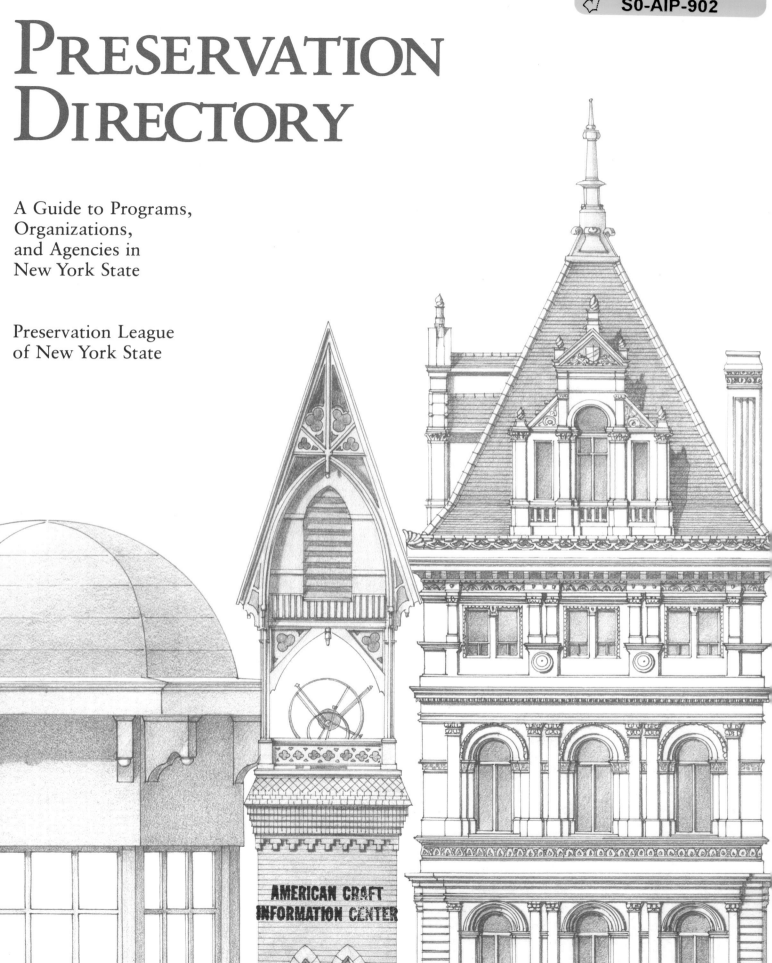

AMERICAN CRAFT
INFORMATION CENTER

The Preservation League of New York State is a private, not-for-profit organization whose primary purpose is to stimulate and encourage public participation in historic preservation throughout the state.

This publication was made possible by major funding from The J.M. Kaplan Fund. Support was also received from the Corning Glass Works Foundation. Government funding for the Preservation League is provided by the Architecture, Planning and Design Program of the New York State Council on the Arts.

Designed by Rich Kraham Design Unit

Cover illustrations by Herb Kashian

Printed in the United States of America

Revised edition

ISBN: 0-942000-06-4

Preservation League of New York State 307 Hamilton Street Albany, New York 12210 518-462-5658

Table of Contents

Introduction

When the Preservation League of New York State published the first edition of its *Preservation Directory* in 1977, the book proved to be an indispensable source of information for those engaged in efforts to save and protect the state's diverse architectural resources. Over the last decade, the dramatic increase in the number of programs, organizations, and agencies addressing preservation concerns is indicative of the rapid growth and change in the preservation field. Preservationists today must be knowledgeable about such varied disciplines as law, finance, historical research, architecture, housing, archeology, planning, and tax policy. Developing the expertise to deal effectively in such areas is a difficult task not only for the professional, who needs to have current information for everyday reference, but also for the volunteer, who frequently does not have the time or resources to conduct adequate research. The Preservation League's purpose in publishing this revised and expanded edition of the *Preservation Directory* is to make a wide range of up-to-date preservation information compiled from numerous sources readily available to a broad audience.

The first part of the *Directory* is divided into five chapters covering international, national, and statewide preservation organizations and programs, as well as federal and state agencies and programs. Entries in these chapters have the potential of assisting preservation activities through publications, technical assistance from staff, grants, and loans. The second part of the *Directory* is divided into five chapters providing an overview of preservation and preservation-related legislation in New York State: state legislative programs; components of an effective local preservation ordinance; technical preservation tools, such as easements, tax incentives, and revolving funds; educational programs; and technical assistance programs in New York State. The final part of the *Directory* contains county-by-county listings of local and regional preservation organizations across the state.

As in any undertaking of this sort, it became necessary to limit the scope of the subject to be covered. For the most part, the Preservation League limited the programs and organizations covered in the *Directory* to those concerned with the preservation and adaptive use of structures and their surroundings, but not their contents. Regional consortia of museums in New York State, listed in the local and regional section of the *Directory*, can provide information on museum-related programs, such as exhibitions and museum operations. In addition, directories published regularly by the American Association for State and Local History and the American Association of Museums provide comprehensive listings of museums across the country. On the other hand, we endeavored to make the chapters on local, state, national, and international preservation programs and organizations as comprehensive as possible, since no other published compilation of them exists. The inclusion of a number of environmental organizations reflects the growing cooperation between preservation and conservation organizations as they address a variety of issues affecting the quality of the built and natural environment.

The Preservation League extends

its sincere appreciation to the numerous organizations, agencies, and individuals that supplied information for and assistance with the *Directory*. Dana Mintzer McClive, formerly Assistant Director of the Preservation League and now an instructor in the Cornell University Department of City and Regional Planning, and Peter D. Shaver have served as editors of the *Directory*. Research was begun by Pamela Jones and was continued by Kristin Cihak, a Yankee Intern cosponsored by the National Trust for Historic Preservation and the Preservation League. Nancy F. Gerber, Wesley Haynes, and Katherine Raub Ridley also made valuable contributions to the *Directory*. This revised edition of the *Directory* is based on the first edition which was edited by Diana S. Waite, then Executive Director of the League. The task of preparing a vast amount of information for publication was admirably undertaken by the League's Administrative Director Carol Walther, Membership Secretary Patricia Hunziker, and Secretary Lucille Doxey.

Publication of the *Directory* was made possible by a generous grant from The J.M. Kaplan Fund. Throughout this undertaking the project has benefited from the guidance and encouragement of Joan K. Davidson, President of the Kaplan Fund, and the Fund's Executive Director Suzanne Davis and Program Officer Anthony C. Wood. Support for the *Directory* has also come from the Corning Glass Works Foundation and the New York State Council on the Arts.

Frederick D. Cawley
Executive Director

Sacred Heart Ukranian Catholic Church (1977), Johnson City. Apollinare Osadca, architect. Drawing by Herb Kashian.

International Organizations and Programs

International Organizations and Programs

The Association for Living Historical Farms and Agricultural Museums

National Museum of American History, Room 5035
Smithsonian Institution
Washington, D.C. 20560
202-357-1300

Founded in 1970, the Association for Living Historical Farms and Agricultural Museums (ALHFARM) is a service organization for those involved in the administration, operation, and management of living historical farms, agricultural museums, and outdoor museums of history and folklife. The organization sponsors an annual meeting and publishes the *Bulletin*, a bimonthly publication containing news of individual and institutional activities, educational and professional training opportunities, classified ads, book reviews, and a running bibliography. *Proceedings* of the annual meetings are also published.

Association for Preservation Technology

P.O. Box 8178
Fredericksburg, Virginia 22404
703-373-1621

The Association for Preservation Technology (APT), organized in 1968, is an international membership association of persons directly and indirectly involved in the systematic application of the knowledge of methods and materials to the maintenance, conservation, and protection of historic buildings, sites, and artifact resources. APT holds annual conferences, workshops, and tours, and publishes a bimonthly newsletter, *Communique*, the quarterly APT *Bulletin*, and an annual *International Membership Directory and Resource Guide*.

New York State Chapter:

P.O. Box 2107
Albany, New York 12220

Founded in 1986, the New York State Chapter enables preservation professionals and others to share information about their work through workshops, lectures, and tours. Membership is open to interested individuals and organizations; members of the New York State Chapter must belong to APT International.

The Association of Junior Leagues

660 First Avenue
New York, New York 10016
212-683-1515

The Association of Junior Leagues (AJL) is an international organization of women committed to improving the quality of life through the effective action and leadership of trained volunteers. Its purpose is exclusively educational and charitable. There are 269 Junior Leagues throughout the U.S., Canada, Mexico, and Great Britain. These groups sponsor projects dealing with many community concerns, including education, cultural enrichment, the arts, historic preservation, and urban revitalization. Leagues also engage in public affairs and advocacy activities. Through testimony, reports, and public statements, the Leagues express their concerns on the environment, women's issues, and cultural needs. The Leagues' policies are set by delegates at an annual conference.

The Conservation Foundation and World Wildlife Fund

1250 24th Street, N.W.
Washington, D.C. 20037
202-293-4800

Since its founding in 1948, The Conservation Foundation has worked to improve the quality of the environment and to promote wise use of the earth's resources. The Foundation conducts interdisciplinary policy research on emerging issues in environmental and resource management, such as environmental dispute resolutions and pollution control. It communicates the findings of its work through books, reports, and newsletters, as well as films, conferences, and workshops. The Conservation Foundation has merged with the World Wildlife Fund, although the programs of the two remain distinct.

Council of Europe

B.P. 431 R6
67006 Strasbourg Cedex
FRANCE
88.61.49.61
Telex Strasbourg 870 943

With a membership of 21 European States, the Council of Europe is the largest European political institution. One of its aims is to improve living conditions and promote human values. A part of its working program deals with the protection and enhancement of historic heritage and the built environment. The Council of Europe has drawn up a Convention for the Protection of the Archaeological Heritage and a Convention for the Protection of the Architectural Heritage of Europe. Recommendations of the Committee of Ministers in the fields of heritage conservation are sent to European governments. Conferences and colloquies are organized and the organization publishes the magazine *A Future for Our Past*.

Environmental Design Research Association

L'Enfant Plaza Station
P.O. Box 23129
Washington, D.C. 20026
301-657-2651

The Environmental Design Research Association (EDRA) is an international, interdisciplinary organization, founded in 1968 by design professionals, social scientists, students, educators, and environmental managers. The purpose of EDRA is to advance the art and science of environmental design research, to improve understanding of the interrelationships between people and their built and natural surroundings, and to help maintain and create environments responsive to human needs and their aesthetic ideals.

Europa Nostra

9 Buckingham Gate
London SW1E 6JP
ENGLAND

Europa Nostra, founded in 1963, is an international federation of associations whose aim is to protect Europe's cultural and natural heritage and to improve the environment. It makes recommendations on environmental and heritage matters to local and regional authorities, parliaments, governments, the Council of Europe, and the European Community. It also gives awards annually to projects which make a significant contribution to the protection of Europe's architectural and natural heritage.

International Centre for the Study of the Preservation and Restoration of Cultural Property

13 Via di San Michele
00153 Rome
ITALY

The International Centre for the Study of the Preservation and Restoration of Cultural Property (ICCROM) encourages basic and applied research in techniques for preserving and restoring historic building fabric. ICCROM promotes the exchange of information among technical and scientific laboratories, architects involved in conservation, and commercial firms that carry out conservation work. ICCROM regularly sponsors technical symposia which bring together individuals from around the world working on particular building conservation problems. The proceedings of these symposia are subsequently published in book form and are available through ICCROM in Rome.

In the United States:
c/o Advisory Council on Historic Preservation
1100 Pennsylvania Avenue
Washington, D.C. 20004
202-786-0503

International Council of Museums

American Association of Museums
1225 I Street, N.W. Suite 200
Washington, D.C. 20005
202-289-1818

The International Council of Museums (ICOM) is a professional organization founded in 1946 and dedicated to the improvement and advancement of the world's museums. Its Paris-based Secretariat and Documentation Center assures the day-to-day running of the organization and the world-wide coordination of its activities and programs.

The United States National Committee of ICOM (AAM/ICOM) has been an integral part of the American Association of Museums since 1973. AAM/ICOM administers memberships of American members of ICOM and coordinates all internationally focused activities of the AAM. ICOM publishes *ICOM News*, *International Museological Bibliography*, *Basic Museum Bibliography*, and *ICOM Education*. The organization also sponsors specialized annual international meetings.

International Council on Monuments and Sites United States Committee

US/ICOMOS
1600 H Street, N.W.
Washington, D.C. 20006
202-842-1866

The United States Committee of the International Council on Monuments and Sites (US/ICOMOS) is a non-governmental, not-for-profit, international, membership organization of professionals and concerned individuals active in the preservation and protection of cultural heritage. As one of 68 national committees forming a world-wide alliance for the study and conservation of historic buildings, districts, and sites, US/ICOMOS assists representatives of other countries in studying preservation techniques, adaptive use, community action, tax incentives, and many other aspects of preservation, conservation, and rehabilitation in the United States. US/ICOMOS carries out international programs of mutual interest under cooperative agreements with the

National Park Service and the National Trust for Historic Preservation. US/ICOMOS' publications include a monthly *Newsletter* and a biannual newsletter entitled *World Heritage. ICOMOS Information*, a quarterly journal published by the ICOMOS Secretariat, contains scholarly articles, technical reports, case studies, news items, a calendar of events, and a review of recent publications.

International Institute for Conservation of Historic and Artistic Works
6 Buckingham Street
London WC2N 6BA
ENGLAND
01-839-5975

The International Institute for Conservation of Historic and Artistic Works (IIC) is concerned with the structure, composition, deterioration, and conservation of the whole field of inanimate objects considered worthy of preservation, whether in museums and libraries or exposed externally. Founded in 1950, it has over 3,000 members in more than 65 countries and includes in its membership professional conservators working independently, outside the ambit of governments and institutions. Members keep abreast of technical advances through personal contact with their colleagues at home and overseas and through IIC's publications, congresses, and groups.

International Union of Architects
51, rue Rayounard
75016 Paris
FRANCE

The International Union of Architects (IUA) was founded in 1948 to unite the architects of all

countries in a union of their national organizations. Its programs and goals include professional training, international cooperation, and professional development of architecture. IUA sponsors seminars for these programs and holds an international conference every three years. Reports and information on IUA's activities are published in the monthly *Newsletter*.

Nature Conservancy
1800 North Kent Street
Arlington, Virginia 22209

The Nature Conservancy is an international conservation organization committed to preserving natural diversity by finding and protecting lands and waters supporting the best examples of all elements of the natural world. Since 1951, the Conservancy and its members have been involved in the preservation of nearly three million acres in 50 states, the Virgin Islands, Canada, Latin America, and the Caribbean. Although some areas are transferred for management to other conservation groups, both private and public, the Conservancy owns and manages a national system of some 900 preserves.

New York Field Office
1736 Western Avenue
Albany, New York 12203
518-869-6959

New York State Chapters:

Adirondack Conservancy
P.O. Box 188
Elizabethtown, New York
12932
518-873-2610

Central New York Chapter
P.O. Box 175
Ithaca, New York 14850

Eastern New York Chapter
1736 Western Avenue
Albany, New York 12203
518-869-0453

Long Island Chapter
250 Lawrence Hill Road
Cold Spring Harbor,
New York 11724
516-367-3225

Lower Hudson Chapter
RFD 2, Chestnut Ridge Road
Mount Kisco, New York 10549
914-666-5365

South Fork/Shelter Island
Chapter
P.O. Box JJJJ
East Hampton, New York 11937
516-324-1330

Organization of American States
Department of Cultural Affairs
Regional Cultural Development Program
1889 F Street, N.W.
Washington, D.C. 20006
202-458-3140

The Organization of American States (OAS), through its Multinational Project for the Protection and Defense of Historic Artistic and Archaeological Heritage, is concerned with the protection, conservation, and safeguarding of cultural heritage. Since 1969, the Regional Cultural Development Program has cooperated with OAS member states in their efforts to rescue, preserve, and protect cultural artifacts from the pre-Colombian, Colonial, and Republican periods in order that a better understanding of the historical process of the peoples of the Americas can be achieved.

Royal Oak Foundation
285 West Broadway, Suite 400
New York, New York 10013
212-966-6565

Founded in 1975, the Royal Oak Foundation is an educational organization established to support the preservation and understanding of Anglo-American cultural heritage. Programs include tours, lectures, exhibitions, conferences, and a newsletter. Since awarding its first grant in 1976, the Foundation has given more than $2.4 million in support of historic preservation and conservation, and has established chapters in seven cities across the country.

Society for American Archaeology

808 17th Street, N.W., Suite 200
Washington, D.C. 20006
202-223-9774

The Society for American Archaeology is a not-for-profit, scientific and educational membership organization founded in 1934 to promote and stimulate interest and research in the archeology of the American continents; and to advocate and aid in the conservation of archeological data. Its quarterly journal, *American Antiquity*, publishes papers on the archeology of the western hemisphere and closely related subjects.

Society for Post-Medieval Archeology

c/o Museum of London
London Wall
London EC2Y 5HN
ENGLAND

The Society for Post-Medieval Archeology was founded in 1967 to promote the study of archeological evidence, both artifactual and architectural, of British and Colonial history from the end of the medieval period until the advent of industrialization. The Society holds conferences and publishes *Post-Medieval Archeology*, an annual journal issued free to members.

World Monuments Fund

174 East 80th Street
New York, New York 10021
212-517-9367

The World Monuments Fund (WMF) is a not-for-profit organization devoted to the worldwide preservation of our artistic and architectural heritage. WMF seeks to complement government support for cultural preservation by planning and carrying out restoration projects in the field and by financing training, research, and public education activities relating to preservation. WMF also works with state agencies and local preservation groups. Founded in 1965, the organization has sponsored over 50 restorations in 15 countries around the world.

Sweetheart Cottage (1880), Thousand Island Park. Drawing by Herb Kashian.

National Organizations and Programs

National Organizations and Programs

America the Beautiful Fund

219 Shoreham Building
Washington, D.C. 20005
202-638-1649

The America the Beautiful Fund (ABF) was founded in 1965 as a private, not-for-profit organization to promote activities that would improve the quality of life in the United States. Through educational programs and advisory services, it supports projects which involve community effort. Its "seed grants" in amounts up to $1,000 offer assistance to isolated and neglected communities across the country. ABF publishes a newsletter, *Better Times*.

American Association for State and Local History

172 Second Avenue North
Suite 102
Nashville, Tennessee 37201
615-255-2971

The American Association for State and Local History (AASLH) is a not-for-profit, educational organization dedicated to advancing knowledge and appreciation of local history in the United States and Canada. Programs include annual meetings, awards, seminars, workshops, a placement service, and an audio-visual training series. AASLH publishes *History News*, a bimonthly magazine; *The History News Dispatch*, a monthly newsletter; technical reports; how-to-do pamphlets; books dealing with all facets of history work; and a directory of historical societies and agencies. AASLH also houses the National Information Center for Local Government Records, a reference and referral service providing basic records management and archives information for local governments.

American Association of Museums

1225 I Street N.W., Suite 200
Washington, D.C. 20005
202-289-1818

The American Association of Museums (AAM) serves and represents museums of all sizes and types throughout the United States—including art museums, natural history museums, historical museums and societies, historic sites and science-technology centers, arboreta, botanical gardens, zoos, art centers, and children's museums. The AAM also serves the individuals who work in museums—including directors, trustees, volunteers, curators, registrars, educators, and security personnel. Programs include accreditation, government affairs, museum assessment, and an annual meeting. Publications include *Aviso*, a monthly newsletter; *Museum News*, a bimonthly magazine; and a national directory of member organizations. The Mid-Atlantic Association of Museums (address below) is the regional affiliate of the American Association of Museums serving New York State.

Mid-Atlantic Association
of Museums
P.O. Box 817
Newark, Delaware
19715-0817
302-731-1424

American Council for the Arts

1285 Avenue of the Americas
3rd Floor
New York, New York 10019
212-245-4510

The American Council for the Arts is an umbrella organization representing state, regional, and local arts agencies. The organization distributes information; publishes books and a magazine; and provides mailing lists for state and community arts councils, regional arts alliances, and related groups.

American Historical Association

400 A Street, S.E.
Washington, D.C. 20003
202-544-2422

The American Historical Association (AHA) is a not-for-profit, membership corporation founded in 1884 for the promotion of historical studies, the collection and preservation of historical manuscripts, and the dissemination of historical research. As the largest historical society in the United States, the AHA conducts an active scholarly and professional program for historians interested in every period and geographical area. The AHA publishes a variety of research materials, offers prizes and fellowships to scholars, sponsors a series of regional teaching conferences across the country, and runs the Institutional Services Program, which offers a collection of useful directories, publications, and other services. In addition, AHA publishes a journal, *The American Historical Review*, and *Perspectives*, a newsletter.

American Institute for Conservation of Historic and Artistic Works

3545 Williamsburg Lane, N.W.
Washington, D.C. 20008
202-364-1036

The American Institute for Conservation of Historic and Artistic Works (AIC) is a not-for-profit, professional organization. AIC was formed to set and uphold standards of professional conduct and to coordinate and advance knowledge and practice in the maintenance and preservation of cultural property. AIC publications include the semi-annual *Journal of the American Institute for Conservation* and a bimonthly newsletter. AIC also sponsors an annual conference of conservation professionals.

American Institute of Architects

1735 New York Avenue, N.W.
Washington, D.C. 20006
202-626-7300

The American Institute of Architects (AIA) represents the interests of architects across the country by helping increase professional competence, promoting public knowledge of their expertise, and making their collective voice heard in lawmaking bodies throughout the country. The AIA works to establish standards of accepted practice, to develop specification systems and techniques useful to architectural firms, and to take stands on relevant social and environmental issues. The AIA sponsors a variety of continuing education programs and an annual meeting, and maintains an extensive architectural library in Washington. It publishes *Architecture* (monthly); a newsletter, *Memo*; and reports.

The AIA's Committee on Historic Resources is concerned with issues related to historic resource conservation, preservation, restoration, adaptive use, and the management of change affecting the cultural environment. It maintains a strong information exchange activity with public and private preservation organizations throughout the country through a network of state and regional preservation coordinators. By means of meetings, conferences, and publications, the Committee is the focus of preservation information and activity within the AIA. A brochure entitled *Guidelines for Historic Preservation* describing the role of the architect in the preservation process, and information on committee activities and membership, is available without charge. Other materials produced by the committee are available through the AIA Press.

The state preservation coordinators representing New York State are:

Giorgio Cavaglieri, FAIA
250 West 57th Street
New York, New York 10107

William C. Shopsin, AIA
280 West 11th Street
New York, New York 10014

See p.48 for information on the New York State Association of Architects / AIA.

American Planning Association

1776 Massachusetts
Avenue, N.W.
Suite 704
Washington, D.C. 20036
202-872-0611
(headquarters)

1313 East 60th Street
Chicago, Illinois 60637
312-955-9100
(for publications)

The American Planning Association (APA), created in 1978 from the merger of the American Society of Planning Officials and the American Institute of Planners, is a national association of professional planners, elected and appointed officials, and developers who are concerned with creating a better planned environment. The Association sponsors conferences, a placement service, and a Planning Advisory Service, which on a subscription basis assists planning agencies and organizations by analyzing issues, answering specific questions, and providing technical reports. APA publishes *Planning* (monthly), *Job Mart* (bimonthly), *Land Use and Zoning Digest*, research reports, and books.

American Society for Conservation Archeology

University Museum
University of Arkansas
Museum Building 202
Fayetteville, Arkansas 72701
501-575-3555

The purpose of the American Society for Conservation Archeology (ASCA) is to promote and coordinate scholarly activities, scientific research, educational programs, and high standards in the preservation and protection of prehistoric and historic archeology. ASCA publishes a bimonthly newsletter.

American Society of Civil Engineers

Committee on the History
and Heritage of American
Civil Engineering
345 East 47th Street
New York, New York 10017
212-705-7671

Founded in 1852, the American
Society of Civil Engineers
(ASCE) is a professional organization whose primary concern is
the continuing education and
professional growth of its
members. ASCE is also concerned with the quality of professional standards, registration of
engineers, the stimulation of
technical research, and the
publication of new technical information. ASCE holds national
conventions and expositions,
technical meetings, seminars, and
conferences, and publishes a
monthly journal, a monthly
newsletter, and technical journals.

The Committee on the History
and Heritage of American Civil
Engineering runs several programs, including a listing of national civil engineering landmarks. The Committee also
selects the recipient of the
History and Heritage Award,
sponsors the publication of a
civil engineering historical series,
and is currently working on an
oral history of American Civil
Engineering. Surveys of local
historic civil engineering landmarks may be carried out by
local chapters of the society.

American Society of Interior Designers

1430 Broadway, 22nd Floor
New York, New York 10018
212-944-9220

The mission of the American
Society of Interior Designers
(ASID) is to improve the quality
of interior design through education, grants, conferences, and
publications. The largest
organization of professional interior designers in the world,
ASID dispenses grants and
scholarships through its Education Foundation; documents
historically, culturally, or
aesthetically significant interiors
through its Significant Interiors
Survey; and honors outstanding
historic preservation projects
through its Interior Design
Project Awards.

The New York Metropolitan
Chapter/ASID publishes *Dia-
logue*, a bimonthly newsletter
which annually features an issue
on historic preservation. The
Historic Preservation and Interiors Committee of the New
York Metropolitan Chapter is
concerned with locating and
evaluating historic interiors,
documentation methods, and
restoration techniques and
materials.

New York Metropolitan
Chapter / ASID
200 Lexington Avenue,
Suite 226
New York, New York 10016
212-685-3480

American Society of Landscape Architects

1733 Connecticut Avenue, N.W.
Washington, D.C. 20009
202-466-7730

Founded in 1899, the American
Society of Landscape Architects
(ASLA) is a professional
organization of landscape
architects. ASLA publishes a
monthly newsletter and handbooks, and rents films and slide
shows on landscape architecture.

New York State Chapters:

New York Upstate Chapter
c/o Frederick J. Holman, ASLA
21 New Wickham Drive
Penfield, New York 14526

New York Chapter
c/o Fred J. Correale
157 Pepperidge Street
Oakdale, New York 11769

American Society of Mechanical Engineers

History and Heritage Committee
345 East 47th Street
New York, New York 10017
212-705-7740

The American Society of
Mechanical Engineers (ASME),
organized in 1880, is a not-for-
profit, educational and technical
organization seeking to encourage the development of new
technologies, while helping to
solve the problems of an increasingly technological society. The
History and Heritage Committee
designates important mechanical
engineering devices as Historic
Mechanical Engineering Landmarks, with the aim of preserving them and raising the public's
awareness of historical engineering achievements. More than
100 landmarks have been designated; nine of them are located
in New York State. The Committee also develops programs that
include films, publications, oral
histories, exhibits, and local inventories of industrial achievement.

The Archaeological Conservancy

415 Orchard Drive
Santa Fe, New Mexico 87501
505-982-3278

The Archaeological Conservancy was formed in 1980 in order to help preserve the nation's rapidly decreasing archeological heritage. Activities of the Conservancy include archeological site identification, acquisition, and preservation, as well as public education.

The Architectural History Foundation

350 Madison Avenue
New York, New York 10017
212-557-8441

The Architectural History Foundation (AHF) publishes scholarly books devoted to architecture and related fields of design. It was begun in 1977 as a not-for-profit institution by a voluntary association of professionals to meet the needs of laymen, students, and teachers by providing publications with the clear illustrations and reliable editing that commercial or academic publications occasionally lack. AHF publishes both original works and historic documents, and has thus far produced 19 titles.

The Association for Gravestone Studies

46 Plymouth Road
Needham, Massachusetts 02192
617-455-8180

The Association for Gravestone Studies (AGS) is a not-for-profit corporation founded in 1977. Through publications, conferences, and exhibits the AGS encourages the preservation of gravestones and promotes research into all aspects of gravestone studies. An annual conference is held during the fourth week in June. Publications include *Markers*, an annual journal, and the quarterly *AGS Newsletter*.

Association of American Geographers

1710 16th Street, N.W.
Washington, D.C. 20009
202-234-1450

The Association of American Geographers (AAG) is a not-for-profit organization founded in 1904 to advance professional studies in geography and to encourage the application of geographic research in education, government, and business. In recent years, the Association has taken an active role in arranging funding for geographic research, strengthening geographic curricula, and increasing public awareness of the discipline. Through media coverage AAG has highlighted the contributions of geographers to the resolution of public issues, the increasing need for geographic education in a global society, and the comprehensive perspective of current geographic research. AAG also recognizes outstanding geographers, publications, and dissertations through an annual awards program. AAG publishes two quarterly journals and a monthly newsletter.

Catalog of Landscape Records in the United States

Wave Hill
657 West 252nd Street
Bronx, New York 10471
212-549-3200

The Catalog of Landscape Records in the United States is a national project established in 1987 to collect information about the location and content of records documenting American landscapes. The Catalog will contain information on a broad range of documents or collections relating to the landscape—including rural, vernacular, or cultural landscapes—although emphasis is placed on designed, manipulated, or managed landscapes for the initial phase of the project. A quarterly newsletter highlighting new additions to the Catalog is available free of charge.

Center for Historic Preservation

Middle Tennessee State University
P.O. Box 80
Murfreesboro, Tenneesee 37132
615-898-2947

The Center for Historic Preservation was founded in 1984 to support the applied public service research requirements of the undergraduate and graduate degree programs in historic preservation at the university. The Center is engaged in national research on the use of computers in historic preservation, and on the use of community resources in the classroom. The Center provides technical assistance on historic preservation problems to a state, regional, and national clientele, and also provides interns for organizations needing qualified temporary personnel. The Center publishes a quarterly newsletter, reports, and case studies.

Classical America

227 East 50th Street
New York, New York 10022
212-753-4376

Classical America, founded in 1968, is dedicated to the study, appreciation, and application of classical expression in the arts. The society seeks to encourage an understanding of the classical tradition, its inherent sense of continuity with the past, and its unique approach to cooperation among all artists in the design professions. The society offers a multi-faceted program of public and professional education that includes an expanding library of both new and reprinted books on past and present classical design; a periodic series of illustrated magazines; unique courses on classical drawing techniques; tours and lectures; and the annual Arthur Ross Awards that highlight the contributions of artists, craftsmen, and patrons in current classical work.

Clearinghouse for Arts Information

Center for Arts Information
1285 Avenue of the Americas, 3rd Floor
New York, New York 10019
212-977-2545

The Center for Arts Information is a national information clearinghouse and research library focusing on cultural policy, economic and other trends in the arts, organizational management, and individual professional development. The library houses a reference collection of 6,500 volumes, extensive files on service and funding agencies and arts management topics, and 300 periodical titles. The Center responds to questions over the phone or in person. For New York City residents, The Center publishes *For Your Information*, a quarterly newsletter.

Council on America's Military Past

P.O. Box 1151
Fort Myer, Virginia 22211
202-479-2258

The Council on America's Military Past, a not-for-profit organization founded in 1966, is concerned with identifying, locating, preserving, and memorializing military installations and units that no longer serve the roles for which they were created. The Council sponsors military history conferences at sites around the country. The Council publishes the quarterly *Periodical: Journal of the Council on America's Military Past*, and a monthly entitled *Headquarters Heliogram*.

The Decorative Arts Trust

106 Bainbridge Street
Philadelphia, Pennsylvania 19147
215-627-2859

The Decorative Arts Trust is a not-for-profit, membership organization created for the study and preservation of decorative arts through an exchange of information, lectures, and seminars. The Decorative Arts Trust sponsors annual meetings and regional seminars on a range of topics, and publishes a quarterly newsletter. The organization also maintains a registry of important lecturers on the decorative arts and serves as a referral service for members interested in program planning, research materials, and the appraisal, identification, or placement of donated decorative arts.

Educational Facilities Laboratories

211 East Seventh Street, Suite 420
Austin, Texas 78701
512-474-7539

Educational Facilities Laboratories (EFL) is a not-for-profit organization that undertakes research and disseminates information about the facilities of public service institutions. These institutions include those concerned with education, the arts, recreation, and health care. EFL's prime concern is with the physical place—school, campus, hospital, museum, library—and the way that place meets the needs of its users in the community, neighborhood, and region. Published studies of particular interest to the preservation field include *The Arts in Found Places; Fewer Pupils/Surplus Space; Surplus School Space: Options and Opportunities; Reusing Railroad Stations* (Books One and Two); *A College in the City: An Alternative;* and *Movie Palaces: Renaissance and Reuse.*

Environmental Action

1525 New Hampshire Avenue, N.W.
Washington, D.C. 20036
202-745-4870

Founded in 1970, Environmental Action (EA) is a not-for-profit organization whose focus is the human environment, including the impact of laws and corporate practices on environmental quality and public health. EA's projects include the Energy Conservation Coalition, which works at state and national levels to promote energy conservation, and the Waste and Toxic Substances Program, which works for action against toxic pollution. Environmental issues are discussed in EA's bimonthly magazine, *Environmental Action.*

Environmental Defense Fund

257 Park Avenue South
New York, New York 10010
212-505-2100

The Environmental Defense Fund is a not-for-profit organization working to protect environmental quality. The organization commissions and publishes reports on a variety of environmental issues and sponsors seminars, conferences, and workshops.

Environmental Law Institute

1616 P Street, N.W. Suite 200
Washington, D.C. 20036
202-328-5150

The Environmental Law Institute (ELI) is a not-for-profit, research and educational institution with an interdisciplinary staff of lawyers, economists, scientists, and journalists. Founded in 1969, ELI works to help achieve national environmental goals. Through programs such as continuing education, the Institute seeks to improve communications among the varied interests in the environmental affairs field. ELI's publications include *The Environmental Law Reporter* and many research reports and monographs. These resources are shared with both environmental professionals and the general public.

The Foundation Center

79 Fifth Avenue
New York, New York 10003
212-620-4230

Chartered in 1956, The Foundation Center is an independent organization that gathers and disseminates factual information on philanthropic foundations. The Center's libraries in New York and Washington contain extensive collections of books, documents, and reports on the foundation field and current files on the activities and program interests of American foundations. The Center has established regional collections at the New York State Library in Albany, at the Buffalo and Erie County Public Library, at the Levittown Public Library, and at the Rochester Public Library. The Center publishes *The Foundation Directory*, which lists foundations and their program interests and is available in many libraries.

Frederick Law Olmsted Association

475 Riverside Drive
New York, New York 10115
212-870-3033

The Frederick Law Olmsted Association, founded in 1972, is a not-for-profit corporation dedicated to Olmstedian principles of park design, environmental conservation, and urban planning. The Association provides assistance in the form of exhibitions, publications, graphic material, research assistance, and other information to the general public, urban planners, park and parkland managers, architects, engineers, scholars, and students. Of particular concern to the Association is the preservation, historic and otherwise, of the landscapes in urban settings and town plans that Frederick Law Olmsted, his colleagues, and disciples have created. Recent Association projects have included the conservation and cataloguing of 1,400 original drawings for Central Park in New York City, and the production of exhibitions, catalogs, and other publications, including a biography of Olmsted's partner Calvert Vaux. The Association works closely with the National Association for Olmsted Parks, and was involved in efforts to designate the Olmsted Home and Office in Brookline, Massachusetts, a National Historic Site.

Friends of Cast Iron Architecture

235 East 87th Street, Box 57
New York, New York 10128
212-369-6004

The Friends of Cast Iron Architecture, founded in 1970, is a not-for-profit organization devoted to encouraging the preservation and restoration of cast-iron architecture in the United States and Canada. In addition to taking stands on preservation issues affecting cast-iron architecture, the organization maintains a file of photographs and slides of cast-iron buildings, and offers assistance on technical aspects of preserving cast-iron structures.

Friends of Terra Cotta

Main Post Office Box 421393
San Francisco, California 94142
415-893-9829

The Friends of Terra Cotta was founded to promote education and research in the preservation of architectural terra cotta and related materials. The organization seeks to raise the awareness of the general public as well as building professionals, and emphasizes the value of and difficulties associated with the preservation of terra cotta.

New York State Branch
c/o Susan Tunick
45 Gramercy Park
New York, New York 10010
212-228-8265

The New York State Branch, founded in 1983, is the only Eastern Seaboard affiliate of the national organization. As such, it is devoted to information sharing with a focus on maintenance, restoration, and replacement techniques. Several publications are available.

Institute for Urban Design

Main Post Office Box 105
Purchase, New York 10577
914-253-9341

The Institute for Urban Design is a professional and civic association exclusively concerned with urban design. The Institute's goal is to improve the physical form of cities through publications and programs and to encourage communication among people concerned with those cities. Publications include *Urban Design Update*, a bimonthly newsletter; *Project Monograph*, a quarterly series; and *Urban Design International*, an annual publication. The Institute convenes an annual conference on urban design each fall and regional conferences each spring.

Institute of Early American History and Culture

P.O. Box 220
Williamsburg, Virginia 23187
804-253-5117

Founded in 1943, the Institute of Early American History and Culture is dedicated to the furtherance of study, research, and publication in the early American period, approximately to the year 1815. The Institute interprets "history and culture" to include the study of the arts, letters, religion, science, and thought, as well as political, military, economic, and social history. The Institute maintains seven major programs: book publication; the publication of the *William and Mary Quarterly*; postdoctoral research; the organization and sponsorship of conferences and symposia; a "clearinghouse" function through its newsletter and other less formal means; documentary research and editing; and editorial apprenticeships and internships.

Land Trust Exchange

1017 Duke Street
Alexandria. VA 22314
(703) 683-7778

The Land Trust Exchange is a national network and service center that works to improve the effectiveness and capacity of local and regional not-for-profit land conservation groups and land trusts. The Exchange provides a variety of educational and technical assistance programs which enable land trusts to do the best job possible in conserving important land resources.

League of Historic American Theatres

1511 K Street, N.W. Suite 923
Washington, D.C. 20005
202-289-1494

The League of Historic American Theatres was founded in 1977 to promote the preservation and use of America's historical theater buildings. Towards this goal, the League offers general information, a forum for discussion, technical information, and historic data specific to the unique problems of restoring and operating an historic theatre facility. Benefits of membership include no-fee consulting, monthly bulletins, an annual conference and theater tour, regional preservation mini-conferences, an annual photographic journal, and other publications. Members include theaters, arts councils, libraries, individuals, and professionals in the preservation/restoration and theater consulting field. The League also owns the Chesley Collection, a permanent archive on American historic theater buildings housed in Princeton University Library's Theatre Collection.

National Alliance of Preservation Commissions

c/o School of
Environmental Design
609 Caldwell Hall
University of Georgia
Athens, Georgia 30602
404-542-1365

The National Alliance of Preservation Commissions is an educational organization concerned with the implementation and administration of effective local landmark ordinances in communities across the United States. Alliance representatives participate in seminars and workshops and provide advice on drafting, enacting, and administering local landmark laws. A newsletter, *The Alliance Review*, provides timely information of interest to members of local landmark commissions.

National Association for Olmsted Parks

P.O. Box 25437
Washington, D.C. 20007
202-362-9511

The National Association for Olmsted Parks (NAOP), founded in 1980, is a not-for-profit, membership organization dedicated to increasing public awareness of significant historic landscapes in the United States. The organization is particularly concerned with Olmsted parks and landscapes, sponsoring annual conferences on various aspects of Olmsted design and associated preservation issues. The organization publishes a quarterly newsletter and is compiling an up-to-date inventory of Olmsted projects by state, a bibliography of published books and articles on Frederick Law Olmsted and the firm he founded, and a list of research projects and theses on Olmsted currently underway at universities around the country.

National Association of Conservation Districts

509 Capitol Court, N.E.
Washington, D.C. 20002
202-547-6223

The National Association of Conservation Districts is a not-for-profit organization representing 3,000 local soil and water conservation districts in the United States and its territories. The organization serves as a single voice in promoting the use of conservation districts as a means of protecting the natural environment and publishes *Tuesday Letter*, a monthly newsletter.

National Association of Counties

440 First Street, N.W., 8th Floor
Washington, D.C. 20001
202-393-6226

The National Association of Counties (NACo) works to improve county government, serves as the national voice for counties, and helps to achieve a public understanding of the role of counties in the intergovernmental system. NACo's main focus is toward the federal government, and it presents the county viewpoint to decision-makers in the White House, Congress, departments, and agencies. NACo also sponsors a program which provides training, research, and technical assistance concerning the major programs and problems of county government. Legislative and technical issues are covered in the monthly *County News*, and periodic briefings and conferences are held as well.

National Association of Historic Preservation Attorneys

612 North Blount Street
Raleigh, North Carolina 27604
919-828-1627

The National Association of Historic Preservation Attorneys (NAHPA) is an association of attorneys with special skill and experience in various areas of historic preservation law. Participating attorneys have knowledge and experience in revolving fund operation, local historic preservation ordinance enactment and enforcement, and the use of tax incentives. NAHPA members are available to speak at or lead seminars for preservation lay people, attorneys, or preservation professionals. Follow-up assistance is also provided for the local implementation of activities suggested by the speaker.

National Association of Housing and Redevelopment Officials

1320 18th Street, N.W.
Washington, D.C. 20036
202-429-2960

The National Association of Housing and Redevelopment Officials (NAHRO) is a not-for-profit association which serves the professionals who work in public housing authorities, redevelopment agencies, and community development agencies throughout the United States. NAHRO is an advocate for efficient and well-funded housing and community development programs, and provides its members with a variety of management and information resources. NAHRO publishes the *NAHRO Monitor*, a biweekly report on issues in housing and community development, and the *Journal of Housing*, a bimonthly magazine which analyzes programs and policies in the housing and community development fields.

National Audubon Society

950 Third Avenue
New York, New York 10022
212-546-9100

Founded in 1905 as an association devoted to the study and protection of bird life, the National Audubon Society is one of the nation's oldest and largest conservation organizations. The Society believes that all life and the Earth's life-support systems—the air, water and land—are interdependent. Through a balanced program of research, education, and action, the National Audubon Society carries out its prime objective of long-term conservation of land, water, wildlife, and other natural resources. A nationwide network of regional offices, local chapters, and sanctuaries, in addition to offices in Washington, D.C., and New York City, assures the success of the Society's local, national, and global conservation initiatives. The Society publishes several renowned publications including its flagship magazine, *Audubon*, and produces an award-winning conservation TV documentary series, "World of Audubon."

National Building Museum

Pension Building
Judiciary Square, N.W.
Washington, D.C. 20001
202-272-2448

The National Building Museum (NBM), mandated by Congress in 1980, celebrates America's past and present architectural achievements. NBM sponsors a national program of exhibitions, films, and publications, bringing news to the public about what is being designed and constructed across America. The museum itself, located in the Pension Building designed by Montgomery C. Meigs in 1881, houses a documentation center which makes available written and visual archives concerning buildings of national significance. The Museum's building information center is developing a national library and technical data bank that will serve the building world. NBM also offers a variety of tours, as well as a quarterly publication entitled *Blueprints*.

National Center for Preservation Law

1233 Twentieth Street, N.W.
Suite 501
Washington, D.C. 20036
202-828-9611

The National Center for Preservation Law was incorporated in New York in 1977 to serve as a national clearinghouse for information about historic preservation law. The National Center published *A Primer on Preservation Law in the State of New York* in 1981 (revised 1985), co-published with The Conservation Foundation the *Handbook of Historic Preservation Law* in 1983, and currently issues a series of "Preservation Law Updates." The National Center has participated in the past in several important court cases involving critical preservation law precedents and actively monitors pending cases to identify those of most importance to the national preservation movement. The "Updates" summarize recent court decisions and analyze developing trends in preservation law from a national perspective. The National Center works closely with communities developing innovative land use regulations designed to protect historic resources.

National Conference of State Historic Preservation Officers

Hall of the States
444 North Capitol Street, N.W.
Suite 332
Washington, D.C. 20001
202-624-5465

The National Conference of State Historic Preservation Officers (NCSHPO) is a not-for-profit, professional association representing State Historic Preservation Officers in the 50 states, 5 territories, and the District of Columbia. The purposes of NCSHPO are: to provide an association of State Historic Preservation Officers for the purpose of facilitating a continuous interchange of information, knowledge, and evolving techniques pertaining to the administration of state and federal preservation programs; to provide for research and development of historic preservation programs as well as legislative proposals for their implementation at the state and federal levels; to establish and maintain effective liaison with federal and state agencies concerned with financing and administering programs in the interest of historic preservation; to establish and maintain effective liaison with the associate members of the National Conference: the National Governor's Association, the National Alliance of Preservation Commissions, the National Trust for Historic Preservation in the United States, Preservation Action, and others concerned with the administration of historic preservation programs; and to elicit widespread citizen support for historic preservation.

National Council for Preservation Education

Department of History
Georgia State University
University Plaza
Atlanta, Georgia 30303
404-658-3255

The National Council for Preservation Education, founded in 1980, encourages and assists in the development and improvement of preservation education programs in the United States and elsewhere. The Council also coordinates efforts related to preservation education with public and private organizations and interested individuals; facilitates the collection, exchange, and dissemination of information and ideas concerning preservation education; and creates public awareness of endeavors in preservation education. Two classes of membership, institutional and associate, are available. Institutional membership is open to any educational institution offering formal education programs involving a sequence of courses in the field of historic preservation, while associate membership is available to any individual, institution, or organization interested in fostering and supporting preservation education.

National Council on Public History

Department of History
West Virginia University
Morgantown, West Virginia
26505
304-293-2421

The National Council on Public History (NCPH) is a not-for-profit organization that seeks to promote the utility of history in society through professional practice. Members include federal historians, archivists, historic preservationists, academics, contract historians, and historians working for agencies of state and local govern-

ment. NCPH has an active Cultural Resources Management Committee (CRM) that seeks to promote history as an integral part of the CRM process. The NCPH journal, *The Public Historian,* and its *Public History News* regularly include articles on historic preservation, and its annual conferences feature sessions on preservation-related topics.

National Institute for Architectural Education

30 West 22nd Street
New York, New York 10010
212-924-7000

The National Institute for Architectural Education (NIAE) is an organization of architects, designers, and educators dedicated to improving the means and methodologies by which both the profession and architectural schools perform their shared purpose of educating architects-to-be. The NIAE regularly sponsors national and international competitions for study and travel, and offers faculty research grants and gifts to schools to conduct competitions. The NIAE also sponsors Career Days in Architecture in selected cities so that high school students, their guidance counselors, and parents can learn more about architecture as a career.

The National Institute for the Conservation of Cultural Property

900 Jefferson Drive, S.W.
A & I 2225
Washington, D.C. 20560
202-357-2295

Since its founding in 1982, the National Institute for Conservation (NIC) has worked to meet the needs of the nation's collections and to assist conservation professionals. NIC sponsors information programs and projects in support of scientific research

and professional training. Through these programs, NIC seeks to provide a center for the exchange of information, to enhance public understanding of conservation, and to increase support for conservation throughout the United States.

National Main Street Center

National Trust
for Historic Preservation
1785 Massachusetts
Avenue, N.W.
Washington, D.C. 20036
202-673-4219

The National Main Street Center was established by the National Trust for Historic Preservation in 1980 to assist states and towns searching for effective and affordable solutions to the problems in their older central business districts. The center offers training courses and technical assistance to selected states and communities interested in integrating history and present needs into an overall downtown revitalization program. The Center also has available a wide variety of technical manuals, booklets, and slide/tape presentations designed for use by civic leaders and public officials to promote downtown revitalization.

National Parks and Conservation Association

1015 31st Street, N.W.
Washington, D.C. 20007
202-944-8530

The National Parks and Conservation Association (NPCA) is the only private, citizen-funded organization devoted to protecting, promoting, and improving the National Park System. NPCA endeavors to keep elected officials and the public informed about problems and needs of the national parks and the threats to their survival. The organization raises money to buy inholdings and create needed new park areas. It seeks to preserve wilderness in the parks as well as important archeological sites, historic buildings, monuments, and battlefields. Through its outreach activities, NPCA encourages research into park wildlife, habitat, and historic preservation. NPCA publishes books, reports, and a bimonthly magazine *National Parks*. See p.47 for information on the New York Parks and Conservation Association.

National Preservation Institute
Pension Building
Judiciary Square, N.W.
Washington, D.C. 20001
202-272-2448

The National Preservation Institute, housed in the National Building Museum, is a not-for-profit, educational corporation chartered in 1980 to carry on a national program of education, training, research, and technical consultation in historic preservation. The Institute sponsors courses and conferences on a variety of preservation issues in Washington, D.C., in cooperation with the National Building Museum, and elsewhere.

National Recreation and Park Association
3101 Park Center Drive
Alexandria, Virginia 22302
703-820-4940

The National Recreation and Park Association (NRPA), founded in 1965, aims to develop a network of park and recreation systems on the local, state, and federal levels to promote mental, physical, and social well-being; to better the social and physical environments through provision of recreation opportunities; and to ease community tensions and urban and rural deterioration through recreation, parks, and leisure. NRPA offers several programs, including on-going professional development opportunities to individuals who work in park and leisure services. NRPA publishes *Parks and Recreation*, a monthly magazine; *Dateline: NRPA*, a monthly newsletter; and *Therapeutic Recreation Journal*, a quarterly. Books and pamphlets are also available.

National Trust for Historic Preservation
1785 Massachusetts Avenue, N.W.
Washington, D.C. 20036
202-673-4000

The National Trust for Historic Preservation is a private, not-for-profit, membership organization chartered by Congress with the responsibility to encourage public participation in the preservation of sites, districts, buildings, and objects significant in American history and culture. In addition to those listed below, the Trust's programs include an extensive library (located at the Architectural School of the University of Maryland, College Park), the annual National Preservation Conference, many other conferences and meetings, a study tour program, the Preservation Honor Awards, and National Historic Preservation Week.

The primary function of the Trust's seven regional and field offices is to provide professional advice on preservation problems through correspondence and field visits; New York inquiries should be directed to the Northeast Regional Office (address below). The National Trust operates a preservation bookshop, which is located at 1600 H Street, N.W., Washington, D.C. 20006, telephone 202-673-4200. The bookshop handles mail orders. The Trust publishes *Historic Preservation*, a bimonthly full-color magazine; *Preservation News*, a monthly newspaper; books by the Preservation Press; *Preservation Law Reporter*; and *Preservation Forum*, a quarterly journal designed to serve the essential network of professionals and organizations who get the work of preservation done.

Members of the Trust's Preservation Forum program are eligible to receive grants and loans from the National Trust's Office of Financial Services, including: Preservation Services Fund, which provides matching grants averaging $1,000 to $1,500 to not-for-profit organizations and public agencies for "start-up" projects; National Preservation Loan Fund, which provides low-interest loans and loan guarantees up to $100,000 to not-for-profits, public agencies, and owners of endangered National Historic Landmarks; and Inner-City Ventures Fund, which provides financial assistance for projects and benefits low- and moderate-income residents of older neighborhoods facing displacement pressures. In New York State, the Trust sponsors the Streb Fund, a funding program for preservation projects of not-for-profit groups. (see Statewide Organizations p.51)

The National Trust owns 17 historic house museums open to the public and administers nine of them:

Aiken House, Charleston, South Carolina

Chesterwood in Stockbridge, Massachusetts

Decatur House in Washington, D.C.

Lyndhurst in Tarrytown, New York

Montpelier, near Charlottesville, Virginia

The Shadows-on-the-Teche in New Iberia, Louisiana

Woodlawn Plantation and the Pope-Leighey House in Mount Vernon, Virginia

The Woodrow Wilson House in Washington, D.C.

Another eight historic house museums are owned by the Trust but are administered by cooperating local not-for-profit organizations:

Belle Grove in Middletown, Virginia

Brucemore in Cedar Rapids, Iowa

Casa Amesti in Monterey, California

Cooper-Molera in Monterey, California

Cliveden in Philadelphia, Pennsylvania

Filoli in Woodside, California

Oatlands near Leesburg, Virginia

The Frank Lloyd Wright Home and Studio in Oak Park, Illinois

The National Trust also owns the Aiken House in Charleston, South Carolina, site of its Southern Regional Office, and 1785 Massachusetts Avenue in Washington, D.C, its headquarters.

Northeast Regional Office National Trust for Historic Preservation 45 School Street, 4th Floor Boston, Massachusetts 02108 617-523-0885

See also the National Main Street Center, p.24.

National Women's Hall of Fame
76 Fall Street, P.O. Box 335 Seneca Falls, New York 13148 315-568-8060

The National Women's Hall of Fame is a not-for-profit, membership institution incorporated in 1969 to honor women who have made outstanding contributions to many areas of American life. The Hall of Fame offers educational programs for schools, community groups, and individuals, and has a research library on women's history available for public use. The Hall of Fame is part of the Women's Rights National Historic Park and the New York State Urban Cultural Park Program.

Natural Resources Defense Council
122 East 42nd Street New York, New York 10168 212-949-0049

The Natural Resources Defense Council (NRDC) is a not-for-profit, membership organization dedicated to protecting America's endangered natural resources and improving the quality of the human environment. NRDC maintains offices in New York, Washington, and San Francisco. NRDC is concerned with monitoring government agencies, scientific research, litigation, and public education in such areas as air and water pollution, nuclear safety, land use, noise, mass transit, forest management, strip mining, and farmland preservation.

Organization of American Historians
112 North Bryan Street Bloomington, Indiana 47401 812-335-7311

The Organization of American Historians (OAH) is a professional society created for the investigation, study, and teachings of American history. The OAH holds an annual meeting in a different city in the United States each spring and has three main publications: the *Journal of American History*, the OAH *Newsletter*, and the annual meeting *Program*. It also publishes pamphlets on topics relevant to the profession, as well as teaching guides and bibliographies.

Partners for Livable Places
1429 21st Street, N.W. Washington, D.C. 20036 202-887-5590

Partners for Livable Places is a not-for-profit, membership organization working with communities across the nation to improve the quality of cultural facilities, open spaces, economic conditions, and the natural environment. The organization offers technical assistance; sponsors conferences, workshops, and seminars; and publishes *PLACE*, a bimonthly illustrated magazine offering news, opinion, and in-depth articles on cultural planning, tourism, historic preservation, urban archaeology, and downtown animation. Partners also has available a number of other publications concerning the quality of the built environment and, in cooperation with the Design Arts Program of the National Endowment for the Arts, runs the Livability Clearinghouse to provide information on grants awarded by this federal agency.

Pioneer America Society

c/o Department of Earth Science
Southeast Missouri
State University
Cape Girardeau, Missouri 63701
314-651-2354

The Pioneer America Society is a not-for-profit, membership organization which identifies, records, and analyzes North American material culture while promoting preservation of the past. The Society publishes a triannual journal, *Material Culture*, and holds an annual meeting at various locations across the United States. A selection of papers presented by the Society's annual meeting is published in *PAST* (Pioneer America Society Transactions) three or four times per year.

Preservation Action

1350 Connecticut Avenue, N.W.
Suite 401
Washington, D.C. 20036
202-659-0915

Preservation Action (PA) is the only national grassroots lobby organized exclusively for historic preservation issues. Through its network of board members, state lobbying coordinators, Tax Task Forces, and individual members, PA works to influence the course of federal historic preservation legislation.

PA works closely with the National Trust for Historic Preservation, the National Conference of State Historic Preservation Officers, and other national groups concerned with historic preservation. Funded and governed solely by its membership, PA is an independent advocate for historic preservation issues.

The Preservation Library and Resource Center

498 South Main Street
Madison, Georgia 30650
404-342-0770

The Preservation Library and Resource Center is a regional organization that publishes *Heritage Education Quarterly*, a national publication for teachers, planners, preservationists, educators, museums, and civic groups, who head community heritage projects. The quarterly journal serves as an information network for heritage education instructors by focusing on "Architecture as a Teaching Tool," "Educational Resources," "Publications," "Impact! Museums/Foundations," and "Downtown—Main Street U.S.A."

Preservation Techniques

1924 Arch Street
Philadelphia, Pennsylvania
19103
215-567-0547

Preservation Techniques is a technical and practical not-for-profit, educational organization which teaches effective methods of maintaining and restoring historic buildings, both inside and out. The organization has available a videotape series entitled *Master Craftsmen at Work*, focusing on the creation, maintenance, and repair of ornamental painting, plaster, wrought iron, slate roofing, and stained glass.

Project for Public Spaces

153 Waverly Place
New York, New York 10014
212-620-5660

Project for Public Spaces (PPS) is a not-for-profit corporation specializing in public space planning, design, and management. PPS has been involved nationwide in projects that improve the relationship between the design and management of public spaces and the way people use them. In privately and publicly funded projects, PPS works with local communities in a joint revitalization process that seeks to increase a city's economic and social viability while preserving the city's unique heritage.

Public Works Historical Society

1313 East 60th Street
Chicago, Illinois 60637
312-667-2200

The Public Works Historical Society is dedicated to documenting and recognizing the achievements of the public works profession. Through its various programs and activities it seeks to improve public understanding, inform and bridge the gap between academic historians and public works practitioners, and increase professionalism. Since its founding in 1975, the Society has published many works in the field and encouraged the production of numerous others. In addition, a quarterly newsletter and a monthly biographical article for the *APWA Reporter* are published. The Society also sponsors symposia and works closely with museums, libraries, and state and local historical societies to enable them to include public works themes and materials in their own programs.

Sierra Club

730 Polk Street
San Francisco, California 94109
415-776-2211

The Sierra Club is a not-for-profit organization concerned with the preservation of the natural environment. Through its chapters, the Club is a voice for conservation efforts aimed at preventing the exhaustion of natural resources. The Club publishes *Sierra*, a bimonthly magazine addressing environmental issues and legislative developments, while individual chapters publish their own newsletters and conduct various activities.

Atlantic Chapter
234 Hudson Avenue
Albany, New York 12210
518-472-1534

Small Towns Institute
P.O. Box 517
Ellensburg, Washington 98926
509-925-1830

The Small Towns Institute is a not-for-profit organization concerned with finding new solutions to the problems facing small communities in the modern world. Through educational and information services, primarily its bimonthly magazine, *Small Town*, the Institute works to improve the quality of life, to keep local citizens up-to-date on national events affecting their communities, and to provide news of innovations which have successfully solved economic and social problems in other towns. The publication includes case studies of communities that have developed projects and programs to help better their quality of life.

Society for Commercial Archeology
National Museum of American History, Room 5010
Washington, D.C. 20560
202-966-8912

The Society for Commercial Archeology is a membership organization concerned with analyzing, recording, and preserving the artifacts and structures, signs and symbols of the American commercial process. The Society promotes public awareness, exchange of information, and encourages the selective conservation of the commercial landscape, including transportation facilities, roadside development, and recreation facilities. Society members participate in conferences and field trips and receive the *SCA News Journal* and special publications.

Society for Historical Archaeology
P.O. Box 231033
Pleasant Hill, California 94523
415-686-4660

The Society for Historical Archaeology (SHA) is a not-for-profit, scientific, and educational organization whose purpose is to promote scholarly research and to disseminate information on the archeology of the modern world (A.D. 1400-present). The main focus of the Society is the era since the beginning of European exploration, especially in the western hemisphere. SHA holds conferences and issues a quarterly newsletter, *Historical Archaeology* (semi-annual), and an annual special publication.

Society for Industrial Archeology
National Museum
of American History
Room 5020
Washington, D.C. 20560
202-357-2058

The Society for Industrial Archeology (SIA) promotes the study and preservation of the physical survivals of our technological and industrial past. SIA encourages and sponsors field investigations, research, recording, and the dissemination and exchange of information on all aspects of industrial archeology. SIA also seeks to increase the awareness of the public, public agencies, and site owners on the advantages of preserving—through continued or adaptive use—structures and equipment of significance in the history of technology, engineering, and industry. SIA holds an annual conference each spring and sponsors a weekend trip each fall. The Society publishes a quarterly newsletter and a journal, along with occasional special publications.

Two chapters of SIA are active in New York State: the Roebling chapter in the New York metropolitan area and the Southern New England chapter in the eastern part of the state.

New York State Chapters:

Roebling Chapter, SIA
c/o Aaron Eisenpress
235 West End Avenue,
14-C
New York, New York
10023

Southern New England
Chapter, SIA
c/o Peter Stott
Box 356
Newton Highlands,
Massachusetts 02161

Society for the Preservation of Old Mills
Gardiner Road, P.O. Box 435
Wiscasset, Maine 04578
207-882-6547

The Society was founded in 1972 to promote interest in old mills and to work toward their preservation. The Society maintains files and a library on mills and related subjects and acts as a clearinghouse on events and publications.

Society of American Historians
610 Fayerweather Hall
Columbia University
New York, New York 10027
212-280-2555

The Society of American Historians was founded in 1939 for the purpose of promoting literary distinction in historical writing. The Society offers several awards annually for outstanding historical literature, as well as a lifetime achievement prize. Along with the American Association for State and Local History, the Society sponsors the magazine *American Heritage*.

Society of Architectural Historians

1232 Pine Street
Philadelphia, Pennsylvania
19107-5944
215-735-0224

The Society of Architectural Historians (SAH) counts among its members professionals and laymen concerned with architecture, its history and preservation. Founded in 1940, the Society serves as an international forum on architecture and the related arts, encouraging scholarly research in the field, and promotes the preservation of significant architectural monuments throughout the world. Programs include annual meetings, tours, awards, and placement service. SAH publishes a bimonthly newsletter and a highly respected quarterly journal and sells other architectural publications.

New York State Chapters:

Turpin Bannister Chapter, SAH
468 Madison Avenue
Albany, New York 12208

Harley McKee Chapter, SAH
25 Hardwood Hill
Pittsford, New York 14534

New York City Chapter, SAH
452 Riverside Drive, #94
New York, New York 10027

Western New York Chapter, SAH
616 City Hall
Buffalo, New York 14202

Other:

Decorative Arts Chapter, SAH
c/o the Brooklyn Museum
200 Eastern Parkway
Brooklyn, New York 11238

Census of Stained Glass Windows in America, SAH
c/o Visual Arts Department
College of Holy Cross
Worcester, Massachusetts
01610

Society of Professional Archeologists

Department of Anthropology
Wake Forest University
Box 7807
Winston-Salem, North Carolina 27109
919-761-5282

The Society of Professional Archeologists was founded in 1976 to foster professional standards among archeologists. The Society maintains a current list of archeologists who meet the qualifications for recognition as professional archeologists and who subscribe to the Society's code of ethics, institutional standards, and standards of research performance.

Temple Hoyne Buell Center for the Study of American Architecture

305 Buell Hall
Columbia University
New York, New York 10027
212-280-8262

The Buell Center was founded in 1982 as part of the Graduate School of Architecture, Planning, and Preservation at Columbia University. Its primary purpose is to advance the study of history, theory, and criticism of American architecture, landscape, and urbanism by assisting and enlarging the community of architectural scholars and practitioners.

Trust for Public Land

116 New Montgomery Street
San Francisco, California 94105
415-495-4014

The Trust for Public Land (TPL) conserves land as a living resource for present and future generations. TPL works closely with urban and rural groups and government agencies to acquire and preserve open space to serve human needs; share knowledge of not-for-profit land acquisitions processes; and pioneer methods of land conservation and environmentally sound land use. TPL's projects are chronicled in its newsletter, *Update*.

Northeast Regional Office
Trust for Public Land
666 Broadway
New York, New York 10012
212-677-7171

Urban Land Institute

1090 Vermont Avenue, N.W.
Suite 300
Washington, D.C. 20005
202-289-8500

The Urban Land Institute (ULI) is a not-for-profit organization concerned with improving the quality of land use planning and development, and with historic preservation and adaptive use. ULI conducts research projects on private development activities in preservation, sponsors workshops, and publishes a monthly magazine as well as quarterly case study reports called *Project Reference File*.

Vernacular Architecture Forum

P.O. Box 283
Annapolis, Maryland 21401
301-974-2438

The Vernacular Architecture Forum (VAF) encourages the study and preservation of all aspects of vernacular architecture and landscapes through inter- and multi-disciplinary methods. VAF publishes a newsletter containing news on current research along with book reviews and bibliographies. The organization also sponsors an annual conference and tours of significant examples of American vernacular architecture.

Victorian Society
in America
219 South Sixth Street
Philadelphia, Pennsylvania
19106
215-627-4252

The Victorian Society was founded to promote an appreciation of all aspects of Victorian art and culture and to encourage the preservation of all things Victorian. A preservation committee is concerned with national issues. Activities include annual meetings, tours, an autumn symposium, and a summer school in England for graduate students and professionals interested in studying Victorian Britain. The Society publishes a bimonthly newsletter and a quarterly magazine, *Nineteenth Century.* Local chapters are active preservation agents.

New York Chapter
Victorian Society in America
217 East 85th Street,
Suite 296
New York, New York 10028

Wilderness Society
1400 I Street, N.W.
10th floor
Washington, D.C. 20005
202-842-3400

Since its founding in 1935, the Wilderness Society has applied itself vigorously to all activities relating to the public lands. The Society provides timely and accurate information and analysis on issues affecting public lands to the Department of the Interior, the U.S. Forest Service and other executive agencies, to Congress, and to the courts. Through the membership, cooperation with other local, state, and national conservation groups, the media, and Society-sponsored workshops and seminars, the Society seeks to educate and encourage concerned citizens to participate in the decision-making process for determining the future of public lands.

Federal Agencies, Departments, and Programs

Buffalo City Hall (1931). George J. Dietel and John J. Wade with Sullivan W. Jones, architects. Drawing by Herb Kashian.

Federal Agencies, Departments, and Programs

Federal Agencies, Departments, and Programs

Advisory Council on Historic Preservation

1100 Pennsylvania
Avenue, N.W.
Suite 809
Washington, D.C. 20004
202-786-0503

The Advisory Council on Historic Preservation, an independent federal agency, was created by the National Historic Preservation Act of 1966 to advise Congress and the President on historic preservation, to encourage public interest in preservation, to recommend studies relating to state and local preservation legislation, and to provide training and education in preservation. Through the Section 106 process, the Council, in cooperation with State Historic Preservation Officers, reviews federal and federally assisted undertakings that have an effect on properties listed in, or that are eligible for, the National Register of Historic Places. The Council annually publishes a *Report to the President and Congress*, overviewing national preservation activity and issues; single copies of the *Report* are available free. A booklet entitled *Section 106, Step-by-Step*, which outlines the Section 106 review process as amended in 1986, is available upon request. The Council also coordinates U.S. membership in the International Centre for the Study of the Preservation and Restoration of Cultural Property, which sponsors technical assistance programs, publications, and training courses (see p.10).

American Battle Monuments Commission

Pulaski Building, Room 5127
20 Massachusetts Avenue, N.W.
Washington, D.C. 20314
202-272-0533

The American Battle Monuments Commission is a small independent agency of the Executive Branch of the federal government. It is responsible for designing, constructing, and maintaining American military burial grounds in foreign countries, and for encouraging the maintenance of American military monuments and markers by their sponsors.

Commission of Fine Arts

708 Jackson Place, N.W.
Washington, D.C. 20006
202-566-1066

The Commission of Fine Arts supplies artistic advice relating to the appearance of Washington, D.C. It reviews the plans for all public buildings, parks, and other architectural elements in the Capital and for private structures in certain areas of the city. The Commission is particularly involved in developing architectural designs that complement Washington's historic structures and districts.

Council on Environmental Quality

722 Jackson Place, N.W.
Washington, D.C. 20006
202-395-5750

The Council on Environmental Quality (CEQ) is the agency administering the environmental review process on the federal level. Under the provisions of the National Environmental Policy Act, major federal actions having a significant effect on the quality of the environment must be evaluated according to the process established by CEQ regulations.

General Services Administration

18th and F streets, N.W.
Washington, D.C. 20405
202-655-4000

The General Services Administration administers the Public Buildings Cooperative Use Act. Its provisions require the federal government to give preference to historic buildings in its leasing and acquisition activities.

Public Buildings Service
202-566-1100

The Public Buildings Service (PBS) is responsible for the design, building or leasing, appraisal, repair, operation, protection, and maintenance of most of the federally controlled buildings in the United States. PBS administers a design program which emphasizes energy conservation, economy of operation, and efficiency and economy in the design-construction process. Additional program emphases include historic preservation, handicapped accessibility, and art-in-architecture.

Institute of Museum Services

Nancy Hanks Center
1100 Pennsylvania
Avenue, N.W.
Washington, D.C. 20506
202-786-0516

The Institute of Museum Services (IMS) was created by Congress in 1976 to help museums improve their basic operations and meet the increasing costs of service to the public, and to better care for the collections entrusted to them. IMS is the only federal agency to regularly support all types and sizes of museums. Its grant programs include General Operating Support, Conservation Project support, and the Museum Assessment Program. All not-for-profit museums in the U.S. are eligible.

Library of Congress
James Madison Building
101 Independence Avenue, S.E.
Washington, D.C. 20540
202-287-5000

The Library of Congress has extensive collections which are universal in scope. Originally established to serve Congress, the Library's range of services has expanded to include the entire governmental establishment in all its branches and the public at large, so that it has become a national library for the United States. Of particular interest to preservationists are the Library's manuscripts collections relating to manifold aspects of American history and civilization. Materials available for research include maps—such as Sanborn Insurance Maps—and views; photographic records from the daguerrotype to the latest news photo, government documents, newspapers, and periodicals from all over the world. Admission to the various research facilities of the Library is free and open to persons over high school age who wish to read in the general reading rooms. Certain collections, like those of the Manuscript, Rare Book, and Special Collections, can be used only by those with a serious purpose for doing so. Among the many other programs of the Library is the American Folklife Center, which carries out programs to support, preserve, and present American folklife through such activities as the collection and maintenance of archives, scholarly research, field projects, performances, exhibitions, festivals, workshops, publications, and audiovisual presentations.

National Archives and Records Administration
Seventh Street and Pennsylvania Avenue, N.W.
Washington, D.C. 20048
202-523-3220

The National Archives and Records Administration is responsible for establishing policies and procedures for managing the records of the United States government. The National Archives assists federal agencies in adequately documenting their activities, administering their records management programs, scheduling their records, and retiring their noncurrent records to Federal Records Centers. The agency also arranges, describes, preserves, and makes available to the public the historically valuable records of all three branches of the federal government. Managing the Presidential Libraries System, assisting the National Historical Publications and Records Commission in its grant program for state and local records and edited publications of prominent Americans, and publishing legislative, regulatory, Presidential, and other public documents are additional activities of this agency.

National Historical Publications and Records Commission
202-523-5384

The National Historical Publications and Records Commission is a statutory commission which makes plans, estimates, and recommendations for historical works and, in cooperation with various non-federal agencies and institutions, gathers and publishes papers and documents important for the study of American history. The Commission awards grants to promote a variety of historically oriented projects, such as archival programs, documentary publications projects, and archival and editorial education. The Publications Program of the Commission provides grant money for printed and microfilm publications of the papers of famous Americans, while the Records Program makes grants to state and local governments, historical societies, archives, libraries, and associations for the preservation, arrangement, and description of historical records.

National Endowment for the Arts
Nancy Hanks Center
1100 Pennsylvania Avenue, N.W.
Washington, D.C. 20506
202-682-5400

Challenge Grants Program
202-682-5436

The Challenge Grants program provides opportunities for arts institutions to strengthen their long-range institutional capacity and stability. The Challenge Grants program supports projects that advance the Arts Endowment's mission to encourage excellence in, access to, and appreciation of, the arts. Two types of grants exist: Challenge III, which supports projects that address artistry, access, appreciation and/or non-federal support; and Challenge II, which provides opportunities for arts institutions to launch major fundraising campaigns that strengthen long-term institutional capacity and enhance artistic quality.

Design Arts Program
202-682-5437

The Design Arts Program (DAP) provides grants for projects promoting excellence in architecture, landscape architecture, urban design, historic preservation, and planning; and graphic, interior, industrial, and fashion design. It also supports projects involving design practice, media, theory, research, and education about design. Design of cities (from the smallest village to the largest metropolis) is of special concern within the Design Advancement Category for individuals and organizations. The Program also offers distinguished designer fellowships, grants to organizations awarding design fellowships, and design program grants to state and regional arts agencies. DAP and the Visual Arts Program jointly solicit applications for exemplary public project collaborations between visual artists and design professionals.

Eligibility: U.S. citizens/permanent residents; tax-exempt organizations, including local and state governments; community/neighborhood organizations; colleges/universities, and independent not-for-profit groups/institutions.

Museums Program
202-682-5442

The Museums Program funds projects of artistic significance in the museum field. All types of museums, as well as some other organizations and museum professionals, are eligible for grants. In general, an organization must have been in operation for at least two years before submitting an application. The Program does not fund new construction or major structural modification of buildings. Grants are awarded for a wide range of projects, including special exhibitions, catalog publication, conservation and maintenance of collections, museum training, and special projects.

National Endowment for the Humanities
Nancy Hanks Center
1100 Pennsylvania Avenue, N.W.
Washington, D.C. 20506
202-786-0438

Challenge Grants Program
202-786-0361

The Challenge Grants Program, jointly funded from federal and non-federal sources, provides grants to institutions and organizations to develop long-term capital resources for the humanities, to improve program quality, and to achieve greater financial stability and growth of resources.

Eligibility: not-for-profit institutions and organizations working within the humanities; colleges and universities; museums; historical and professional societies; research libraries; advanced study centers; medical organizations; university presses; educational, cultural and community groups.

Museums and Historical Organizations Program
Division of General Programs
202-786-0284

This program provides grants to assist cultural institutions in the planning and implementation of interpretive programs that use cultural and artistic artifacts to convey and interepret the humanities to the public.

Eligibility: Museums; historical societies; not-for-profit organizations; libraries; professional organizations; colleges and universities; any branch of state or local government.

Neighborhood Reinvestment Corporation
Federal Home Loan Bank Board
1325 G Street, N.W.,
Suite 800
Washington, D.C. 20005
202-376-2400

The Neighborhood Reinvestment Corporation (NRC) is a congressionally chartered corporation which launches a variety of community revitalization projects in low-income neighborhoods across the country. Working principally with the Neighborhood Housing Services of America, Inc., NRC aids in financing these projects by providing housing rehabilitation loans to low-income families who are seldom able to meet normal underwriting criteria. In addition, NRC helps local, state-chartered neighborhood revitalization organizations across the country to organize public-private partnerships, set up loan funds, hire staff, and develop fundraising strategies.

Small Business Administration
1441 L Street, N.W.
Washington, D.C. 20416
202-653-6365

The purpose of the Small Business Administration is to aid, counsel, assist, and protect the interests of small businesses; ensure that small business concerns receive a fair portion of government purchases, contracts, and subcontracts, as well as of the sales of government property; make loans to small business concerns, state and local development companies, and the victims of floods and other catastrophies; and license, regulate, and make loans to small business investment companies.

Smithsonian Institution

Office of Museum Programs
Arts and Industries Building,
Room 2235
Washington, D.C. 20560
202-357-3101

The Office of Museum Programs (OMP) of the Smithsonian Institution provides training, services, information, and assistance for the professional enhancement of museum personnel and institutions throughout the United States and abroad. OMP offers museum training workshops, both in Washington, D.C., and on-site; arranges for internships and short-term visits by professionals; produces and distributes audiovisual presentations on conservation theory, preventive care and practice, and educational programming; provides training, technical assistance, and consultation services for Native American museums; maintains a comprehensive museum reference center open and available to museum professionals, students, and researchers; produces publications on museum-related topics; and conducts conferences, group projects, and special seminars on museum careers, training, and practices. OMP's programs and services are available free or at nominal cost to the museum community.

U.S. Department of Agriculture
14th Street and Independence Avenue, S.W.
Washington, D.C. 20250-0100
202-447-2791

The Department of Agriculture works to improve and maintain farm income, and develop and expand markets abroad for agricultural products. The Department administers various programs intended to help cure poverty, hunger, and malnutrition, and works to enhance the environment and protect natural resources. Rural development, credit, and conservation programs are some of the Department's key methods for carrying out national growth policies.

Farmers Home Administration
Office of Rural
Development Policy
202-447-3631

The Farmers Home Administration (FmHA), an agency within the Department of Agriculture, provides credit for those in rural America who are unable to get credit from other sources at reasonable rates and terms. FmHA provides financial aid and management assistance through a wide variety of loan programs. Of particular interest to preservationists are FmHA Rural Housing Loans available to low-income families for the purpose of constructing, buying, and repairing homes and building sites in open country and in small rural communities with populations of not more than 10,000 and in rural towns of 10,000 to 20,000. Loans are also made through this program to private, not-for-profit corporations, consumer cooperatives, state or local public agencies, and individuals or organizations operating on a profit or limited profit basis to provide rental or cooperative housing in rural areas for persons of low and moderate income.

National Forest Service
P.O. Box 96090
Washington, D.C. 20090-6090
202-447-3760

The National Forest Service has the responsibility for federal leadership in forestry. Its mission is to provide a continuing flow of natural resource goods and services to help meet the needs of the nation, and to contribute to the needs of the international community. The National Forest Service manages the 156 national forests, 19 national grasslands, and 17 land stabilization projects in the National Forest System. Construction of roads, trails, picnic, water-sport, skiing, and other facilities on National Forest System lands is regulated by the National Forest Service.

U.S. Department of Commerce
14th Street and Constitution Avenue, N.W.
Washington, D.C. 20230
202-377-2000

The Department of Commerce encourages, serves, and promotes the nation's international trade, economic growth, and technological advancement. The Department offers assistance and information in a variety of areas. Of particular interest are the Department's programs designed to improve the understanding and benefits of the earth's physical environment and oceanic resources.

Center for Building Technology
Building 226, Room B250
Gaithersburg, Maryland 20899
301-975-5903

The Center for Building Technology (CBT) is the national building research laboratory. It works cooperatively with other organizations, private and public, to improve building practices and increase the productivity and international competitiveness of the construction industry. It conducts laboratory, field, and analytical research. It develops technologies to predict, measure, and test the performance of building materials, components, systems, and practices. This knowledge is required for responsible and cost-effective decisions in the building process and cannot be obtained through proprietary research and development. CBT does not promulgate building standards or regulations, but its research results are widely used in the building industry and adopted by governmental and private organizations that have standards and codes responsibilities.

Economic Development Administration
105 South Seventh Street,
1st floor
Philadelphia, Pennsylvania
19106
215-597-7893

Title I of the Public Works Employment Act provides employment opportunities through federal funding of state and local capital projects in areas of high unemployment. The Act provides funding for the construction of public facilities, including public buildings, water and sewer lines, streets, pavements, and health, education, and social services facilities; and their renovation, repair, or other improvement. Grants may not be used for the acquisition of any interest in real property, or for the maintenance costs. All projects to be funded must be completed within two years; construction must begin within 90 days of project approval. The program is funded annually, and is announced in the *Federal Register*.

National Oceanic and Atmospheric Administration
Coastal Zone Management Program
Washington, D.C. 20230
202-377-2985

The mission of the National Oceanic and Atmospheric Administration (NOAA) is to explore, map, and chart the global ocean and its living resources and to manage, use and conserve those resources; to describe, monitor, and predict conditions in the atmosphere, ocean, sun, and space environment; to issue warnings against impending destructive natural events; to assess the consequences of inadvertent environmental modification over time; and to manage and disseminate long-term environmental information. Through its Coastal Zone Management Program, NOAA provides federal leadership in promoting wise and balanced management of the nation's coastal zone.

National Technical Information Service
5285 Port Royal Road
Springfield, Virginia 22161
703-487-4650

The National Technical Information Service (NTIS) is a self-supporting federal agency which operates on a cost recovery basis to bring the benefits of government-sponsored research and development activities to American business and industry. NTIS offers a technical report collection covering subjects such as building industry technology, photography, and civil engineering, a collection of software programs, and summaries of technical reports dating back to 1946. NTIS publishes 26 newsletters annually to report new research entering their collection.

U.S. Department of Education

College Work-Study Program
P.O. Box 84
Washington, D.C. 20044
800-333-4636

This program funds educational institutions for jobs for needy students. The students may be employed to work for the school, or for a not-for-profit organization. The program covers 80% of the salary, which must equal at least the minimum wage. The school or organization pays 20% of the salary, plus social security benefits.

Eligibility: Educational institutions, including four-year colleges, junior colleges, community colleges, business schools, certain vocational schools, and public and private not-for-profit organizations. Students must apply to the institution they are attending. Organizations should contact a participating educational institution.

U.S. Department of Housing and Urban Development
451 Seventh Street, S.W.
Washington, D.C. 20410
202-755-6422

Community Development Block Grants

Community Development Block Grants supply direct funding to communities for projects to improve urban living conditions through housing and environmental changes. Block Grants fund such preservation-related activities as surveys of cultural resources; studies for the adoption of regulatory or protective ordinances; establishment of financial programs, including low interest loans and grants for the rehabilitation of historically and architecturally significant structures; easement programs; and establishment of revolving funds for the acquisition, rehabilitation, and disposition of historic properties. Block Grants can also be used to match National Park Service Historic Preservation Grants-in-Aid.

Eligibility: Metropolitan cities, urban counties, certain units of local government, suburban areas. Other groups should consult local governments for project funding.

New York Regional Offices:

Albany Area Office
U.S. Department of Housing and Urban Development
Leo W. O'Brien
Federal Building
North Pearl Street
Albany, New York
12207-2395
518-472-3567

Buffalo Area Office
U.S. Department of Housing and Urban Development
107 Delaware Avenue
Statler Building
Buffalo, New York 14202-2986
716-846-5755

New York Area Office
U.S. Department of Housing and Urban Development
26 Federal Plaza
New York 10278-0068
212-264-8068

U.S. Department of the Air Force

The Pentagon
Washington, D.C. 20330
202-545-6700

The Department of the Air Force is responsible for providing an Air Force that is able, in conjunction with the other Armed Forces, of preserving the peace and security of the United States. For information on Air

Force history, contact the following address:

Office of Air Force History
Bolling Air Force Base
Washington, D.C. 20332
202-767-5764

U.S. Department of the Army

The Pentagon
Washington, D.C. 20310
202-545-6700

The mission of the Department of the Army is to organize, train, and equip active duty and reserve forces for the preservation of peace, security, and the defense of the United States. For information on Army history, contact the following address:

U.S. Army
Center of Military History
Pulaski Building
Washington, D.C.
20314-0200
202-272-0291

U.S. Army Corps of Engineers
20th Street and Massachusetts Avenue, N.W.
Washington, D.C. 20314
202-272-0001

The U.S. Army Corps of Engineers performs the full cycle of real property activities (requirements, programming, acquisition, operation, maintenance, and disposal); manages and executes engineering, construction, and real estate programs for the Army and the U.S. Air Force; and performs research and development in support of these programs. These programs include planning, design, construction, operation and maintenance, and real estate activities related to rivers, harbors, and waterways; and administration of laws for protection and preservation of navigable waters and related resources such as wetlands.

U.S. Department of the Interior

National Park Service
U.S. Department of the Interior
P.O. Box 37127
Washington, D.C. 20013-7127

Archeological
Assistance Division
202-343-4105

This office is responsible for conducting a nationwide program for the salvage of archeological remains. It develops policies, standards, and procedures for professional conduct and archeological research methods, and advises governmental agencies, historical and archeological societies, and commissions on archeological matters. The Division issues permits for archeological exploration on federally controlled lands.

Historic American
Buildings Survey
202-343-9625

Since 1933, the Historic American Buildings Survey (HABS) has recorded detailed building studies, including measured drawings, photographs, and architectural and historical data, for a national architectural archive. The program is administered by the National Park Service in cooperation with the American Institute of Architects and the Library of Congress, which is the repository of the records. Recording projects are conducted jointly with state and local governments and with private organizations. HABS gives particular priority to preservation through documentation of historic buildings threatened by demolition or alteration. Other criteria are listed in the brochure *HABS*. Copies of HABS records may be ordered from the Photo Duplication Service, Library of Congress, Washington, D.C. 20540. *Historic America: Buildings, Structures, and Sites,* the first comprehensive guide to the HABS collection since 1941, is available from the Superintendent of Documents, Government Printing Office, Washington, D.C. 20402, by requesting publication # 03-000-00149-4.

Historic American
Engineering Record
202-343-9625

Since 1969, the Historic American Engineering Record (HAER) has documented significant examples of the engineering profession's many branches (civil, mechanical, architectural, electrical, hydraulic, etc.) States, local governments, and private organizations may sponsor a HAER project.

A cooperative program with the Library of Congress and the American Society of Civil Engineers, HAER operates primarily through the regional survey, determined by geographic factors, and the industrial survey, determined by the type of industry. Also documented are historic sites and structures threatened with imminent demolition. Criteria for inclusion in HAER are listed in *HAER,* a free brochure. All records (drawings, photographic and photogrammetric records, historical research, and technical documentation) are stored in the Library of Congress.

Leasing Program
202-343-8145

In 1984, the National Park Service began to lease historic properties as a means to protect these cultural resources while keeping direct government expenses within reasonable limits. As authorized by Section 111 of

the National Historic Preservation Act of 1966, as amended in 1980, the National Park Service leases selected historic properties to individuals, groups, or organizations who assume the responsibility of rehabilitating and maintaining the property. Leasing historic property, both structures and agricultural land, enhances the scenic qualities and cultural landscape of the park area. In addition, any proceeds from these leases are used to maintain, repair, and preserve National Park Service historic property and to defray the costs of administering the program.

Leasing historic properties involves four general steps: selecting and evaluating a property, developing lease documents and offering the property for lease, negotiating with potential lessees, and managing the property under lease. To qualify as a candidate for the leasing program, a property must be owned by the federal government, listed or determined eligible for listing in the National Register of Historic Places, and not appropriate or necessary for park administration, operations, interpretation, employee housing, concessions, and the like. The qualifications of proposers are evaluated by the National Park Service to assure that prospective lessees have the financial resources to carry out the terms of the lease, experience in rehabilitating historic property and managing projects of similar uses, and the ability to assure the long-range success of the lease arrangements.

National Historic
Landmarks Program
History Division
202-343-8163

The 1935 Historic Sites Act authorizes the Secretary of the Interior to identify historic sites and buildings of national significance. Potential landmarks are evaluated by the National Park System Advisory Board, and are recommended to the Secretary for designation. Upon the owner's agreement to adhere to accepted preservation precepts, the designation is recognized by the award of a bronze plaque. All National Historic Landmarks are included in the National Register of Historic Places, and are listed in the History Division's publication, *Catalogue of National Historic Landmarks.*

National Natural
Landmarks Program
202-343-9528

National Natural Landmarks are areas which represent important examples of the nation's natural history. Areas such as Round Lake in Onondaga County and the Petrified Gardens in Saratoga County, along with other significant areas in New York State and around the country, contain ecological or geological features of such distinctive quality as to be of national significance and worthy of designation as National Natural Landmarks. More than 500 areas have been designated by the Secretary of the Interior since 1962. The areas are listed in the National Registry of Natural Landmarks, published by the National Park Service.

National Natural Landmark designation may be given to publicly or privately owned sites or to sites where there is a combination of land ownership types.

The program exists to help identify and encourage the preservation of these significant areas. The objectives of the program are: 1) to encourage the preservation of sites illustrating the geological and ecological character of the United States; 2) to enhance the scientific and educational value of sites thus preserved; 3) to strengthen public appreciation of natural history; and 4) to foster a greater concern for the conservation of the nation's natural heritage.

National Park System
202-343-9536

The National Park System of the United States comprises 337 areas covering some 79 million acres in 49 states, the District of Columbia, Guam, Puerto Rico, Saipan, and the Virgin Islands. Although best known for its scenic parks, more than half the areas of the National Park System preserve places and commemorate persons, events, and activities important in the nation's history. These range from archeological sites associated with prehistoric Indian civilizations to sites related to the lives of modern Americans. Historical areas are customarily preserved or restored to reflect their appearance during the period of their greatest historical significance.

National Park System areas in New York State associated with significant persons and/or events are listed below. Check with each site for visiting hours.

Castle Clinton National
Monument
Manhattan Sites
National Park Service
26 Wall Street
New York, New York 10005

Eleanor Roosevelt National
Historic Site
249 Albany Post Road
Bellfield Headquarters
Hyde Park, New York 12538

Federal Hall National Memorial
Manhattan Sites
National Park Service
26 Wall Street
New York, New York 10005

Fort Stanwix
National Monument
112 East Park Street
Rome, New York 13440

General Grant
National Memorial
Manhattan Sites
National Park Service
26 Wall Street
New York, New York 10005

Hamilton Grange
National Memorial
287 Convent Avenue
New York, New York 10031

Home of Franklin D. Roosevelt
National Historic Site
249 Albany Post Road
Bellfield Headquarters
Hyde Park, New York 12538

Martin Van Buren National
Historic Site
Box 545, Route 9H
Kinderhook, New York 12106

Sagamore Hill National
Historic Site
Cove Neck Road, Box 304
Oyster Bay, New York 11771

Saratoga National Historic Park
R.D. 2, Box 33
Stillwater, New York 12170

Statue of Liberty/Ellis Island
National Monument
Liberty Island
New York, New York 10004
(Also in New Jersey)

Theodore Roosevelt Birthplace
National Historic Site
28 East 20th Street
New York, New York 10003

Theodore Roosevelt Inaugural
National Historic Site
641 Delaware Avenue
Buffalo, New York 14202

Vanderbilt Mansion National
Historic Site
249 Albany Post Road
Bellfield Headquarters
Hyde Park, New York 12538

Women's Rights National
Historical Park
P.O. Box 70
Seneca Falls, New York 13148

National Register of
Historic Places
Interagency Resources Division
202-343-9536

The National Register lists the nation's properties that are officially designated as worthy of preservation, including archeological or historical sites, districts, buildings, and objects:

a. that are associated with events that have made a significant contribution to the broad patterns of our history; or

b. that are associated with the lives of persons significant in our past; or

c. that embody the distinctive characteristics of a type, period, or method of construction, or that represent the work of a master, or that possess high artistic values, or that represent a significant and distinguishable entity whose components may lack individual distinction; or

d. that have yielded, or may be likely to yield, information important in prehistory or history.

Properties are usually nominated to the Register by the State Historic Preservation Officer. Listing in the Register provides certain protection from federally financed, licensed, or assisted projects. Projects in the Register also qualify for certain federal tax benefits.

Preservation Assistance Division
202-343-9573

The Division is responsible for developing and disseminating technical information on the preservation and restoration of cultural properties; advising federal agencies on the preservation and maintenance of such properties; reviewing the transfer of surplus federal property for historic monument purposes; and advising preservation grantees on preservation methods. The Division monitors projects assisted by Historic Preservation Grants-in-Aid for compliance with federal regulations. Technical Preservation Services, a branch of the Preservation Assistance Division, publishes *Preservation Briefs*, a series of technical leaflets on building conservation, as well as technical reports, preservation case studies, *Preservation Tech Notes*, and tax incentive program information.

National Park Service Regional Office for New York State residents (For information on federal tax incentives and other Park Service publications):

Mid-Atlantic Regional Office
U.S. Custom House
Room 251
Second and Chestnut streets
Philadelphia, PA 19106
215-597-1578

U.S. Geological Survey
National Center
Reston, Virginia 22092
703-648-4460

The U.S. Geological Survey prepares and sells topographic maps that are useful for conducting surveys of historic resources, and are required as part of National Register documentation. If copies of the desired quadrangles are not available locally, they may be ordered from the U.S. Geological Survey, Branch of Distribution, Box 25286, Federal Center, Denver, Colorado 80225.

U.S. Department of the Navy
The Pentagon
Washington, D.C. 20350
202-545-6700

The primary mission of the Department of the Navy is to protect the United States by the effective prosecution of war at sea including, with its Marine Corps component, the seizure or defense of advanced naval bases; to support, as required, the forces of all military departments of the United States; and to maintain freedom of the seas. For information on Navy history, contact the following address:

U.S. Navy Library
Naval Historical Center
Washington Naval Yard
Washington, D.C.
202-433-4131

U.S. Marine Corps
Department of the Navy
Washington, D.C. 20380-0001
202-694-2500

The primary mission of the Marine Corps is to provide Fleet Marine Forces of combined arms, together with supporting air defense of advanced naval bases and for the conduct of such land operations as may be necessary to carry out this goal. For information on Marine Corps history, contact the following address:

History and Museums Division
Washington, D.C. 20380
202-433-2273

U.S. Department of Transportation
400 Seventh Street, S.W.
Washington, D.C. 20590
202-366-4000

The U.S. Department of Transportation (DOT) establishes the nation's overall transportation policy. Under its umbrella there are nine administrations whose jurisdictions include highway planning, development, and construction; urban mass transit; railroads; aviation; and the safety of waterways, ports, and oil and gas pipelines. Decisions made by DOT in conjunction with the appropriate state and local officials strongly affect other programs such as land use planning, energy conservation, scarce resource utilization, and technological change. The Department administers one of the strongest preservation tools at the federal level. Popularly known as "Section 4(f)" of the Transportation Act, it prohibits the Secretary of Transportation from approving any project requiring the use of land from an historic site unless the Secretary can show that there is no feasible and prudent alternative to its use and that the project includes all possible planning to minimize harm to the site.

Federal Highway Administration
202-366-0630

The Federal Highway Administration (FHWA) is a three-tiered organization consisting of headquarters, regions, and divisions. The headquarters and regional offices provide guidance to division offices which are the primary contacts with the state and local transportation agencies. For certain programs, local officials share responsibilities with the state. The division offices review and approve projects, monitor the states' programs, and provide technical assistance. The FHWA performs bridge inspections and surveys, prepares plans, and supervises construction of facilities to serve public lands. The FHWA also provides technical assistance to foreign countries and oversees the major research programs in the highway field.

New York State
Regional Office
Region 1
Leo W. O'Brien Federal
Building, Room 729
Clinton Avenue and
North Pearl Street
Albany, New York 12207
518-472-6476

Federal Railroad Administration
202-366-0881

The Federal Railroad Administration is the center of federal government activities on railroads, and the primary federal spokesperson on rail issues. The Administration promulgates and enforces rail safety regulations, administers railroad financial assistance programs, and conducts research and development in support of improved railroad safety.

Urban Mass Transit Administration
202-366-4043

The missions of the Urban Mass Transit Administration are to assist in the development of improved mass transportation facilities, equipment, techniques, and methods; to encourage the planning and establishment of area-wide urban mass transportation systems where they are cost-effective; to provide assistance to state and local governments in financing such systems; and to encourage private sector involvement in local mass transportation systems.

Statewide Organizations and Programs

Syracuse Savings Bank (1876), Syracuse. Joseph Lyman Silsbee, architect. Drawing by Bonnie Glasser.

Statewide Organizations and Programs

Statewide Organizations and Programs

Alliance of New York State Arts Councils

P.O. Box 6128
Stewart International Airport
New Windsor, New York 12550
914-564-6462

The Alliance of New York State Arts Councils, Inc., is a not-for-profit, membership organization chartered in 1975. Its purpose is to strengthen New York State arts councils and other arts organizations to help create an environment in which the arts can thrive at the local, state, and national levels. The Alliance serves as a resource for members and other local arts service organizations by operating the Professional Arts Management Services Program, designed to provide information and referrals, individually tailored management assistance, publications, and consultations. Additional services, such as technical assistance and special publications, are available. The Alliance also publishes *Update*, a monthly bulletin; a quarterly; *The Alliance Handbook*, a pamphlet series for arts managers; and an arts councils directory.

Association of Municipal Historians

123 Fonda Road
Waterford, New York 12188
518-237-1416

The Association of Municipal Historians is an alliance of city, village, and town historians across New York State. The Association serves the needs of the historians through two annual statewide workshops and a newsletter, *Empire Exchange*. Eight regional offices of the Association hold workshops and programs for local constituencies of members.

Association of Towns of the State of New York

146 State Street
Albany, New York 12207
518-465-7933

The Association of Towns of the State of New York, organized in 1933, acts as an agency of the towns of New York State in devising ways for obtaining greater economy and efficiency in government. The Association compiles and publishes information relative to town government, suggests and develops improved administrative methods, assists in training town officers, and provides a medium for the exchange of ideas and experiences. The services provided by the Association to its members are largely educational in character. During the legislative sessions, the Association advises its members, by weekly bulletins, of legislation affecting towns and counties. At the end of the sessions a digest of new laws is distributed. Also, six monthly bulletin services are maintained for town officials and town and county attorneys. The Association provides its members with continuous advisory services on specific town and county problems, sponsors statewide training schools for various town and county officers, and holds an annual conference.

Business Council of New York State

152 Washington Avenue
Albany, New York 12210
518-465-7511

The Business Council is a statewide business organization which lobbies the State Legislature and state government for the interests of its members. The Council's program calls for tax cuts, more assistance to small businesses, and better job training programs. The Council publishes *Business/New York*.

Canal Society of New York State

c/o Onondaga Historical Association
311 Montgomery Street
Syracuse, New York 13202
315-428-1862

The Canal Society is a private, membership organization concerned with the history of the canals of New York State. The Society sponsors day-long excursions to canal sites twice a year and also maintains research files and a library.

County Historians Association of New York State

c/o Susan L. Conklin
Genessee County Historian
131 West Main Street
Batavia, New York 14020
716-343-4727

The County Historians Association is an alliance of officially appointed historians of the 62 counties in New York State. The Association provides members with information pertinent to their duties through an annual fall meeting, workshops, and *CHAT*, a quarterly newsletter.

Dutch Barn Preservation Society

P.O. Box 176
Rensselaer, New York 12144
518-477-9132

The Dutch Barn Preservation Society is a newly formed not-for-profit group organized to study, record, and help preserve the architectural form described as the New World Dutch Barn. This barn still dots the Hudson, Mohawk, and Schoharie valleys, and other areas of Dutch and German settlement, but its numbers are decreasing. The Society arranges local programs, sponsors trips to measure and photograph barns, and publishes a newsletter. The Society plans to raise funds for preservation programs.

Empire State Crafts Alliance

511 Broadway
Saratoga Springs, NY 12866
518-584-1819

The Empire State Crafts Alliance (ESCA) is a statewide organization devoted to fostering a better understanding and greater appreciaton of New York State crafts. Its members include artists, educators, designers, architects, and others who value the beauty of handmade works. ESCA sponsors an annual conference as well as occasional seminars, and publishes *inForm*, a bimonthly newsletter.

Energy Conservation and Facilities Management Corporation

148 Madison Avenue
New York, New York 10016
212-481-0240

The Energy Conservation and Facilities Management Corporation (ECF Management) is a not-for-profit agency which helps other not-for-profit groups in New York City's five boroughs, Westchester County, and Long Island upgrade and manage their buildings more efficiently. Begun as a project of the New York Community Trust and separately incorporated in 1984, ECF Management operates several loan funds and provides a variety of technical assistance services.

Loans are available for up to $100,000 at 8% to 10% interest for construction projects that improve energy efficiency. ECF also provides interest-free loans for up to $10,000 to finance plan reviews and audits. To apply, an organization must submit its financial statements for the past three years plus a description of the proposed renovation, con-

struction, or energy conservation project.

Other ECF services include assistance in obtaining qualified engineers, architects, or contractors; review of plans for renovation and bids for construction; assistance in developing reports on building needs for use in grant proposals; a youth contracting program for weatherization; and a Building Upgrading and Maintenance Program (BUMP), which is designed to aid not-for-profits in developing plans for on-going building maintenance and energy savings. ECF also serves as a consultant for the Not-for-Profit Energy Conservation Program (see p.50).

Environmental Planning Lobby

33 Central Avenue
Albany, New York 12210
518-462-5526

The Environmental Planning Lobby (EPL), formed in 1969, is a statewide, not-for-profit organization working in the Legislature and with state agencies on behalf of sound environmental policies. EPL has played a role in the passage of many environmental laws, including the Environmental Quality Bond Act and the State Environmental Quality Review Act. EPL publishes news on environmental issues in a bimonthly newsletter, and sponsors an annual statewide environmental conference.

Film/Video Arts

817 Broadway
New York, New York 10003
212-673-9361

Film/Video Arts is a media arts center which provides low-cost film and video services to individuals and organizations. Services include rental of production and exhibition equipment; facilities for editing, sound transfer and mixing, film-to-tape transfer, and screenings; a training program with beginning and advanced courses; and financial assistance for New York State not-for-profit organizations for film exhibitions.

Gallery Association of New York State

Box 345, Route 12B
Hamilton, New York 13346
315-824-2510

The Gallery Association of New York State (GANYS) is a cooperative network of over 260 not-for-profit, exhibiting institutions in New York State and the surrounding region. GANYS provides traveling exhibitions, film programs, fine art insurance, art transport, design and fabrication services, and publications to member institutions. GANYS receives major funding from the New York State Council on the Arts.

New York Archaeological Council

c/o Dean Snow
SUNY at Albany
1400 Washington Avenue
Albany, New York 12222
518-399-7257 (h)

New York Archaeological Council (NYAC) is a not-for-profit organization composed of professional archeologists with a concern for the history and prehistory of New York State. The Council meets three times a year and deals with professional issues relating to public information, education, legislation, publication, preservation planning, cultural resource management, treatment of human remains, and collections inventories.

New York Council for the Humanities

198 Broadway, 10th Floor
New York, New York 10038
212-233-1131

Organized in 1975, the New York Council for the Humanities (NYCH) is an independent, publicly supported organization, funded by grants from the National Endowment for the Humanities and private foundations as well as contributions from individuals and corporations.

Through its competitive grants programs, the Council makes awards to not-for-profit organizations such as community groups, museums, libraries, and cultural centers to support projects which bring together scholars and public audiences. Projects funded by NYCH include conferences, lecture series, films, walking tours, and symposia. The common denominator in all NYCH-sponsored projects is an emphasis on "the humanities": history, literature, archeology, linguistics, and history and criticism of the arts. Not-for-profit organizations, institutions, and groups are eligible to apply.

New York Folklore Society

P.O. Box 250
Nassau, New York 12062

The New York Folklore Society is a private, not-for-profit, membership organization that is devoted to the study, preservation, documentation, and dissemination of folklore and folk arts in New York State. It publishes *New York Folklore,* a biannual scholarly journal, and a quarterly newsletter.

New York Foundation for the Arts

5 Beekman Street, Suite 600
New York, New York 10038
212-233-3900

The New York Foundation for the Arts (NYFA) was established in 1971 to work with the arts community throughout New York State to develop and facilitate arts programs in all disciplines. The Foundation collaborates with government agencies, foundations, corporations, local communities, and individuals to further the careers and work of contemporary artists. NYFA provides grants and services to creative artists through five programs: the Artists' Fellowship Program, the Artists in Residence Program, the Artists' New Works Program, the Communications Program, and the Revolving Loan Program (for organizations).

New York Land Institute

P.O. Box 365
Albany, New York 12201
518-465-7412

The New York Land Institute, a not-for-profit organization formed in 1979, is concerned with the wise development of New York's land resources for the fair service of all the people and interests of New York State. The Institute is dedicated to providing a forum for the exchange of ideas between environmentalists, land developers, attorneys, architects, planners, state and local government officials, the financial community, and concerned citizens. Institute activities include publication of a monthly, *New York Land Report*, the bimonthly *SEQR Report*, and, for associate members, the bimonthly *New York Land Forum.* The Institute also regularly sponsors a range of continuing professional education programs on a variety of land use topics. A specialized publication usually accompanies each program which the Institute conducts.

New York Parks and Conservation Association

35 Maiden Lane, P.O. Box 309
Albany, New York 12201
518-434-1583

The New York Parks and Conservation Association (NYPCA) was founded in 1985 as a chapter of the National Parks and Conservation Association. A not-for-profit, membership organization, NYPCA is dedicated to protecting and promoting New York's parks, open spaces, and cultural resources. They publish a newsletter, *Greenspace*, that provides information about park activities and programs across the state.

New York Planning Federation

301 South Allen Street
Albany, New York 12208
518-489-8116

The New York Planning Federation was organized in 1938 to provide educational programs related to regional, urban, rural, and local planning; to improve planning practices and effective administration; to serve as a clearinghouse on planning; and to promote community and regional planning in New York State. The Federation holds annual meetings and seminars and publishes a bimonthly newsletter.

New York State Agricultural Society

c/o Lee A. Traver
Box 350B, RD 4
Troy, New York 12180
518-286-3061 (h)

The New York State Agricultural Society is dedicated to promoting a healthy agricultural environment, supporting activites which create a better image of agriculture, and discussing new agricultural trends. The Society annually recognizes four Century Farm families who have operated the same farm for over 100 years; conducts an annual forum; recognizes journalists for excellence in reporting agricultural information; cosponsors the Empire State Food and Agriculture Leadership Institute; and is represented on the Cornell University Board of Trustees.

New York State Archeological Association

84 Lockrow Avenue
Albany, New York 12205
518-459-4209

The New York State Archeological Association is a not-for-profit organization comprised of thirteen chapters and a membership extending across the United States and Canada. The Association is dedicated to the preservation and recovery of archeological data, particularly for research on the Indians of New York State. The membership comprises many amateur archeologists, in addition to professionals. Its activities include meetings, conferences, lectures, workshops, and the publication of occasional research monographs. Individual chapters often also publish chapter bulletins.

New York State Association for Olmsted Parks

373 Lincoln Parkway
Buffalo, New York 14216
716-875-4713

The New York State Association for Olmsted Parks organizes tours, lectures, and workshops which promote preservation and public appreciation of the many Olmsted-designed landscapes in New York State.

New York State Association of Architects/AIA

235 Lark Street
Albany, New York 12210
518-449-3334

The New York State Association of Architects (NYSAA) is the state component of the American Institute of Architects (p.16). Through its legislative program, the Association serves as a liaison between New York State architects and the Legislature and state agencies. Some local chapters have preservation of-

ficers and a preservation committee. Local chapters with staffs are listed below:

Central New York Chapter/AIA
Executive Secretary
1509 Park Street
Syracuse, New York 13208
315-475-3162

Eastern New York Chapter/AIA
Executive Secretary
235 Lark Street
Albany, New York 12210
518-465-3191

Long Island Chapter/AIA
Component Executive Secretary
P.O. Box 59
Albertson, New York 11507
516-333-6303

New York Foundation for Architecture
New York Chapter/AIA
Executive Secretary
457 Madison Avenue
New York, New York 10022
212-838-9670

Rochester Chapter/AIA
Executive Secretary
Brewster/Burke House
130 Spring Street
Rochester, New York 14606
716-232-7650

Staten Island Chapter/AIA
Executive Vice President
3711 Richmond Road
Staten Island, New York 10306
718-979-0337

Westchester/Mid Hudson/AIA
Component Executive
RR2, Box 119C
South Salem, New York 10590
914-533-6240

New York State Association of Renewal and Housing Officials

Executive Park Tower
Albany, New York 12203
518-482-2931

The New York State Association of Renewal and Housing Officials (NYSARHO) is a professional, not-for-profit organization of individuals, public agencies, private companies, suppliers, and affiliated or interested professionals who work with subsidized housing and community development programs in New York State. Founded in 1960, NYSARHO sponsors two annual statewide conferences and regional workshops, and publishes a monthly newsletter which comments on pertinent federal and state legislation and reports on subsidized housing and community development activities throughout the state. During the legislative session NYSARHO also publishes a biweekly legislative report.

New York State Bar Association

Environmental Section Committee on Historic Preservation, Parks and Recreation (see below for contact)

The Committee on Historic Preservation, Parks and Recreation is a unit of the Environmental Section of the New York State Bar Association. The Committee meets regularly throughout the year to consider current issues and the legal questions they generate in the areas of historic preservation and parks law. The Committee comments on relevant bills pending before the Legislature. It provides analysis on matters of agency practice and regulations. Although membership on the Committee is limited to attorneys who are members of the New York State Bar Association, interested visitors are welcome at meetings. For further information, contact either of the co-chairs: Judith LaBelle, Berle, Kass and Case, 45 Rockefeller Plaza, Room 2350, New York, NY 10020, 212-765-1800; or Katherine Raub Ridley, Preservation League of New York State, 307 Hamilton Street, Albany, NY 12210, 607-722-4568.

New York State Conference of Mayors and Other Municipal Officials

119 Washington Avenue
Albany, New York 12210
518-463-1185

The New York State Conference of Mayors (NYCOM), established in 1910, is an advocacy group for cities and villages in New York State. NYCOM represents the interests of its members before the State Legislature and state agencies, advises mayors on municipal issues, and provides ongoing education and training for local officials. NYCOM publishes a bimonthly bulletin, *Municipal Bulletin*; and two newsletters, *NYCOM News* and *Legislative Update*.

New York State Conservation Council

8 East Main Street
Ilion, New York 13357
315-894-3302

The New York State Conservation Council is a representative statewide organization, affiliated with the National Wildlife Federation, primarily devoted to the wise use, conservation, aesthetic appreciation, and restoration of wildlife and other natural resources.

New York State Historical Association

Lake Road, P.O. Box 800
Cooperstown, New York 13326
607-547-2533

The New York State Historical Association (NYSHA) is a not-for-profit, educational organization chartered in 1899 to stimulate an awareness and appreciation of the past. NYSHA operates Fenimore House and the affiliated Farmer's Museum.

It also maintains a research library and sponsors a junior program, fellowhips, awards, and Seminars on American Culture which are held each summer. The Association publishes a quarterly journal, *New York History*; a magazine, *Heritage*; and other materials, including books and pamphlets.

New York State Recreation and Park Society

119 Washington Avenue
Albany, New York 12210
518-463-1232

The New York State Recreation and Park Society (NYSRPS), established in 1940, is an independent, not-for-profit, public interest, professional, membership association. NYSRPS sponsors programs in areas such as professional development/education and professional certification. The Society holds conferences, runs continuing education programs for leisure service professionals, and offers a professional referral service. NYSRPS's publications include *Voice* magazine, issued four times a year; *Therapeutic Recreation Newsletter*; and occasional bulletins on new programs offered by the Society and New York State.

New York State Rural Housing Coalition

150 State Street
Albany, New York 12207
518-434-1314

The New York State Rural Housing Coalition is a statewide network of rural housing and community development professionals and organizations. Safe, sanitary and affordable housing for all low- and moderate-income rural New Yorkers is the Coalition's goal. Through the publication of a *Rural Housing Resource Book* annually, and the biweekly production of its newsletter, *Rural Delivery*, the Coalition provides continuing information on the state and federal resources available for rural housing and community development efforts. An annual conference, regional meetings, and other sessions sponsored by the Coalition provide training and networking opportunities for rural housing and community development practitioners. Technical assistance in the form of basic research and funding application packaging is available from the coalition. Through its Affordable Housing for Rural New York (AHRNY) Program, the Coalition provides administrative support to organizations participating in the state's Affordable Home Ownership Development Program. By mid-1987, AHRNY was aiding in the administration of approximately $6 million (1,084 units) in local affordable housing efforts around the state.

Not-for-Profit Energy Conservation Program of New York State

The New York Community Trust
415 Madison Avenue
New York, New York 10017
212-758-0100

The Not-for-Profit Energy Conservation Program of New York State was created by the State Legislature in 1986 to support energy conservation programs and services for not-for-profit organizations in New York State. Sixteen community foundations throughout the state are serving as partners with the New York State Energy Office for the program. The New York Community Trust is coordinating the effort statewide and has information on the participating local foundations.

Each community foundation has its own deadlines for distributing a portion of the $15 million set aside for the program. Any not-for-profit organization with 501(c)(3) status, including religious groups, is eligible to apply. Grants assist such activities as technical studies, audits, workshops, training, financial planning, and loan packaging. Grants may not be used to purchase or install energy conservation equipment but may be used to reduce the interest rate on loans.

Open Space Institute

122 East 42nd Street
Room 1901
New York, New York 10168
212-949-1966

The Open Space Institute provides funding for grassroots environmental projects across New York State to help local communities preserve their environment.

Preservation League of New York State

307 Hamilton Street
Albany, New York 12210
518-462-5658

The Preservation League of New York State is a not-for-profit, membership organization founded in 1974 to safeguard the multitude of historic architectural resources across New York State. From its base in Albany, the League functions as an advocate for preservation legislation. The League also publishes a quarterly newsletter; maintains a film lending library and collection of resource materials; produces technical preservation leaflets, manuals, films, and slide/tape programs; and sponsors workshops and seminars on a variety of preservation topics. Other League activities include an annual statewide preservation conference, a legal services pro-

gram offering professional advice on a variety of preservation-related legal issues, and operation of a technical assistance program providing in-house and on-site advice on a variety of preservation and public policy issues. Through the New York State Coalition of Local Landmark and Historic District Commissions, the League also provides specialized services to those concerned with regulating preservation activity at the local level.

Publishing Center for Cultural Resources

625 Broadway
New York, New York 10012
212-260-2010

The Publishing Center is a not-for-profit corporation which assists not-for-profit educational organizations with economical and effective publications. The Center will provide aid on those aspects of publishing which an organization cannot perform due to lack of personnel, skills, space, or equipment—assisting with editing, design, production, and distribution of publications. The Center also sponsors cooperative press runs which bring high quality postcard and notecard printing within reach of small institutions.

Sacred Sites and Properties Fund

New York Landmarks
Conservancy
141 Fifth Avenue, 3rd Floor
New York, New York 10010
212-995-5260

The Sacred Sites and Properties Fund is a matching grant program for the preservation of religious buildings and related sites located in the State of New York. Grants of up to $15,000 are available to plan and execute restoration work on properties and sites owned by religious institutions. All restoration work must meet the U.S. Secretary of the Interior's Standards for Rehabilitation.

To qualify for a grant from the Sacred Sites and Properties Fund, a property must be 1) located in New York State; 2) owned by a religious institution; and 3) designated a local landmark or in a designated local historic district, or individually listed in the National Register of Historic Places or located within a National Register historic district. Any property located within a historic district must contribute to the character of the historic district. In some cases, properties that have not yet obtained local landmark or National Register status will be considered for funding. Grant applications are available from the Landmarks Conservancy. There are three grant cycles per year; check with the Landmarks Conservancy for current application deadlines.

Streb Fund

Field Representative
Northeast Regional Office
National Trust for Historic Preservation
45 School Street
Boston, Massachusetts 02108
617-523-0885

The Streb Fund is an additional funding program within the Preservation Services Fund administered by the National Trust for Historic Preservation (p.25) enabling not-for-profit groups in New York State to obtain professional advice on preservation projects. Eligible activities include, but are not limited to, hiring consultants, sponsoring preservation conferences, designing and implementing innovative preservation programs, and undertaking planning activities that will lead to the implementation of a specific preservation project. Bricks and mortar projects are not eligible. Grants

range from $1,000 to $1,500, and applications are due October 1, February 1, and June 1.

Volunteer Lawyers for the Arts

1285 Avenue of the Americas, 3rd floor
New York, New York 10019
212-977-9270

Volunteer Lawyers for the Arts (VLA) was founded in 1969 to provide the arts community with free legal assistance and comprehensive legal education. Artists and arts organizations with arts-related problems that are unable to afford legal counsel are eligible for VLA's legal services. Over 900 attorneys in the New York area now volunteer their time to artists through VLA on such matters as copyright, contracts, and not-for-profit incorporation and tax exemption. To apply, prospective clients must call VLA and be screened. If they meet VLA guidelines, they will be scheduled for an appointment with the staff attorney at VLA's offices. If the problem is not handled by a staff attorney, VLA will try to match the client with a volunteer attorney. VLA also offers a nationwide program of educational services, including conferences, seminars, workshops, books, a newsletter, and a journal. VLA is a part of a network of 38 independent volunteer lawyers for the arts organizations.

Other VLA-affiliated organizations in New York State are:

Albany
VLA Program
518-449-5380

Buffalo
Arts Council in Buffalo and Erie County
716-856-7520

Huntington
Huntington Arts Council
516-271-8423

Poughkeepsie
Dutchess County Arts Council
914-454-3222

Ontario County Courthouse (1858), Canandaigua. J. Foster Warner, architect. Drawing by Herb Kashian.

State Agencies, Departments, and Programs

State Agencies, Departments, and Programs

Department of Agriculture and Markets

Agricultural Districts Program
One Winners Circle
Albany, New York 12235
518-457-2715

The purpose of agricultural districts is to protect and enhance agricultural land as a viable segment of the state's economy, and as an economic and environmental resource of major importance. Districting also benefits communities by containing urban sprawl, assuring open space and green belts, and retaining rural character. The creation of agricultural districts limits local regulations that unreasonably restrict farming within the district, limits the exercise of eminent domain and the advance of public funds that would facilitate non-farm land uses within the district, and also provides for real property agricultural value assessment. A free handbook, *How to Create an Agricultural District*, is available.

Department of Economic Development

Division of Tourism
One Commerce Plaza
Albany, New York 12245
518-474-4116 or
1-800-225-5697

The Division of Tourism issues publications designed to promote the tourist business in New York State, including annual and seasonal guidebooks to New York City and upstate New York, which provide listings of historic properties, events, and tours. Deadline for submission is from two to six months prior to publication dates; copies are available free. The Division also offers advisory services to organizations on promoting historic sites in their communities, and maintains files of photographs and slides, which are available to the public on a limited basis. Regional offices are located in Albany, Buffalo, Kingston, Jericho, New York City, and Lake Placid.

Education Department

Bureau of Educational Facilities Planning
Cultural Education Center
Room 3090
Albany, New York 12230
518-474-3906

This office approves plans and specifications for the erection, repair, enlargement, and remodeling of school buildings in all public school districts in New York State, except those in New York City. Section 3602 of the Education Law limits the aid available from state funding sources to rehabilitate and remodel school buildings to one-half the cost of construction of a new building, which would offer similar space and features. Bureau staff is available for consultation on rehabilitation, adaptive use, code enforcement, and feasibility studies.

Eligibility: Public school districts.

State Archives and Records Administration
Cultural Education Center
Room 10A46
Albany, New York 12230
518-474-1195

A function of the Archives is to strengthen statewide historical records programs. The office acquires, preserves, and makes available for reference by state officials and others, those official records whose historical or other value warrants continued preservation. The Archives also provides records management advice and assistance to all local governments in the state, except New York City.

Records Center
Office of General Services
Building 21
State Campus
Albany, New York 12226
518-457-3171

The Records Center is responsible for storing and, when appropriate, for disposing of inactive records relating to the operations of state government. Records of lasting value are stored at the Center, prior to being transferred for preservation to the State Archives.

State Historical Records Advisory Board
State Archives
Cultural Education Center
Room 10A46
Albany, New York 12230
518-474-1195

The State Historical Records Advisory Board plans and coordinates statewide historical records programs. It reviews and evaluates all applications for funding made to the National Historical Publications and Records Commission (NHPRC). Eligible are: not-for-profit organizations, institutions, and state and local governments. NHPRC makes grants for gathering, arranging, describing, and preserving significant historical records. Types of projects eligible for funding include surveying, accessioning, preservation, reproduction, records use, archival techniques, and feasibility studies. Funding priorities within New York State are described in the brochure, *Information for New York Applicants to the National Historical Publications and Records Commission's Records Grant Program*, available free from the State Historical Records Advisory Board.

State Library
Cultural Education Center
7th Floor
Empire State Plaza
Albany, New York 12230
518-474-7646

The State Library maintains a collection of 2,500,000 bound volumes, as well as a wealth of related materials; included are outstanding collections of materials on state and local history, and on American architecture. In addition to many rare books, the library has the microfilm publication, *American Architectural Books*, which includes all books listed in Helen Park's *Architectural Books Available in America Before the Revolution* and Henry-Russell Hitchcock's *American Architectural Books Published in America Before 1895*. Also of note are the microfilm version of the *Index of American Design*, as well as extensive trade catalogues and newspapers. The Library offers photocopying and microfilming of materials in its collections.

Clearinghouse for Paper Preservation and Restoration
Associate Librarian
Collections Management/
Preservation
State Library
Cultural Education Center
Empire State Plaza
Albany, New York 12230
518-474-5146

The Clearinghouse provides information and referral services to libraries, historical societies, archival agencies, and museums on the subject of paper preservation, including architectural drawings. The Clearinghouse also gathers information on paper preservation being carried on within the state, including microfilming, reprinting, and preservation of original records.

Manuscripts and Special Collections
State Library
Cultural Education Center
Empire State Plaza
Albany, New York 12230
518-474-6282

This section maintains special collections, including manuscripts, maps, atlases, prints, photographs, broadsides, posters, sheet music, postcards, rare books, and pamphlets. Such materials are lent to other libraries and museums for use in exhibits, under appropriate environmental and security conditions. The section answers inquiries about New York State history, cartographic studies, historical, scientific, genealogical, and other subjects that are supported by its collections, and makes available photocopy, photostat, and microfilm materials from the collections. The section also provides advisory services for conserving historical documentation. Discussion is welcomed regarding potential donations of historical materials related to New York State history. Free brochures describing the section's resources and services are available.

State Museum

Division of Research and Collections

Historical Survey

—Historical Research
Cultural Education Center
Room 3099
Empire State Plaza
Albany, New York 12230
518-474-5375

This office offers advisory services on the fundamentals of organizing a new historical society, including constitutions and bylaws, and on society programs and methods of managing collections. Research is conducted on a variety of subjects relating to the state history and the State Museum collections. A Research Residency Program provides funding to students and scholars to support research programs in New York State history. Relevant publications, which are available free, include *Guide to Drafting a Historical Society Constitution, Guide to Applying for a Charter,* and *Basic Curatorial Responsibilities in the Small Historical Society.* The office serves as a coordinator with and adviser to county and local historians. The office also provides advisory services to the public on historical markers. Maintenance of state markers along state roads and other state property is the responsibility of the state Department of Transportation; maintenance of other markers is the responsibility of the owner of the property on which they are located. Single copies of a booklet on the state's areawide (not local) markers are available upon request. The office will arrange to have markers cast or damaged ones repaired.

—Curatorial Unit
Cultural Education Center
Room 3097
Empire State Plaza
Albany, New York 12230
518-474-5353

The Curatorial Unit locates and acquires objects for the collections of the State Museum; these objects include some building elements. The Bureau also assists other museums through a limited program of loans of exhibits and objects.

Anthropological Survey

Cultural Education Center
Room 3122
Empire State Plaza
Albany, New York 12230
518-474-5813/473-1503

The Anthropological Survey deals with the identification and description of aboriginal cultures, and historic cultural resources in New York State. Its activities include field reconnaissance, excavation, analysis, and interpretation of data and artifacts collected from these sites, and a highway salvage program. The office conducts an annual field research program, and cooperates with summer field schools sponsored by SUNY-Oneonta and other State University programs. The office also offers technical consultations to the public and to other state agencies. Research is published in the New York State Museum's *Bulletin* and *Memoir* series, and independent journals. A Research Residency Program provides funding to graduate students and scholars to support research projects in biology, geology, history, or anthropology of particular value and interest to New York State.

—Archeological and
    Paleontological Collectors
    Permits

State laws stipulate that permits are required for the examination, excavation, or gathering of archeological and paleontological objects located on state-owned lands (including underwater lands). Permits must be signed first by the Education Department, and countersigned by the agency having jurisdiction over the land. Permits are customarily issued annually, on April 1, for a period not exceeding one year. Eligible applicants for archeological permits are qualified staff members of recognized universities, research institutions, colleges, or museums; also individuals not affiliated with the foregoing institutions, who are considered professionally qualified by this office.

—Cultural Resources
    Survey Program

This program, carried out in cooperation with the state Department of Transportation and other state agencies in response to the mandates of federal and state law, locates, evaluates, and recovers prehistoric and historic archeological resources within designated construction areas. This office coordinates field surveys to identify structures and archeological sites, and consults with state agencies on proposals to protect, or mitigate impact on, those properties. The office also provides consultation services to other state agencies regarding potential impact on archeological resources.

**State University of
New York**

New York State
Sea Grant Institute
Dutchess Hall
State University of New York
Stony Brook, New York
11794-5000
516-632-6905

Operated jointly by the State University of New York and Cornell University, the Sea Grant Institute initiates research, education, and advisory service efforts on coastal issues pertaining to New York's marine and Great Lakes shores and harbors. Programs include publications, a traineeship program, matching research grants, and conferences. Advisory Service Offices are located in Brockport, East Aurora, Ithaca, New City, Oswego, Plainview, Riverhead, and Stony Brook. A list of publications and audio-visual materials is available upon request.

College of Environmental
Science and Forestry

Center for Community Design
    and Planning

Faculty of Landscape
Architecture
State University of New York
Syracuse, New York 13210
315-470-6541

The Center for Community Design and Planning (CCDP) is organized to promote public awareness and understanding of design and planning values for communities, and the role of design and planning professionals in community development processes. The CCDP serves to identify and facilitate faculty and student opportunities for community projects and applied research. The CCDP engages in a wide variety of problems generally encompassed within the fields of land use planning and design at site and community scales.

School of Continuing
    Education

State University of New York
Syracuse, New York 13210
315-470-6891

The College of Environmental Science and Forestry provides educational opportunities to extramural audiences in many areas of environmental concern. The School offers services for planning and conducting short courses, conferences, seminars, and workshops, in cooperation with professional societies, industry, and state and federal agencies. Recent courses of interest to preservationists include wood deterioration by insects, environmental impact, and urban and regional planning.

Department of Environmental Conservation

Bureau of Environmental Analysis

General Project Review Section
Division of Regulatory Affairs
New York State Department of
Environmental Conservation
50 Wolf Road
Albany, New York 12233
518-457-2224

The National Environmental Policy Act of 1969 (NEPA) requires federal agencies to prepare an environmental impact statement for federally assisted projects that will have a significant impact on the environment; included in this review are federally assisted local projects. The Department of Environmental Conservation (DEC) coordinates the review of environmental impact statements for the state, when it funds, approves, or directly undertakes the action. Historic properties are one of the environmental elements that must be considered during NEPA review. NEPA review is coordinated with review under the compliance procedures of the federal Advisory Council on Historic Preservation; Advisory Council procedures also apply to federally assisted projects that do not require an environmental impact statement.

Cultural Resource Section

New York State Department of
Environmental Conservation
50 Wolf Road, Room 440
Albany, New York 12233
518-457-3811

This office provides project review services for compliance with the National Historic Preservation Act (NHPA) on wastewater treatment construction grant projects, funded by DEC and the United States Environmental Protection Agency. It also offers guidance and assistance to other DEC program areas, regarding compliance with the NHPA. Through the Division of Regulatory Affairs and the Agency Preservation Officer, the Cultural Resource Section's project review services also assist DEC units and programs in complying with the State Historic Preservation Act and the cultural resource management aspects of the State Environmental Quality Review Act.

Environmental Management Council Program

Bureau of Community Affairs
New York State Department of
Environmental Conservation
50 Wolf Road, Room 507
Albany, New York 12233
518-457-0849

The Environmental Conservation Law authorizes the creation of county and regional environmental management councils by the governing body of any county in the state. The councils' purpose is to serve within the structure of county government, as advisory, coordinating, planning, educational, and reviewing agencies, to assist in the protection, preservation, and enhancement of the environment's quality. Councils are authorized to conduct surveys, studies, and research, and must undertake a natural resources inventory, including buildings and structures, which can aid in the preparation of zoning and master plans, as well as in project review and environmental impact studies. DEC reimburses councils for a portion of their expenses. Details and a model local law that may be used to establish a county council are available free.

Environmental Quality Review Section

Division of Regulatory Affairs
New York State Department of
Environmental Conservation
50 Wolf Road
Albany, New York 12233
518-457-2224

The State Environmental Quality Review Act (SEQR) helps government and the public to protect and improve the environment. DEC is responsible for the implementation of SEQR. Under SEQR, environmental as well as social and economic factors must be considered in decision making at all levels of state and local government. The law requires that all agencies determine whether their actions will have a significant impact on the environment, including historic resources. If so, an environmental impact statement must be prepared so that SEQR may examine all reasonable alternatives to reduce or avoid adverse environmental impacts related to a proposed action. SEQR encourages communication between government agencies, project sponsors, and the public.

The SEQR *Handbook*, available free, includes information on administrative procedures for local government, and guidelines for preparing environmental impact statements. For additional information on SEQR, see the SEQR entry on page 80.

State Forest Preserve
Division of Lands and Forests
Bureau of Preserve Protection
and Management
New York State Department of
Environmental Conservation
50 Wolf Road
Albany, New York 12233
518-457-7430

This office is responsible for the care, custody, and control of lands within the State Forest Preserve, which contains nearly three million acres of state land within Greene, Sullivan, Ulster, Delaware, Saratoga, Warren, Washington, Essex, Clinton, Franklin, Hamilton, Fulton, Herkimer, Lewis, Oneida, and St. Lawrence counties. Most of this state-owned land is within the 'blue line' of the Adirondack and Catskill parks. In accordance with Article 14 of the state Constitution, Forest Preserve lands are designated "to be forever kept as wild forest lands." Two historic sites are maintained by the state within the Adirondack Park: the John Brown Farm and Grave, near Lake Placid, and Crown Point Reservation, on Lake Champlain.

By State Forest Preserve legislation enacted by the State Legislature and signed by the Governor in 1983, DEC is mandated to maintain a policy not to acquire or accept ownership of historically significant structures in the parks, since that acquisition would bring their future into conflict with the "forever wild" provision of the State Constitution. The law also sets forth a procedure for state use of historic resources in the forest preserves which already are under state ownership.

State Nature and Historical Preserve Trust
Division of Lands and Forests
Bureau of Preserve Protection
and Management
New York State Department of
Environmental Conservation
50 Wolf Road
Albany, New York 12233
518-457-7433

The Trust consists of unique lands and waters outside the State Forest Preserve areas which have special importance because of their natural beauty, wilderness character, or geological, ecological, or historical significance. The Board of Trustees is composed of the Commissioner of Environmental Conservation, the Commissioner of Parks, Recreation and Historic Preservation, the Chairman of the State Council of Parks and Recreation, and four members appointed by the Governor. The main function of the Board is to recommend real property to be included in the Preserve; nominations of property are accepted from the public. This program is used to protect selected areas of major significance, rather than to acquire large areas.

Executive Department

Adirondack Park Agency
P.O. Box 99
Ray Brook, New York 12977
518-891-4050

The Adirondack Park Agency (APA), an independent bipartisan body within the state Executive Department, was created in 1971 to protect the natural resources and to ensure a stable economic base in the six-million-acre Adirondack Park. The APA administers the Adirondack Park State Land Master Plan; Adirondack Park Land Use and Development Plan; New York State Wild, Scenic, and Recreational

Rivers System Act (on private land); and the Freshwater Wetlands Act. Major decisions, regarding land-use plans and regional projects, are made by the APA's 11-member board at monthly meetings open to the public.

Although many new land uses are controlled by local governments, the APA has independent review and permit jurisdiction over significant regional projects and alteration of critical resources. Permits are required for single-family homes in remote resource management areas. The APA's Division of Regulatory Programs manages project review for new regional land uses, which require permits, as outlined in *A Citizen's Guide to Land Use Regulations*. The APA's Division of Planning provides regional and local planning assistance to local governments, as outlined in *A Citizen's Guide to Adirondack Community Planning*. The facilities of the new Division of Adirondack Park Interpretive Programs, scheduled to open in 1988, will provide nature education and travel information.

Division of the Budget
New York State Clearinghouse
Division of the Budget
State Capitol
Albany, New York 12224
518-474-1605

Under general authorization of Presidential Executive Order 12372, the State Clearinghouse administers intergovernmental reviews of federal funding applications. Applicants for federal assistance under a wide variety of programs should send project summaries in the prescribed form to the State Clearinghouse, and to the clearinghouse or other review agency covering the locality in which the proposed project is to be based. Reviews are conducted on state and local levels. The State Clearinghouse sends project information to state review agencies; these have about 30 days to comment on any project within their jurisdiction. The local administering agency follows a parallel procedure with regard to local review agencies. Most projects pass without comment. When the State Clearinghouse issues a clearance letter for each project, that letter must accompany the project sponsor's application to the federal grantor agency as evidence of compliance with intergovernmental review requirements. An annual list of federal aid programs requiring intergovernmental review is published in the *Catalogue of Federal Domestic Assistance*, Appendix I; similar information is also contained in the application package materials sent to prospective applicants by federal grantor agencies.

Division of Housing and Community Renewal
State of New York Division of Housing and Community Renewal
P.O. Box 2085
38-40 State Street, 7th Floor
Campus Plaza
Albany, New York 12207
518-474-8580

Division of Housing and Community Renewal (DHCR) is responsible for supervising state-aided public, limited dividend, and limited profit housing. DHCR also supervises state-aided urban renewal projects, services the uniform building code, and administers rent control and rent stabilization programs throughout New York State, including New York City.

Community Development

Neighborhood Preservation Companies Program

The Neighborhood Preservation Companies Program (NPC) provides not-for-profit community organizations with funds for the administrative and planning costs associated with housing and community development activities. The maximum annual award is $100,000. Contracts may be renewed annually up to an aggregate amount of $650,000, unless otherwise mandated by the State Legislature. Each NPC is required to provide a match of ⅓ of its contract funds and to work towards self-sufficiency. As of 1986, there were 220 NPC's in New York State.

Rural Areas Revitalization Program

Under the Rural Areas Revitalization Program, not-for-profit organizations may apply for up to $100,000 to fund a portion of the expenses of a specific community revitalization project. Eligible activities include specific work for the revitalization and improvement of a rural area through creation, preservation, or improvement of housing resources or commercial facilities; restoration or improvement of public facilities or other aspects of the area environment; related community preservation or renewal activities; or any combination.

Applications are evaluated by DHCR's Office of Rural Development for the extent to which they meet several criteria, including project readiness and financial feasibility, leveraging, community impact, applicant capability, alternative and innovative technology, and affirmative action.

Rural Preservation Companies Program

This program gives the DHCR authority to contract with rural, not-for-profit organizations (Rural Preservation Companies or RPC's) which perform housing preservation and community renewal activities. RPC's engage in a wide variety of activities, including general housing rehabilitation and renovation; revolving loan funds; planning and surveys; and technical assistance.

The public funds available to RPC's are for administrative purposes only, and are individually limited on an annual basis to a maximum of $100,000 and on a lifetime basis to $650,000. The funds must be matched by a local share equal to at least ⅓ of the state grant. These administrative funds give not-for-profit organizations the ability to implement housing and community development plans and services in rural areas. As of 1986, there were 84 RPC's in New York State.

Urban Initiatives Program

The purpose of the Urban Initiatives Program is to assist the efforts of eligible not-for-profit, community-based organizations in distressed urban areas of New York State in community preservation and revitalization efforts, by providing funding for costs of Urban Initiatives Projects, and to foster the most effective use of public and private resources. Under this program, the DHCR executes contracts with selected eligible community organizations for "hard costs" related to innovative approaches to neighborhood revitalization that address the improvement of physical conditions of local communities. To be eligible, projects must be located in municipalities with a population of 20,000 or more.

Housing Trust Fund Corporation

The Housing Trust Fund Corporation, a public benefit corporation, was created in the spring of 1985 to administer the Low Income Housing Trust Fund. Applicants must be not-for-profit corporations or charitable organizations or their subsidiaries, housing development fund companies, low-income individuals, or municipalities, and must propose projects or programs in eligible areas. Applicants may apply for funds to rehabilitate a specific project which they own or intend to acquire, or they can apply to act as administrators of local housing trust fund programs under which they select and supervise the rehabilitation of projects owned by other eligible applicants. The Trust Fund can provide up to $40,000 per unit to rehabilitate vacant or under-utilized residential property, or convert vacant non-residential property to residential use for occupancy by low-income homesteaders, tenants, tenant-cooperators, or condominium owners. Proposals are reviewed by the Corporation, which selects those which are consistent with the intent of the legislation and which best meet its other criteria for funding.

**New York State
Council on the Arts**
915 Broadway
New York, New York 10010
212-614-2962

Architecture, Planning and Design Program

The Architecture, Planning and Design Program is particularly concerned with design issues in New York State. It provides funding for projects that show a high degree of programmatic quality in, and treat interrelationships among, the fields of architecture; architectural history;

landscape architecture; urban and rural planning; urban design; historic preservation; graphic, industrial, and interior design; and architectural documentation. Project support is available for, but not limited to, such areas as exhibitions, publications, slide shows and videotapes, historic landscape reports, historic structures reports and surveys, research, archival / conservation projects, feasibility studies, workshops, and sponsored projects. Support is also available for ongoing activities of those organizations that were created specifically to deal with the quality of the state's designed environment. Applications are accepted once annually; the deadline is March 1. An additional source of funding administered by the Architecture, Design and Planning Program is the Capital Initiative. Begun in 1987, grants are available for capital improvements to not-for-profit arts facilities.

Decentralization Program

The Decentralization Program enables selected local arts councils, county governments, and regional advisory boards to regrant New York State Council on the Arts (NYSCA) funds for arts events in their communities. Funds may be distributed to avocational organizations, community theatres, orchestras, dance companies, choral groups, historical societies, and other groups which conduct programs for the benefit of the general public. For information on the local regranting agency in your area, contact the Decentralization Program.

Folk Arts Program

The Folk Arts Program supports activities that extend opportunities for presenting the traditional arts, enhance public understanding of these traditions, and help to sustain the vitality of the living cultural heritage of New York State. The Program is especially interested in identifying and assisting folk artists of high artistic quality who exemplify the knowledge and skills required to practice their traditions. Support is available for a variety of projects focusing on material folk culture such as traditional crafts, visual arts, architecture, and the adornment and transformation of the built environment. Application deadline: March 1.

Museum Aid Program

The Museum Aid Program provides grants for museums, zoos, botanical gardens, and organizations performing services for museums. Funds are provided in two categories: program support and ongoing operational support. Program support, for which all institutions are eligible, funds exhibitions, collections care, educational and interpretive programs, personnel development, consultants, collaborative programs among several institutions, and salaries. Ongoing operational support provides funds for general operations. Application deadline: March 1.

Office of General Services
Real Property Planning and Utilization Group
Corning Tower Building
26th Floor
Empire State Plaza
Albany, New York 12242

This program manages state-owned real estate and negotiates leases for commercial space throughout the state. It is also responsible for the custody and sale of the state's surplus lands and facilities. In addition to basic housekeeping, the office provides such other services for real property as engineering and space planning, design and construction, and real property planning and utilization. It also administers food service contracts, parking and security services, and the promotion of tourism and conventions at the Empire State Plaza.

Office of Parks, Recreation and Historic Preservation
Agency Building 1
Empire State Plaza
Albany, New York 12238

Divison for Historic Preservation

Bureau of Historic Sites

New York State Office of Parks, Recreation and Historic Preservation
Peebles Island State Park
Waterford, New York 12188
518-237-8643

The Bureau of Historic Sites is responsible for the management, preservation, and interpretation of 34 state-owned historic sites. Through its administrative offices and technical services facilities at Peebles Island, it provides the sites with guidance and assistance in the areas of archeology, collection care and management, landscape and architectural restoration, exhibit design and fabrication, research, and interpretation.

Individuals or organizations seeking general information in these subject areas may contact the Bureau, or the Regional Historic Preservation Supervisors at the Office of Parks, Recreation and Historic Preservation regional offices listed below. Friends organizations exist for many of the state historic sites

(see under localities in regional and local organizations listings.)

NYSOPRHP
Allegany Region
Salamanca, New York 14779
716-354-2535
Allegany, Cattaraugus, Chautauqua counties

NYSOPRHP
Central Region
Clark Reservation
Jamesville, New York 13078
315-492-1756
Broome, Chenango, Cortland, Delaware, Herkimer, Madison, Oneida, Onondaga, Oswego, Otsego counties

NYSOPRHP
Finger Lakes Region
Taughannock Falls State Park
Trumansburg, New York 14886
607-387-7041
Cayuga, Chemung, Ontario, Schuyler, Seneca, Steuben, Tioga, Tompkins, Wayne, Yates counties

NYSOPRHP
Genesee Region
One Letchworth Park
Castile, New York 14427
716-493-2611
Genesee, Livingston, Monroe, Orleans, Wyoming counties

NYSOPRHP
Long Island Region
P.O. Box 247
Babylon, New York 11702
516-669-1000
Nassau, Suffolk counties

NYSOPRHP
New York City Region
1700 Broadway
New York, New York 10019
212-977-8257
Bronx, Kings, New York, Queens, Richmond counties

NYSOPRHP
Niagara Frontier Region
Prospect Park
Niagara Falls, New York 14303
716-278-1761
Erie, Niagara counties

NYSOPRHP
Palisades Interstate Park Region
Bear Mountain, New York 10911
914-786-2701
Orange, Rockland, Sullivan, Ulster counties

NYSOPRHP
Saratoga-Capital District Region
Saratoga Spa State Park
P.O. Box W
Saratoga Springs, New York 12866
518-584-2000
Albany, Fulton, Greene, Montgomery, Renssealer, Saratoga, Schenectady, Schoharie, Warren, Washington counties

NYSOPRHP
Taconic Region
Staatsburg, New York 12580
914-889-4100
Columbia, Dutchess, Putnam, Westchester counties

NYSOPRHP
Thousand Islands Region
Keewaydin State Park
Box 247
Alexandria Bay, New York 13607
315-482-2593
Clinton, Essex, Franklin, Hamilton, Jefferson, Lewis, St. Lawrence counties

The following is a list of state-owned historic sites:

Central Region

Burroughs Memorial
State Historic Site
Roxbury, New York 12474

Fort Ontario
State Historic Site
P.O. Box 102
Oswego, New York 13126
315-343-4711

Herkimer Home
State Historic Site
Box 631
Little Falls, New York
13365-0631
315-823-0398

Hyde Hall
State Historic Site
RD 2, Box 578
Cooperstown, New York 13326
607-547-8704

Lorenzo
State Historic Site
RD 2
Cazenovia, New York 13035
315-655-3200

Oriskany Battlefield
State Historic Site
Route 69, RD 1, Box 275
Oriskany, New York 13424

Von Steuben Memorial
State Historic Site
Remsen, New York 13438
315-831-3034

Finger Lakes Region

Ganondagan
State Historic Site
P.O. Box 239
Victor, New York 14564-0239
716-924-5848

Parrott Hall
State Historic Site
Geneva, New York 14456

Long Island Region

Walt Whitman
State Historic Site
246 Walt Whitman Road
Huntington Station,
New York 11746
516-427-5240

Niagara Region

Old Fort Niagara
State Historic Site
Box 169
Youngstown, New York 14174
716-745-7611

Palisades Region

Fort Montgomery
State Historic Site
Fort Montgomery, New York
10922

Knox's Headquarters
State Historic Site
P.O. Box 207
Vail's Gate, New York 12584
914-561-5498

New Windsor Cantonment
State Historic Site
P.O. Box 207
Vail's Gate, New York 12584
914-561-1765

Senate House
State Historic Site
296 Fair Street
Kingston, New York 12401
914-338-2786

Stony Point Battlefield
State Historic Site
P.O. Box 182
Stony Point, New York 10980
914-786-2521

Washington's Headquarters
State Historic Site
84 Liberty Street
P.O. Box 1783
Newburgh, New York 12550
914-562-1195

Saratoga/Capital Region

Bennington Battlefield
State Historic Site
RD 2, P.O. Box 11-W
Hoosick Falls, New York 12090
518-686-7109

Crailo
State Historic Site
9½ Riverside Avenue
Rensselaer, New York 12144
518-463-8738

Crown Point
State Historic Site
RD 1, Box 219
Crown Point, New York 12928
518-597-3666

Grant Cottage
State Historic Site
Mt. McGregor
Wilton, New York 12866
518-587-8277

Guy Park
State Historic Site
366 West Main Street
Amsterdam, New York 12010
518-842-7550

Johnson Hall
State Historic Site
Hall Avenue
Johnstown, New York 12095
518-762-8712

Rexford Aqueduct
State Historic Site
Rexford, New York 12148

Schoharie Crossing
State Historic Site
P.O. Box 140
Fort Hunter, New York 12069
518-829-7516

Schuyler Mansion
State Historic Site
32 Catherine Street
Albany, New York 12202
518-434-0834

Taconic Region

Clermont
State Historic Site
RD 1, Box 215
Germantown, New York 12526
518-537-4240

Clinton House
State Historic Site
P.O. Box 88
Poughkeepsie, New York 12601
914-471-1630

John Jay Homestead
State Historic Site
P.O. Box AH
Katonah, New York 10536
914-232-5651

Mills Mansion
State Historic Site
Staatsburg, New York 12580
914-889-4100

Olana
State Historic Site
RD 2
Hudson, New York 12534
518-828-0135

Philipse Manor Hall
State Historic Site
P.O. Box 496
Yonkers, New York 10702
914-965-4027

Thousand Islands Region

John Brown Farm
State Historic Site
John Brown Road
Lake Placid, New York 12946
518-523-3900

Sackets Harbor Battlefield
State Historic Site
505 West Washington Street
P.O. Box 27
Sackets Harbor, New York
13685
315-646-3634

Field Services Bureau

New York State Office of Parks,
Recreation and Historic
Preservation
Agency Building 1
Empire State Plaza
Albany, New York 12238
518-474-0479

The Field Services Bureau administers federal and state
preservation programs in New
York State as authorized by the
National Historic Preservation
Act of 1966 and the New York
State Parks and Recreation Law,
Section 14.09. The Bureau maintains a close relationship with a
number of federal, state, and
local preservation organizations,
including the National Park Service, which sets standards for
preservation activities nationwide.

The Bureau is responsible for
statewide preservation planning
to ensure that the state's historic
resources—historical, architectural, archeological, and
cultural—are identitifed and pro-
tected. The programmatic
responsibilities for this protection
fall into four units within the
Bureau. All units can be con-
tacted at the above address and
telephone number.

—Survey, Planning and
Registration Unit

The Survey, Planning and
Registration Unit is responsible
for the identification and evaluation of historic resources as well
as the nomination of eligible
resources to the National and

State Registers of Historic Places.
In addition, this unit administers
the Certified Local Government
program, which provides funding
to qualified local governments
for historic preservation activities.

—Certified Local
Government Program

Since 1966, when Congress
established a preservation program for the United States, the
national historic preservation
program has operated as a
decentralized partnership between the federal government and
the states. The success of this
relationship prompted Congress
to expand the partnership to
provide for participation by local
governments. The National
Historic Preservation Act
Amendments of 1980 (P.L.
96-515) direct the Secretary of
the Interior to certify qualified
local governments, upon application and upon the recommenda-
tion of the State Historic Preservation Officer, to participate in
this partnership and specifies
several requirements which local
governments must meet to
qualify for certification.

The main inducements for local
government participation in the
Certified Local Government
(CLG) Program are that a CLG
competes only with other CLG's
for subgrant monies which com-
prise at least 10% of the state's
total federal historic preservation allocation, and a CLG has
significant authority delegated to
it, particularly in the area of National Register nominations. Certified Local Government sub-
grants are awarded on a 50%
matching basis and may be used
for "planning" activities which
further the goals of identification, evaluation, registration,
and protection of a community's
cultural resources. Eligible

activities include comprehensive survey, preparation of research and documentation to nominate property to the National Register, and publication of design guidelines and other informational materials concerning the preservation of local historic structures.

In order to qualify for certification, cities, towns, villages, and counties in New York State must operate a historic preservation program that includes:

1. a local historic preservation ordinance for designating and protecting historic properties;

2. an adequate and qualified historic preservation review commission;

3. a system for the survey and inventory of historic properties; and

4. a process to ensure adequate public participation in the local historic preservation program.

Local governments can apply for certification at any time; applications for subgrant monies are available to Certified Local Governments in October of each year and must be submitted by December. Grant awards are made in March.

—National Register of Historic Places

The National Register of Historic Places, established by the National Historic Preservation Act of 1966, is the official listing of the nation's cultural resources that are worthy of preservation. The National Register includes districts, structures, buildings, archeological sites, or objects of national, state, and local significance. Listing on the National Register makes properties eligible for consideration for state and federal historic preservation grants and provides pro-

tection through a review procedure at the state and federal levels. These procedures evaluate the effect of federally financed, assisted, or licensed undertakings upon properties. Properties proposed for nomination are reviewed by the New York State Board for Historic Preservation, and recommended to the Commissioner of Parks, Recreation and Historic Preservation, who, as the State Historic Preservation Officer, places the property on the State Register and forwards the nomination to the National Register of Historic Places. *The National Register*, a leaflet describing the program, is available from the Bureau. *The National Register of Historic Places* (stock no. 024-005-00645-1; 961 pp.), which describes all properties listed as of December 31, 1974, is available from the U.S. Government Printing Office (G.P.O.), Washington, D.C. 20402. A cumulative listing of all properties is published each February in the *Federal Register* and additions are published on the first Tuesday of each month; these are also available from the G.P.O. A booklet describing New York State entries, *The National Register of Historic Places in New York State, The First Five Years 1969-1973*, is available from the New York State Office of Parks, Recreation and Historic Preservation.

Eligibility: Proposal of properties for nomination to the National Register should be made to this Bureau after a comprehensive survey of the community has been completed. Evaluation criteria, which are established by the federal Department of the Interior, are listed on p.40.

—Statewide Inventory of Historic Resources

Because surveys of historic resources are critical to the implementation of preservation programs, this office coordinates a statewide survey of historic resources. The staff is available for consultations with and field visits to volunteer groups, public agencies, and individuals who are interested in surveying their own communities. The *Historic Resources Survey Manual*, which provides guidelines for undertaking a local survey, is available free of charge, as are state inventory forms. The long-range objective of the survey is to record all historic resources—districts, structures, buildings, and archeological sites—which are more than 50 years old; the inventory encompasses structures and sites representing a wide variety of historical themes (e.g., transportation, settlement, industry, etc.). Survey files are available for public use in Albany.

—Project Review Unit

The Project Review Unit reviews projects which are funded, licensed, or assisted by federal agencies and which may have an impact upon historic resources in New York State. In an advisory capacity, the Commissioner of Parks, Recreation and Historic Preservation, in his appointed role as the State Historic Preservation Officer (SHPO), provides comments to federal agencies during the compliance process outlined in the procedures established by the federal Advisory Council on Historic Preservation. All federal agencies must comply with the Advisory Council's procedures by identifying historic and cultural resources within a project area and by weighing the effects, if any, of the project upon those resources; the agency must also consult with the SHPO concerning its findings. *The Advisory Council's Procedures for the Protection of Historic and Cultural Properties,* reprinted from the *Federal Register,* are available upon request.

The Commissioner also consults with other state agencies if a state funded, licensed, or assisted project will have an impact upon historic and cultural resources listed or determined eligible for the State and National Registers of Historic Places or which are in the Statewide Inventory. A list of State Agency Preservation Officers responsible for monitoring such projects starts on p.75. The review process includes a discussion of alternatives, as well as the adoption of mitigating measures when appropriate. This consultation is carried out in accordance with Section 14.09 of the New York State Parks, Recreation and Historic Preservation Law.

As the state agency responsible for the coordination of the state's historic preservation programs, including the encouragement and assistance of local preservation programs, the New York State Office of Parks, Recreation and Historic Preservation offers advice and comment to both the public and private sectors regarding concerns for cultural resources. This input is especially useful given the need for local level decision making under the State Environmental Quality Review Act (SEQR).

—Technical Services Unit

The Technical Services Unit administers the federal tax incentive program developed to encourage private investment in the nation's historic resources. Since 1976 more than 1,500 buildings have been rehabilitated in New York State under this program. Additionally, the unit conducts technical reviews for other Bureau units, as well as provides technical assistance to the public on appropriate rehabilitation, restoration, and new construction projects.

—Grants/Field Unit

The Grants/Field Unit, established as a result of the passage of the Environmental Quality Bond Act in 1986, administers the historic preservation grant program, as well as provides field representation for all Bureau programs. Under the Bond Act, historic preservation projects are receiving funding as part of a $250 million allocation for land acquisition, municipal and urban cultural parks, and historic preservation.

—Historic Preservation Matching Grant Program of the Environmental Quality Bond Act

The Historic Preservation Matching Grant Program of the Environmental Quality Bond Act provides grant assistance for a variety of historic preservation projects. To receive grant assistance, a historic building, object, or site must be listed in the State or National Register of Historic Places at the time of application. Eligible applicants are municipalities and not-for-profit organizations with an ownership interest in an historic property. Projects which will achieve the grant program goal of preservation, protection, and improvement of significant historic properties in New York State are eligible for assistance. Criteria for project selection are: physical condition and need, performance and long-term protection, significance of the property, project planning, project impact, project finances and match, and preservation technology.

These grants are matching grants and can be up to 50% of eligible project costs, less any federal or state funds in the project. An applicant may receive a grant commitment based on financial need and the proposed fundraising plan, and will be given up to one year to to raise the match. Types of match include cash, force account labor, donated labor, donated equipment, donated supplies, and materials.

For general information, copies of the regulations, and applications, contact the Regional Grants Representative in your NYSOPRHP regional office (see page 62), or contact the Field Services Bureau of NYSOPRHP in Albany. For projects in the Adirondack and Catskill forest preserves, contact:

Grants Representative
ENCON Region
Room 611
50 Wolf Road
Albany, NY 12233
518-457-6310

New York State Board for Historic Preservation

Chairman, State Board for Historic Preservation c/o Deputy Commissioner for Historic Preservation New York State Office of Parks, Recreation and Historic Preservation Agency Building 1 Empire State Plaza Albany, New York 12238 518-474-0468

The duties of this Board are to advise the Commissioner of Parks, Recreation and Historic Preservation on policy matters affecting historic preservation and the state historic sites; to provide expert consultation on historic site management, development and interpretation; to review and make recommendations on nominations to the National and State Registers; and to review and advise the Commissioner on the statewide comprehensive survey and plan for historic preservation. The Board's meetings are open to the public and are held at least four times a year. Members of the Board are the Commissioner of Education, Chairman of the Council on the Arts, Chairman of the State Council of Parks and Recreation, and eight members appointed by the Governor for terms of four years.

State Council of Parks,
Recreation and
Historic Preservation

Chairman
New York State Council of Parks, Recreation and Historic Preservation
c/o Commissioner of New York State Office of Parks, Recreation and Historic Preservation
Agency Building 1
Empire State Plaza
Albany, New York 12238
518-474-0468

The New York State Council of Parks, Recreation and Historic Preservation is composed of the chairmen of the eleven regional park commissions, the Commissioner of Parks, Recreation and Historic Preservation, the Commissioner of the Department of Environmental Conservation, and the Chairman of the State Board for Historic Preservation. The Council reviews and makes recommendations regarding the policy, budget, and statewide plans of the Office of Parks, Recreation and Historic Preservation, and submits reports for the Governor. It also acts as an advisory agency on all matters affecting parks, recreation, and historic preservation.

Urban Cultural Park Program

New York State Office of Parks, Recreation and Historic Preservation
Agency Building 1
Empire State Plaza
Albany, New York 12238
518-473-2375

Unlike the traditional notion of a park as a "green space," an urban cultural park (UCP) links main streets, historic neighborhoods, industrial complexes, and natural resources into a recreational experience that tells the story of the people who settle and live in New York's cities and villages. Nine cultural themes illustrating components of New York State's history are represented in the parks: natural environment, defense, maritime trade, business and capital, transportation, labor and industry, immigration and migration, reform movements, and flowering of culture.

The Urban Cultural Park Program has four goals: to preserve important resources, to educate citizens about the relationship of the area to urban life, to encourage recreational use, and to provide a catalyst for economic development. The Urban Cultural Parks Advisory Council, consisting of state officials, appointed local officials and citizens, assists in carrying out these goals.

As of July, 1987, 14 UCP's had been designated by state legislation. UCP's which have had their management plans approved by the New York State Office of Parks, Recreation and Historic Preservation are eligible for local assistance grants for acquisition and development projects, and educational and promotional programming. Under provisions of the Environmental Quality Bond Act, UCP communities are eligible for up to 100% state funding for interpretive/visitor center facilities which will serve as a focal point in visitor orientation and education. UCP communities may also apply for 50% matching grants under the historic preservation and municipal park programs of the Bond Act.

The following is a list of urban cultural parks in New York State and their associated themes:

Albany: Business and Capital and Transportation

Buffalo: Flowering of Culture

Hudson-Mohawk: Labor and Industry

Kingston: Transportation
New York City: Maritime Trade and Immigration

Ossining: Reform Movements

Rochester: Natural Environment

Sackets Harbor: Defense

Saratoga Springs: Natural Environment

Schenectady: Labor and Industry

Seneca Falls: Reform Movements

Susquehanna: Immigration and Migration; Labor and Industry

Syracuse: Business and Capital

Whitehall: Defense

For further information see listings of regional and local organizations.

St. Lawrence-Eastern Ontario Commission

317 Washington Street
Watertown, New York 13601
315-785-2460

The primary purpose of the agency is to insure the "optimum conservation, protection, preservation, development, and use of the unique scenic, esthetic, historic, ecological, recreational, economic, and natural resources of the St.Lawrence-Eastern Ontario area." This area includes the 23 towns and two cities (Oswego and Ogdensburg) in St. Lawrence, Jefferson, Oswego, and Cayuga counties, which border the St. Lawrence River and eastern Lake Ontario. The Commission offers staff consultations in the areas of land use planning, zoning, mapping, and historic district and landmarks ordinances, as well as audio-visual materials and publications on land-use planning.

Eligibility: Towns, villages, and cities within the St. Lawrence-Eastern Ontario area.

State Board of Equalization and Assessment

Agency Building 4
Empire State Plaza
Albany, New York 12223
518-474-1700

The State Board's main responsibilities are to establish equalization rates for local governments and to help them improve property tax administration. The Board also provides training for Assessors, and offers advisory appraisals on complex properties, assistance in the installation of computer-assisted administrative systems, and extensive help in the completion of revaluation programs.

Department of Labor

Job Training Partnership Council

Governor Alfred E. Smith
Office Building
17th Floor
P.O. Box 7015
Albany, New York 12225
518-474-6014

The Council advises the Governor on policy and program matters related to the federal Job Training Partnership Act (JTPA), and on the coordination of JTPA with related education, training, and economic development initiatives. JTPA provides funds to service delivery areas, state agencies, and community organizations for training, placement, and supportive services for economically disadvantaged youth and adults, dislocated workers, and others.

Department of Law

Environmental Protection Bureau

New York State
Department of Law
120 Broadway
New York, New York 10271
212-341-2450

This Bureau has jurisdiction over litigation and legislation involving all aspects of environmental law. The Bureau has litigated issues involving landmarks, and intervened in the litigation over New York City's landmark designation of Grand Central Station.

Natural Heritage Trust

Agency Building 1
Empire State Plaza
Albany, New York 12238
518-474-0427

The Natural Heritage Trust was established as a public benefit corporation to receive and administer private gifts, devises, and bequests of real and personal property donated to further conservation, outdoor recreation, and historic preservation purposes. The Commissioner of Environmental Conservation, the Commissioner of Parks, Recreation and Historic Preservation, and the Chairman of the State Council of Parks are the three members of the Board of Trustees. The Trust is empowered to acquire property; to furnish services and materials required to manage, preserve, restore, maintain, and improve property under its jurisdiction; and to undertake research and make reports related to conservation and historic preservation.

New York State Commission on the Restoration of the Capitol

Governor Alfred E. Smith Office Building
P.O. Box 7016
Albany, New York 12225
518-473-0341

The New York State Commission on the Restoration of the Capitol (Capitol Commission) was created in 1979 in order to bring together experts in architecture, preservation, planning, the arts, and business to prepare a historic structure report and a restoration and rehabilitation plan for the New York State Capitol. In accordance with *The Master Plan for the New York State Capitol*, completed by the Commission in 1982, the Executive Chamber has been restored and plans are underway for a major restoration of the Assembly Chamber.

Department of Public Service

Office of Energy Conservation and Environment
New York State Department of Public Service
Agency Building 3
Empire State Plaza
Albany, New York 12223
518-474-8702

The Public Service Commission is responsible for the regulation of electric power, gas, telephone, and water utilities, which have been granted monopoly franchises under the laws of New York State. In addition to its many energy conservation responsibilities, the Office of Energy Conservation and Environment administers the Commission's regulatory activities pertaining to environmental protection, including historic resources. The Office seeks to protect historic properties and archeological sites that would be affected by the construction of power plants and transmission lines.

The Commission's policy requires a utility company to make available, on a matching grant basis, a maximum of 2% of the cost of a new transmission facility right-of-way for the development and administration of appropriate portions of the right-of-way for public outdoor recreational and educational uses. These may include such preservation elements as the development or interpretation of historic or archeological sites along the right-of-way.

Eligibility: Sponsors include municipalities, special local districts, and quasi-public, not-for-profit organizations approved by the Commission.

Department of State

Division of Cemeteries
New York State
Department of State
162 Washington Avenue
Albany, New York 12231
518-474-6226

Under the supervision of the Cemetery Board, the Division of Cemeteries adminsiters the provisions of the law dealing with cemetery corporations, including incorporation and acquisition of land.

Division of Coastal Resources and Waterfront Revitalization
New York State
Department of State
162 Washington Avenue
Albany, New York 12231
518-474-3643

The state Coastal Management Program was developed in response to the federal Coastal Zone Management Act of 1972, and the state Waterfront Revitalization and Coastal Resources Act of 1981. It is designed to preserve, protect, and develop statewide coastal resources, with consideration for ecological, cultural, historic, and esthetic values, as well as for the need of economic development. Coastal communities should prepare Local Waterfront Revitalization Programs (LWRP) that incorporate the protection of historic resources in coastal areas, consistent with state and local programs. The New York State Coastal Zone is defined as the shores of Long Island, the Hudson River up to Troy, the St. Lawrence and Niagara Rivers, and lakes Erie and Ontario. State legislation, in 1986, expanded the LWRP to include communities on the state's major inland waterways and provided funds and technical assistance to economically distressed municipalities for preparing and

implementing local waterfront programs.

Eligibility: Grants are made to eligible municipalities; limited grants are available to public and private groups for implementing state coastal policies.

Division of Economic Opportunity

Community and Neighborhood Assistance Program

Division of Economic Opportunity
New York State
Department of State
162 Washington Avenue
Albany, New York 12231
518-474-5700

The Community and Neighborhood Assistance Program (CNAP) of the Department of State provides assistance to all entities which are concerned with economic development of depressed communities in New York State. CNAP provides technical assistance and guidance to community action agencies, not-for-profit organizations, and local governments. Activities supported by CNAP include organizing neighborhood area groups; identifying federal, state, local, and private funds; packaging community and economic development projects; and coordinating public, private, and philanthropic resources.

Office for Local Government Services

New York State
Department of State
162 Washington Avenue
Albany, New York 12231
518-473-3355

This Office is concerned with all aspects of land use planning and regulation, including zoning and historic preservation. Legal and technical assistance is provided directly and through advisory opinions, meetings, lectures, seminars, and publications, on such topics as adaptive use, code enforcement, architectural design review, neighborhood conservation, streetscape improvements, and historic district and landmark ordinances. The Office also provides training and technical assistance in the resolution of local government management and organizational issues, in the conduct of government consolidation studies, and in intermunicipal cooperation and information systems. A slide/tape program, entitled *Adaptive Use: Survival of the Fittest,* offers examples and advice on finding new uses for old buildings. On a limited basis, Department lawyers also present programs on the legal aspects of preservation, and provide assistance.

State of New York Mortgage Agency

260 Madison Avenue
New York, New York 10016
212-696-9590

State of New York Mortgage Agency (SONYMA) is a public benefit corporation formed in 1970 to provide affordable housing for New York State residents. SONYMA offers below market mortgages through the sale of tax exempt revenue bonds. Proceeds from the sale of these bonds are used to purchase mortgages originated by a network of participating lenders statewide. SONYMA mortgages are available to purchasers of existing and newly constructed homes at fixed rate for a maximum of thirty years with a 5% minimum downpayment.

Beneficiaries of this program must be first-time homebuyers, except in targeted, economically distressed neighborhoods. 20%

of SONYMA's mortgage funds are allocated to these target areas; additionally, ⅓ of SONYMA's funds are earmarked for specific new construction projects.

Temporary State Commission on Tug Hill

State Office Building
317 Washington Street
Watertown, New York 13601
315-785-2380

Created in 1972, the Temporary State Commission on Tug Hill prepares and disseminates information on issues, problems, and opportunities relevant to land use planning and local government technical assistance programs in the Tug Hill region. The Commission is also involved in providing planning assistance to towns and villages adjacent to the Tug Hill area that are impacted by the rapid expansion of Fort Drum.

Department of Transportation

Canal Maintenance
Waterways Maintenance Division
Department of Transportation
State Office Campus
Building 5, Room 216
Albany, New York 12232
518-457-4407

The Department of Transportation (DOT) maintains the state Barge Canal; in some areas, sections of older canals are used as feeders for the Barge Canal. Regional offices of DOT offer advisory services on the maintenance of other canal remains in the state. Contact the pertinent Regional Waterway Maintenance Engineer:

Region 1
New York State Department
of Transportation
84 Holland Avenue
Albany, New York 12208

Region 2
New York State
Department of Transportation
State Office Building
207 North Genesee Street
Utica, New York 13501

Region 3
New York State Department
of Transportation
333 East Washington Street
Syracuse, New York 13202

Region 4
New York State Department
of Transportation
1530 Jefferson Road
Rochester, New York 14623

Region 5
New York State Department
of Transportation
Buffalo State Office Building
125 Main Street
Buffalo, New York 14203

Environmental Analysis Bureau
Cultural Resources
New York State Department
of Transportation
Building 5, Room 303
State Office Campus
Albany, New York 12232
518-457-5672

This office administers the Department of Transportation's (DOT) cultural resources evaluation program, which is designed to ensure that DOT is in full compliance with state and federal historic preservation laws and regulations.

Map Information Unit
New York State Department
of Transportation
Building 4, Room 105
State Office Campus
Albany, New York 12232
518-457-3555

The Unit handles sales of various Department of Transportation (DOT) map series, and functions as a centralized source of data on mapping and aerial photography in New York State. The

Unit maintains data, including free descriptive literature when available, on governmental and commercially produced materials and answers inquiries on various types of maps and photography; inquiries should be specific. DOT sells copies of maps, in the series listed below, which may be helpful in preparing local surveys of historic resources and in preservation plans. Order forms, index maps, and a descriptive brochure are available on request. Maps available include: 1:24,000 series planimetric and topographic maps, 24"x 30," scale 1" = 2000'. These maps are based on the U.S. Geological Survey's topographic maps, but include revised and additional data.

1:9,600 series planimetric maps, scale 1" = 800'. This series provides large scale coverage of all cities and villages in New York State, except New York City, and of other selected developed areas. This series consists of two map formats. Urban Area Maps, 36"x 48", cover the state's larger urban areas, except New York City; several sheets are often required for complete coverage of an urban area. The Village/ Hamlet Atlases, 24" x 36," cover smaller communities, and are published for individual counties, or for regions of two or more counties.

New York State Atlas, 11" x 17," scale 1" = approx. 4 mi., four-colored. Includes comprehensive place index. Each page (some are fold-outs) shows one or more counties. Complete atlas and individual pages are available.

New York State Capitol (1867-99), Albany. Thomas Fuller, H.H. Richardson, Leopold Eidlitz, and Isaac G. Perry, architects. Drawing by Herb Kashian.

State Legislative Programs

State Legislative Programs

State Historic Preservation Act of 1980

The State Historic Preservation Act (SHPA) establishes historic preservation as a policy of New York State government and sets forth a series of programs and mechanisms through which that policy is to be carried out. The major provisions of the bill are:

■ a statewide inventory of historic properties

■ the creation of a State Register of Historic Places

■ a survey by the Office of General Services (OGS), the state's landlord, of all historical and cultural properties under state control

■ preservation and maintenance of historic properties under state control

■ a review process to assess the impact of state-assisted projects on historic properties and to avoid or mitigate adverse impact

■ first priority use by state agencies of buildings with historic, architectural, or cultural significance

■ additional responsibilities for the State Board for Historic Preservation

The Office of Parks, Recreation and Historic Preservation (OPRHP) is designated in the act as the coordinating agency; additional preservation responsibilities lie with all state agencies, offices, departments, commissions, boards, public benefit corporations, public authorities, and municipalities.

Responsibilities of State Government

Statewide Inventory of Historic Properties

The SHPA calls for a statewide inventory of all publicly and privately owned historic properties which may qualify for listing in the State or National Registers of Historic Places. The Commissioner of Parks, Recreation and Historic Preservation is responsible for preparing and maintaining this inventory with the assistance of the more than 80 agency preservation officers (APO's) who are responsible for each agency's compliance with the SHPA, and with the cooperation of municipal preservation officers and the private sector. (Section 14.07, OPRHP Law)

Under the State Historic Preservation Act of 1980, every agency and department within New York State government is required to monitor its own actions which potentially could have an adverse impact on historic properties listed in the State and/or National Registers of Historic Places. Each department and agency has an APO on staff responsible for carrying out this mandate. The APO's for all agencies and departments are listed below:

Adirondack Park Agency
Cecily Bailey
P.O. Box 99
Ray Brook, New York 12977
518-891-4050

Office of Advocate for the Disabled
V. Paul Smith
Deputy Advocate
Agency Building 1
Empire State Plaza
Albany, New York 12223
518-474-2825

Office for the Aging
Lee Lakritz
Aging Services Representative
Agency Building 2
Empire State Plaza
Albany, New York 12223
518-474-7252

Department of Agriculture and Markets
James L. Burnes
Director of Administration
Capital Plaza
1 Winners Circle
Albany, New York 12235
518-457-2737

Division of Alcoholic Beverage Control (State Liquor Authority)
Robert E. Doyle
Commissioner
Twin Towers, Suite 1806
99 Washington Avenue
Albany, New York 12210
518-474-4696

Division of Alcoholism and Alcohol Abuse
Joe Landrigan
Director, Bureau of Standards and Certification
194 Washington Avenue
Albany, New York 12210
518-474-5121

Division of Audit and Control
Adam Ciesinski
Supervising Attorney
A.E. Smith State Office Building
Albany, New York 12236
518-474-6033

Banking Department
Ernest Kohn
2 Rector Street
New York, New York 10006
212-618-6548

Division of the Budget
Rudy F. Runko
Deputy Director
State Capitol
Albany, New York 12224
518-474-2127

Office of Business Permits
Robert Schweikert
Deputy Director
A.E. Smith State Office Building
Albany, New York 12225
518-474-7321

Commission on Cable Television
William Huff
Administrative Officer
Corning Tower
Empire State Plaza
Albany, New York 12223
518-474-4993

Capital District Transportation
Barry D. Bowman
Public Information Specialist
110 Watervliet Avenue
Albany, New York 12206

Department of Civil Service
Joy Smith
State Campus
Albany, New York 12239
518-457-2645

Department of Commerce
Elaine Kerner
Executive Assistant to the
Commissioner
230 Park Avenue
New York, New York 10169
212-949-0573

Commission of Investigation
Charles W. Segal
270 Broadway, 26th Floor
New York, New York 10007
212-577-0700

Commission on Correction
Stephen Chinlud
Chairman
Corning Tower
Empire State Plaza
Albany, New York 12223
518-474-1416

Consumer Protection Board
Stephen Kohn
Administrative Officer
Twin Towers
99 Washington Avenue
Albany, New York 12210
518-474-3797

Department of
Correctional Services
Francis Sheridan, AIA
Director of Facilities Planning
and Development
Building 2
Correctional Services
State Campus
Albany, New York 12226
518-457-8144

New York State
Council on the Arts
Anne H. Van Ingen
Architecture, Planning
and Design
915 Broadway
New York, New York 10010
212-614-2987

Council on Children & Families
Nicholas Forte
Corning Tower, 28th Floor
Empire State Plaza
Albany, New York 12223
518-474-1533

Crime Victims
Compensation Board
Geraldine Jordan
Chairman
270 Broadway, Room 200
New York, New York 10007
212-587-5137

Division of Criminal
Justice Services
Frank J. Rogers
Commissioner
Susan Jacobsen
Director, Office of Crime
Prevention (Commissioner's
Proxy)
Executive Park Tower
Stuyvesant Plaza
Albany, New York 12203
518-457-1260

Developmental Disability
Isabell Mills
Deputy Executive Director
Agency Building 1
Empire State Plaza
Albany, New York 12223
518-474-3655

Dormitory Authority
Joseph Raggio
Assistant Architect
Arlen E. Kuehnert
Assistant Engineer
Alternate
Normanskill Boulevard
Elsmere, New York 12054
518-475-3000

Education Department
James Blendell
Education Building
Room 147
Washington Avenue
Albany, New York 12234
518-474-7770

State Board of Elections
Richard J. Murray
Administrative Officer
Twin Towers
99 Washington Avenue
Albany, New York 12210
518-474-6336

Governor's Office of
Employee Relations
Nancy Hodes
James B. Northrup
Executive Deputy Director
Agency Building 2
Empire State Plaza
Albany, New York 12223
518-474-6988

New York State Energy Office
Delaine Jones
Director, Bureau of Codes and
Standards
Agency Building 2
Empire State Plaza
Albany, New York 12223
518-474-4988

Energy Research and
Development Authority
Michael D. Morgan
Deputy Counsel
Agency Building 2
Empire State Plaza
Albany, New York 12234
518-465-6251

Department of Environmental
Conservation
J. Winthrop Aldrich
Special Assistant to the
Commissioner
50 Wolf Road
Albany, New York 12233
518-457-6557

New York State Environmental
Facilities Corporation
Terence P. Curran
Executive Director
50 Wolf Road
Albany, New York 12233
518-457-4222

State Board of Equalization
and Assessment
Kathy Gustafson
Special Assistant to the
Executive Director
Agency Building 4
Empire State Plaza
Albany, New York 12223
518-473-6917

Commission on Legislative
Expenditure Review
Sanford E. Russell
Director
111 Washington Avenue
Albany, New York 12210
518-474-1474

Facilities Development
Corporation
Suzanne Charles
44 Holland Avenue
Albany, New York 12208
518-474-2155

Office of General Services
James Gallagher
Director, Facilities Procurement
and Allocation
Corning Tower
Empire State Plaza
Albany, New York 12242
518-474-2494

Department of Health
Dave Smith
Corning Tower
Empire State Plaza
Albany, New York 12237
518-474-5073

Higher Education Services
Corporation
Delores Cross
Twin Towers
99 Washington Avenue
Albany, New York 12255
518-474-5592

Division of Housing and
Community Renewal
Myron Holtz
Acting Deputy Commissioner
for Housing
1 Fordham Plaza
Bronx, New York 10458
212-519-5817

New York State Housing
Finance Agency
Eugene Myers
3 Park Avenue
New York, New York 10016
212-686-9700

State Division of Human Rights
James McNamara
Assistant Commissioner
2 World Trade Center
New York, New York 10037
212-488-7646

Insurance Department
Lloyd Franks
Agency Building 1
Empire State Plaza
Albany, New York 12223
518-474-6848

Job Development Authority
Grover B. Tarbox
Plannning and Coordination
One Commerce Plaza
Albany, New York 12210
518-474-7580

State Commission on
Judicial Conduct
Diane Eckert
Agency Building 1
Empire State Plaza
Albany, New York 12238
518-457-1258

Department of Labor
Philip Ross
Industrial Commissioner
Milton M. Tinkle
Labor Department Building
State Campus
Albany, New York 12240
518-457-1258

State Labor Relations Board
Marianna O'Dwyer
Executive Secretary
Building 12
State Campus
Albany, New York 12240
518-457-2724

Department of Law
Alexandra York
Assistant Attorney General
Environmental Protection Bureau
120 Broadway
New York, New York 10271
212-341-2476

Law Revision Commission
Michael J. Hutter
Executive Director
488 Broadway
Albany, New York 12207
518-474-1181

Law Reporting Bureau
John Fitzpatrick
Twin Towers
99 Washington Avenue
Albany, New York 12210
518-474-8211

Temporary State Commission
on Lobbying
Louis J. Cotrona
Executive Director
Twin Towers
99 Washington Avenue
Albany, New York 12210
518-474-7126

Division of the Lottery
Lorin Spiegal
Swan Street Building
Core 1
Empire State Plaza
Albany, New York 12223
518-474-0091

Office of Mental Health
Karen Nicholson
75 New Scotland Avenue
Albany, New York 12208
518-474-5802

Office of Mental Retardation
and Developmental Disabilities
Frederick Richmond under
Charles Herendeen, Director of
Capital Services
44 Holland Avenue
Albany, New York 12229
518-474-0372

Metropolitan Transit Authority
Andrew C. Hyde
347 Madison Avenue
New York, New York 10017
212-878-7027

Division of Military
and Naval Affairs
LTC Maurice M. Savage
Environmental Officer
330 Old Niskayuna Road
Latham, New York 12110-2224
518-786-4551

State of New York
Mortgage Agency
John J. Thompson
Director
111 Washington Avenue
Albany, New York 12210
518-432-2591

Department of Motor Vehicles
Bienvenida Baez
Deputy Commissioner for
Management Services
Swan Street Building
Empire State Plaza
Albany, New York 12228
518-474-2955

Office of Parks, Recreation and
Historic Preservation
Ivan Vamos
Agency Building 1
Albany, New York 12238
518-474-0468

Division of Parole
Robert FitzJames
Senior Parole Officer
Training Division
1450 Western Avenue
Albany, New York 12203
518-457-7636

New York Power Authority
Leona Johnpoll
10 Columbus Circle
Coliseum Tower
New York, New York 10019
212-397-7433

Division of Probation and
Correctional Alternatives
Jack Berry
Deputy Director
60 South Pearl Street
Albany, New York 12207
518-473-0684

Permanent Commission on
Public Employee Pension and
Retirement Systems
Joseph Metz
Executive Director
270 Broadway, Room 804A
New York, New York 10007
212-587-5033

Public Employment
Relations Board
Pat Bredenko
Thomas Joyner
50 Wolf Road, Room 502
Albany, New York 12205
518-457-2922

Public Service Commission
Robert Vessels
Director, Office of
Environmental Planning
Agency Building 3
Empire State Plaza
Albany, New York 12223
518-474-2530

Commission on Quality of Care
for the Mentally Disabled
Gary Masline
Twin Towers
99 Washington Avenue
Albany, New York 12210
518-473-7538

Racing and Wagering Board
Ronald Sommer
Director, Bingo Relations
400 Broome Street
New York, New York 10013
212-219-4226

New York State Science &
Technology Foundation
Mary W. Laub
Deputy Executive Director
Twin Towers
99 Washington Avenue
Albany, New York 12210
518-474-4349

Department of Social Services
T. Pat Bartlett
Director, Office of
Support Services
40 North Pearl Street
Albany, New York 12243-0001
518-474-9489

Board of Social Welfare
Robert B. Keyes
Agency Building 1
Empire State Plaza
Albany, New York 12223
518-432-2641

Office of Special Projects
& Protocol
Ellen Danziger
Frederica S. Neuman
Director
4 Burnett Boulevard
Poughkeepsie, New York 12603
914-431-5913

Office of the State Comptroller
Barry Isenberg
Director of Fiscal Planning and
Management
A.E. Smith State Office Building
Albany, New York 12236
518-474-5512

Department of State
James K. VanDervort
Director, Community Affairs
Donald Croteau
Director of Operations
NYS Board for Historic
Preservation (proxy)
162 Washington Avenue
Albany, New York 12231
518-474-1967

Division of State Police
Captain Hanford Thomas
Division A.D. Section
Robert D. Quick
First Deputy Superintendent
State Police Headquarters
State Campus
Albany, New York 12226
518-457-6710

State University
Construction Fund
Jay Pollard
Director of Physical Plant
Support Services
SUNY—Office of Capital
Facilities
State University Plaza
P.O. Box 1946
Albany, New York 12201
518-443-5582

State University of New York
Central Administration
Oscar E. Lanford
Vice Chancellor for Capital
Facilities
State University Plaza
Albany, New York 12246
518-473-1134

Division of Substance
Abuse Services
John Cavallaro
Philip Joyce
Coordinator of Technical
Assistance
55 West 125th Street
New York, New York 10027
212-870-8464

Supreme Court
Appellate Division
Third Department
John J. O'Brien, Clerk
Box 7288, Capitol Station
Albany, New York 12224
518-474-3609

Department of Taxation
and Finance
John P. McKenna
Deputy Commissioner for
Administration
Building 9
State Campus
Albany, New York 12227
518-457-1404

Thruway Authority
Bernard G. William
P.O. Box 189
Albany, New York 12201
518-436-2946

Department of Transportation
Keith Q. Smith
Director, Environmental
Analysis Bureau
Building 5
State Campus
Albany, New York 12232
518-457-5672

Urban Development Corporation
Gail S. Port
Deputy General Counsel
1515 Broadway
New York, New York
10036-8960
212-930-9000

Division of Veterans' Affairs
William Crandall
194 Washington Avenue
5th Floor
Albany, New York 12210
518-474-3752

Welfare Research
Virginia Sibbison
Executive Director
112 State Street
Albany, New York 12207
518-432-2563

Worker's Compensation Board
Andrew J. Kean, Jr.
Administrative Officer
100 Broadway, Menands
Albany, New York 12241
518-474-6670

Division for Youth
Paul H. Arndt
Director of Facilities Planning
and Development
84 Holland Avenue
Albany, New York 12208
518-473-0487

State Register of Historic Places

Sites, buildings, structures and objects of historic, architectural or cultural significance are to be listed in the State Register of Historic Places. All buildings in, or nominated to, the National Register are automatically listed in the State Register. Procedures and criteria for listing and the public notification process are found in Section 14.07 of the OPRHP Law and Section 427.3 and 427.4 of Title 9 of New York Code of Rules and Regulations.

Preservation and Maintenance of Historic Properties Under State Control

State agencies are to administer historic and cultural properties under their control in a spirit of stewardship and trusteeship for future generations. They are directed to inventory historic properties under their jurisdiction and to provide for the maintenance of historic properties through preservation, rehabilitation, or restoration. State agencies are also to consult with the Commissioner of Parks, Recreation and Historic Preservation before transferring, altering, or demolishing National or State Register Properties. (Section 63, Public Buildings Law)

Protection of Properties Listed or Eligible for Listing in the State and National Registers of Historic Places

All projects that are funded, licensed, or approved by the state are subject to review by the Commissioner of Parks, Recreation and Historic Preservation if it appears that any aspect of the project may or will cause any change in the quality of any historic, architectural, archeological, or cultural property that is listed in the State Register or National Register of Historic Places or is eligible for listing in the State Register. This review is to be conducted as early in the planning stages as practicable. State agencies are to explore fully all feasible and prudent plans which avoid or mitigate adverse impacts on such property. OPRHP is to publish an annual report outlining state agency actions affecting historic properties, proposed alternatives, and results of the review process. Copies may be requested from the Office of Parks, Recreation and Historic Preservation, Agency Building 1, Empire State Plaza, Albany, New York 12238. (Section 14.09, OPRHP Law)

State Use of Historic Buildings

State agencies are to give first priority to utilizing both state-owned and privately owned historic properties when considering acquisition or leasing of space for state use. Owners of properties in, or eligible for listing in, the State Register of Historic Places can register their interest in state purchase or lease of their property with the Office of General Services. Contact the Commissioner of General Services, Tower Building, Empire State Plaza, Albany, N.Y. 12238, or the Commissioner of Parks, Recreation and Historic Preservation, Agency Building 1, Empire State Plaza, Albany, N.Y. 12238. (Section 64, Public Buildings Law)

State Board for Historic Preservation

The State Historic Preservation Act increased membership on the State Board and broadened its responsibilities. The Commissioner of Environmental Conservation and the Secretary of State are appointed to the existing Board, which also includes the Commissioner of Education, the Chairman of the New York State Council on the Arts, the Chairman of the State Council on Parks, and eight members appointed by the governor with expertise in the fields of history, architecture, archeology, and other related professional disciplines. The Board's principle function is to provide an independent voice on preservation issues. In this capacity it may comment upon federal and state projects that might have an impact upon historic resources. In addition, the Board reviews and recommends properties for listing in the State and National Register. Individuals can be apprised of properties that the State Board will consider for listing by contacting the New York State Office of Parks, Recreation and Historic Preservation or consulting the New York State Register, which is published on a weekly basis and contains information on various state activities. For futher information, contact Publications Bureau, Department of State, 162 Washington Avenue, Albany, New York 12231. (Section 11.03, OPRHP Law)

Responsibilities of Individuals and Municipalities

The policy outlined in the SHPA preamble applies to municipalities and individuals as well as to state agencies. Municipalities are given the opportunity to participate in the state's historic preservation program in a number of ways. The chief executive officer of each municipality is designated as the municipal preservation officer (MPO) and is charged with coordinating local preservation activities within that jurisdiction. MPO's are asked to work with the Commissioner of Parks, Recreation and Historic Preservation on development of a statewide preservation plan and, in addition, are requested to prepare a local preservation report on the status of the municipality's preservation programs and on future plans for preservation efforts. Municipalities and individuals may also suggest nominations to the National and State Registers and comment upon nominated resources.

State Environmental Quality Review Act

The State Environmental Quality Review Act (SEQR) requires all state agencies and municipalities to prepare environmental impact statements on actions they propose or approve which may have a significant effect on the environment. Implementing regulations define actions affecting a National or State Register site, or one proposed for listing in the National Register by the State Board for Historic Preservation, as actions likely to require an impact statement. Regulations also define as a significant effect actions which impair the character or quality of important historic, archeological, or architectural resources or existing neighborhood character.

SEQR is at once broader and more narrow than the New York State Historic Preservation Act. SEQR is broader because it applies to actions undertaken by local communities; the New York State Historic Preservation Act applies only to actions of state agencies. SEQR is more narrow than the New York State Historic Preservation Act because it does not apply to properties eligible for the State Register, but only to those actually listed in the Register.

SEQR requires written documentation that the environmental impacts of proposed actions have been considered. Environmental documents are generally prepared by the agency proposing the project. The New York State Historic Preservation Act, on the other hand, triggers a face-to-face discussion between representatives of the state agency proposing the project and the New York State Historic Preservation Office.

How a Bill Becomes a Law in New York State

The New York State legislature consists of two houses, the Senate and the Assembly. The legislative session opens on the first Wednesday after the first Monday in January and continues until both houses have agreed upon a mutual termination date, usually in June.

Each house of the Legislature is headed by officers. In the Senate, the presiding officer is the lieutenant governor, who performs a ceremonial function. The real power is in the hands of the majority leader who is elected by the members of the majority party. There are also elected leaders of the minority parties in both the Senate and the Assembly. In the Assembly, the presiding officer is the speaker, who is elected by all members of the Assembly and is usually a member of the majority political party.

Much of the work of the Legislature occurs in the Senate and the Assembly committees.

Every elected representative is assigned to several committees. There are three types of committees in the Legislature—standing, select, and joint. Standing committees in each house have professional staff members. Select and joint legislative committees, which are created by a joint resolution of both houses, study a specific issue and make recommendations to the Legislature. Only standing committees are able to introduce legislation.

The most important committee in each house is the Rules Committee, which is headed by the Senate majority leader and the Assembly speaker, respectively. All bills submitted to the Legislature after the bill filing deadline, usually during March, must be introduced through this committee. The Senate Finance Committee and the Assembly Ways and Means Committee are also very important because they are concerned with bills involving the expenditure of state funds. Most legislation concerned with preservation issues will be referred to the Assembly Housing, Environmental Conservation, and Commerce and Tourism committees, or the Senate Conservation, Recreation and Environment Committee, and Housing and Urban Development Committee.

Legislative proposals are called bills. To become law, a bill must be passed in the same form by both the Senate and the Assembly and then be signed by the governor. The life of a bill can be simplified as follows: The bill

1) is introduced by a member of the Senate or Assembly and given a number;

2) assigned to committee;

3) if reported out of committee, referred to the floor for a vote by that house;

4) if passed by that house, referred to the other house;

5) assigned to the other house's corresponding committee;

6) if reported out of committee, referred to the floor for a vote by the other house;

7) referred to a conference committee if two different versions of a similar bill are passed in each house;

8) forwarded to the governor for signature or veto.

The first page of a bill contains much useful information, including the bill number and the house in which the bill is introduced. The sponsor's name is included along with the committee to which the bill has been assigned. A memorandum summarizing the proposed legislation in simplified terms is available from the office of the bill sponsor and the committee chairman. A bill's status can be determined by contacting the Assembly Information Office or the Senate Hotline. A bill on its "first reading" means it has been only introduced by its sponsor. Once a bill is reported out of committee, it is on its "second reading." At this stage, the bill is placed on the Assembly or Senate calendar for consideration. Once a bill is ready to be voted on, it is on its "third reading."

Most legislation is approved by a majority of the house's total membership. Home rule bills, appropriation bills, and overriding the governor's veto require a two-thirds majority vote.

Once a bill has been passed by both houses, it is sent on to the governor, who has ten days to act upon it. During the hectic final days of the legislative session, this limit is increased to thirty days following the last day of the session. If the governor takes no action on a bill, it automatically becomes law; if he vetoes a bill, an explanation is usually provided. Once a bill becomes law, it is forwarded to the secretary of state to be printed in the session laws for that year.

Recommended reading: "New York State Legislature," a pamphlet available for $0.38 from the League of Women Voters, 119 Washington Avenue, Albany, New York 12210.

State Legislative Directory

To call your Assembly representative in Albany,	telephone 518-455-4218
To call your senator in Albany,	telephone 518-455-2800
To obtain a copy of a bill,	telephone or write to your Senator or Assembly representative
To determine the status of a bill in the Assembly or in the Senate,	telephone 1-800-342-9860. You must provide the bill number.
To write your senator or Assembly representative,	The Hon. _____ State Senate (The Assembly) Legislative Office Building Albany, NY 12247 (12248) Dear Senator (Assemblywoman, Assemblyman):

If you do not know the number of your district or the name of your elected representative, contact the local board of elections or your local League of Women Voters.

Federal Legislative Directory

To call your congressman (woman) or senator in Washington,	telephone 202-224-3121
To obtain a copy of a bill in the House of Representatives or Senate,	write House Document Room, United States Capitol, Washington, DC, 20515, or Senate Document Room, United States Capitol, Washington, DC 20510. You must provide the bill number and enclose a return address label.
To write your congressman (woman)	The Hon. _____ House of Representatives Washington, DC 20515 Dear Congressman (woman):
To write to your senator,	The Hon. _____ Russell Senate Office Building Washington, DC 20510 Dear Senator:

Local Preservation Legislation

Testimonial Gateway (1908), Mohonk Mountain House, New Paltz. James E. Ware, architect. Drawing by Herb Kashian.

Local Preservation Legislation

Local Preservation Legislation

Components of a Local Preservation Law

With more than 100 local preservation laws already on the books in New York State, appreciation for the ability of such a law to save historic properties is on the rise. Now more than ever before, local preservation activists and municipal officials have realized that the future of their historic and architectural heritage is in their own hands. While state and federal preservation laws provide advice on actions carried out by public agencies, it is only locally enacted laws that can determine how a building is treated by its private owner.

Whether a community has a population of 400 or 7,000,000, the essential elements of a local preservation law are the same. Every law should contain at a minimum:

1. **Purposes clause.** This clause establishes the broad framework and goals of the law which follows. Although these clauses tend to be seen as just so much flowery language, they should be carefully drafted. If the actions of a commission are ever challenged, the court may look back to this clause to determine whether the actions fall within the law's broad framework. Purposes should be firmly grounded in "public welfare" considerations, such as protection of historic heritage, quality of life, and economic growth. Purely aesthetic considerations should be touched on lightly, if at all.

2. **Designation process and criteria.** Designation criteria are the standards for determining which buildings are landmarks and which are not. Criteria should be carefully enunciated so that if a designation is ever challenged, the court will have a set of standards against which to measure the designation. Laws which make designations simultaneously with passage of the law itself often lack these criteria. Chances are this kind of designation was also done without the necessary preliminary step of compiling a record to justify designation.

The designation process should be spelled out in the law as well. It should always include notice to property owners (individual, written notice is best), as well as a public hearing.

3. **Permit process and criteria.** This is the heart of any local preservation law. This section should spell out the commission's powers in reviewing changes to designated properties. Powers may range from advisory only to the vesting of approval/disapproval authority in a local commission. The types of changes requiring review should be enumerated and should allow for a wide variety of situations: exterior alterations, restoration, demolition, new construction, and moving of buildings should all be covered. Review should not be limited to buildings, but should include important contributing elements such as light fixtures, signs, sidewalks, fences, steps, paving, landscaping, and other exterior elements.

The criteria the commission will use in reviewing proposed changes must also be carefully specified. Adherence to these criteria is vital if decisions are to be consistent and objective. Criteria are a good response to the all-too-frequent allegation that a commission is making purely subjective, aesthetic judgments.

The procedure for obtaining a permit should be spelled out. Careful attention should be paid to the information an applicant must submit. Hastily drawn sketches on the backs of napkins should never be deemed a sufficient basis for the commission's judgments. Any time limit within which the commission must decide applications should run only from receipt of a *completed* application. Commission decisions should always be in writing, with specific reference to the criteria relied on in reaching its decision.

4. **Hardship.** If an applicant can demonstrate that denial of his application will result in a hardship, he is entitled to proceed with his proposed project (at least to the extent necessary to alleviate his hardship). Hardship is usually defined as inability to earn a reasonable return, if the property is a commercial one, or prevention of the owner's charitable purpose, if the property is in not-for-profit ownership. The presence of a hardship clause is vital to the constitutionality of every local preservation law. Without this safety valve to allow relief when designation becomes too burdensome on an owner, the law could be deemed a taking of private property without compensation and consequently a violation of the Fifth Amendment of the Constitution.

The process for obtaining a finding of hardship should be described. The burden of proof falls on the applicant, and commissions should not be afraid to require an owner to prove hardship through documentation. They need not rely on the owner's verbal assertion of hardship at a commission meeting. In addition, hardship criteria should not be confused with permit criteria. The fact that a property is a vital and contributing part of the historic district is not a ground for denial of hardship. Conversely, allegations of hardship should not be considered at the permit stage.

5. Maintenance Requirement.
Well thought out laws generally contain an affirmative maintenance clause requiring owners to keep their properties in good repair. Without such a clause, the municipality may be helpless to prevent "demolition by neglect" or deterioration of a building's historic fabric which may not violate the building code but which nonetheless causes loss of significance.

6. Enforcement. Every law should contain a process for enforcing its provisions, as well as a penalties clause if the law is violated. Penalties range from fines (usually accumulated per day the violation continues) to imprisonment. Among the more imaginative and effective penalties is the requirement that owners violating the law be required to restore the property to its condition prior to the violation. A meaningful penalties section can do much to encourage compliance with the law.

When local preservation laws are understood as breaking down into these essential components, they become more comprehensible. Many variations are possible on the basic pattern, but each law should contain at least these elements as a minimum.

The following model historic preservation ordinance / local law is suitable for use at the local municipal level. It contains all the essential elements discussed above as well as several additional options. The model law provides a starting point for a community wishing to protect its architectural heritage. Any law adopted should be tailored to the specific needs of a community and reviewed by a local attorney to insure that it is consistent with the local statutory framework.

Model Historic Preservation Ordinance / Local Law

AN ORDINANCE relating to the establishment of landmarks or historic districts in the Village / Town / City of _____

Section 1. Purpose

It is hereby declared as a matter of public policy that the protection, enhancement, and perpetuation of landmarks and historic districts is necessary to promote the economic, cultural, educational, and general welfare of the public. Inasmuch as the identity of a people is founded on its past, and inasmuch as _____ has many significant historic, architectural, and cultural resources which constitute its heritage, this act is intended to:

(a) protect and enhance the landmarks and historic districts which represent distinctive elements of _____'s historic, architectural, and cultural heritage;

(b) foster civic pride in the accomplishments of the past;

(c) protect and enhance _____'s attractiveness to visitors and the support and stimulus to the economy thereby provided; and

(d) insure the harmonious, orderly, and efficient growth and development of the village / town / city.

Section 2. Historic Preservation Commission

There is hereby created a commission to be known as the _____ Historic Preservation Commission.

(a) The commission shall consist of _____ members to be appointed, to the extent available in the community, by the mayor as follows:

> at least one shall be an architect;
>
> at least one shall be a historian;
>
> at least one shall be a licensed real estate broker;
>
> at least one shall be an attorney;
>
> at least one shall be a resident of an historic district;
>
> at least one shall have demonstrated signficant interest in and commitment to the field of historic preservation evidenced either by involvement in a local historic preservation group, employment, or volunteer activity in the field of historic preservation, or other serious interest in the field;
>
> and all members shall have a known interest in historic preservation and architectural development within the Village / Town / City of _____.

(b) Commission members shall serve for a term of four years, with the exception of the initial term of one of the _____ members which shall be one year, one which shall be two years, and one which shall be three years.

(c) The chairman and vice chairman of the commisssion shall be elected by and from among the members of the commission.

(d) The powers of the commission shall include:

    (i) employment of staff and professional consultants as necessary to carry out the duties of the commission;

    (ii) promulgation of rules and regulations as necessary for the conduct of its business;

    (iii) adoption of criteria for the identification of significant historic, architectural, and cultural landmarks and for the delineation of historic districts;

    (iv) conduct of surveys of significanct historic, architectural, and cultural landmarks and historic districts within the village/town/city;

    (v) designation of identified structures or resources as landmarks and historic districts;

    (vi) acceptance on behalf of the village/town/city government of the donation of facade easements and development rights, and the making of recommendations to the village/town/city government concerning the acquisition of facade easements or other interests in real property as necessary to carry out the purposes of this act;

    (vii) increasing public awareness of the value of historic, cultural, and architectural preservation by developing and participating in public education programs;

    (viii) making recommendations to village/town/city government concerning the utilization of state, federal, or private funds to promote the preservation of landmarks and historic districts within the village/town/city;

    (ix) recommending acquisition of a landmark structure by the village/town/city government where its preservation is essential to the purposes of this act and where private preservation is not feasible;

    (x) approval or disapproval of applications for certificates of appropriateness pursuant to this act.

(e) The commission shall meet at least monthly, but meetings may be held at any time on the written request of any two of the commission members or on the call of the chairman or the mayor.

(f) A quorum for the transaction of business shall consist of _____ of the commission's members, but not less than a majority of the full authorized membership may grant or deny a certificate of appropriateness.

Section 3. Designation of Landmarks or Historic Districts

(a) The commission may designate an individual property as a landmark if it:

    (i) possesses special character or historic or aesthetic interest or value as part of the cultural, political, economic, or social history of the locality, region, state, or nation; or

    (ii) is identified with historic personages; or

    (iii) embodies the distinguishing characteristics of an architectural style; or

    (iv) is the work of a designer whose work has significantly influenced an age; or

    (v) because of unique location or singular physical characteristic, represents an established and familiar visual feature of the neighborhood.

(b) The commission may designate a group of properties as a historic district if it:

    (i) contains properties which meet one or more of the criteria for designation of a landmark; and

    (ii) by reason of possessing such qualities, it constitutes a distinct section of the village / town / city.

The boundaries of each historic district designated henceforth shall be specified in detail and shall be filed, in writing, in the village / town / city clerk's office for public inspection.

(c) Notice of a proposed designation shall be sent by registered mail to the owner of the property proposed for designation, describing the property proposed and announcing a public hearing by the commission to consider the designation. Where the proposed designation involves so many owners that individual notice is infeasible, notice may instead be published at least once in a newspaper of general circulation at least _____ days prior to the date of the public hearing. Once the commission has issued notice of a proposed designation, no building permits shall be issued by the building inspector until the commission has made its decision.

(d) The commission shall hold a public hearing prior to designation of any landmark or historic district. The commission, owners, and any interested parties may present testimony or documentary evidence at the hearing which will become part of a record regarding the historic, architectural, or cultural importance of the proposed landmark or historic district. The record may also contain staff reports, public comments, or other evidence offered outside of the hearing.

(e) The commission shall forward notice of each property designated as a landmark and the boundaries of each designated historic district to the offices of the _____ County Clerk for recordation.

Section 4. Certificate of Appropriateness for Alteration, Demolition or New Construction Affecting Landmarks or Historic Districts

No person shall carry out any exterior alteration, restoration, reconstruction, demolition, new construction, or moving of a landmark or property within a historic district, nor shall any person make any material change in the appearance of such property, its light fixtures, signs, sidewalks, fences, steps, paving, or other exterior elements visible from a public street or alley which affect the appearance and cohesiveness of the historic district, without first obtaining a certificate of appropriateness from the historic preservation commission.

Section 5. Criteria for Approval of a Certificate of Appropriateness

(a) In passing upon an application for a certificate of appropriateness, the historic preservation commission shall not consider changes to interior spaces, unless they are open to the public, or to architectural features that are not visible from a public street or alley.

The commission's decision shall be based on the following principles:

    (i) properties which contribute to the character of the historic district shall be retained, with their historic features altered as little as possible;

    (ii) any alteration of existing properties shall be compatible with its historic character, as well as with the surrounding district; and

(iii) new construction shall be compatible with the district in which it is located.

(b) In applying the principle of compatibility, the commission shall consider the following factors:

(i) the general design, character, and appropriateness to the property of the proposed alteration or new construction;

(ii) the scale of proposed alteration or new construction in relation to the property itself, surrounding properties, and the neighborhood;

(iii) texture, materials, and color and their relation to similar features of other properties in the neighborhood;

(iv) visual compatibility with surrounding properties, including proportion of the property's front facade, proportion and arrangement of windows and other openings within the facade, roof shape, and the rhythm of spacing of properties on streets, including setback;

(v) the importance of historic, architectural, or other features to the significance of the property.

Section 6. Certificate of Appropriateness Application Procedure

(a) Prior to the commencement of any work requiring a certificate of appropriateness, the owner shall file an application for such a certificate with the historic preservation commission. The application shall contain:

(i) name, address, and telephone number of applicant;

(ii) location and photographs of property;

(iii) elevation drawings of proposed changes, if available;

(iv) perspective drawings, including relationship to adjacent properties, if available;

(v) samples of color or materials to be used;

(vi) where the proposal includes signs or lettering, a scale drawing showing the type of lettering to be used, all dimensions and colors, a description of materials to be used, method of illumination, and a plan showing the sign's location on the property;

(vii) any other information which the commission may deem necessary in order to visualize the proposed work.

(b) No building permit shall be issued for such proposed work until a certificate of appropriateness has first been issued by the historic preservation commission. The certificate of appropriateness required by this act shall be in addition to and not in lieu of any building permit that may be required by any other ordinance of the Village / Town / City of _____.

(c) The commission shall approve, deny, or approve the permit with modifications within _____ days from receipt of the completed application. The commission may hold a public hearing on the application at which an opportunity will be provided for proponents and opponents of the application to present their views.

(d) All decisions of the commission shall be in writing. A copy shall be sent to the applicant by registered mail and a copy filed with the village / town / city clerk's office for public inspection. The commission's decisions shall state the reasons for denying or modifying any application.

Section 7. Hardship Criteria

(a) An applicant whose certificate of appropriateness for a proposed demolition has been denied may apply for relief on the ground of hardship. In order to prove the existence of hardship, the applicant shall establish that:

    (i)   the property is incapable of earning a reasonable return, regardless of whether that return represents the most profitable return possible;

    (ii) the property cannot be adapted for any other use, whether by the current owner or by a purchaser, which would result in a reasonable return; and

    (iii) efforts to find a purchaser interested in acquiring the property and preserving it have failed.

(b) An applicant whose certificate of appropriateness for a proposed alteration has been denied may apply for relief on the ground of hardship. In order to prove the existence of hardship, the applicant shall establish that the property is incapable of earning a reasonable return, regardless of whether that return represents the most profitable return possible.

Section 8. Hardship Application Procedure

(a) After receiving written notification from the commission of the denial of a certificate of appropriateness, an applicant may commence the hardship process. No building permit or demolition permit shall be issued unless the commission makes a finding that a hardship exists.

(b) The commission may hold a public hearing on the hardship application at which an opportunity will be provided for proponents and opponents of the application to present their views.

(c) The applicant shall consult in good faith with the commission, local preservation groups, and interested parties in a diligent effort to seek an alternative that will result in preservation of the property.

(d) All decisions of the commission shall be in writing. A copy shall be sent to the applicant by registered mail and a copy filed with the village / town / city clerk's office for public inspection. The commission's decision shall state the reasons for granting or denying the hardship application.

Section 9. Enforcement

All work performed pursuant to a certificate of appropriateness issued under this ordinance shall conform to any requirements included therein. It shall be the duty of the building code enforcement officer to inspect periodically any such work to assure compliance. In the event work is found that is not being performed in accordance with the certificate of appropriateness, or upon notification of such fact by the historic preservation commission, the building code enforcement officer shall issue a stop work order and all work shall immediately cease. No further work shall be undertaken on the project as long as a stop work order is in effect.

Section 10. Maintenance and Repair Required

Nothing in this ordinance shall be construed to prevent the ordinary maintenance and repair of any exterior architectural feature of a landmark or property within a historic district which does not involve a change in design, material, color, or outward appearance.

No owner or person with an interest in real property designated as a landmark or included within a historic district shall permit the property to fall into a serious state of disrepair so as to result in the deterioration of any exterior architectural feature which would, in the judgment of the historic preservation commission, produce a detrimental effect upon the character of the historic district as a whole or the life and character of the property itself.

Examples of such deterioration include:

(a) deterioration of exterior walls or other vertical supports;

(b) deterioration of roofs or other horizontal members;

(c) deterioration of exterior chimneys;

(d) deterioration or crumbling of exterior stucco or mortar;

(e) ineffective waterproofing of exterior walls, roofs, or foundations, including broken windows or doors;

(f) deterioration of any feature so as to create a hazardous condition which could lead to the claim that demolition is necessary for the public safety.

Section 11. Violations

(a) Failure to comply with any of the provisions of this ordinance shall be deemed a violation and the violator shall be liable to a fine of not less than _____ nor more than _____ for each day the violation continues.

(b) Any person who demolishes, alters, constructs, or permits a designated property to fall into a serious state of disrepair in violation of this ordinance shall be required to restore the property and its site to its appearance prior to the violation. Any action to enforce this subsection shall be brought by the village / town / city attorney. This civil remedy shall be in addition to and not in lieu of any criminal prosecution and penalty.

Section 12. Appeals

Any person aggrieved by a decision of the historic preservation commission relating to hardship or a certificate of appropriateness may, within _____ days of the decision, file a written application with the village / town / city board of trustees for review of the decision.

Local Landmark and Historic District Commissions

The following list of communities with local legislation for landmark and historic district designation and for design review has been compiled either from responses received by the Preservation League to questionnaires or from lists compiled by other groups working with local commissions and design review boards. The list is in no way meant to be exhaustive, nor does inclusion on the list necessarily imply any judgment about the quality of the legislation in a community or its compliance with the standards of any particular program.

Albany
City of Albany Historic Sites Commission
City Planning Office
City Hall
Albany, New York 12207
518-434-5190
established: 1966
staff: 1

Amityville
Amityville Board of Zoning
Building Inspector's Office
c/o Board of Trustees
Amityville, New York 11701

Babylon
Town of Babylon Department of Planning and Development
200 East Sunrise Highway
Lindenhurst, New York 11757

Bedford
Bedford Village Historic District Review Commission
Town House
321 Bedford Road
Bedford Hills, New York 10507
914-666-3137
established: 1972
staff: part-time

Bellport
Board of Architectural Review
Bellport, New York 11713

Binghamton
City of Binghamton Commission on Architecture and Urban Design
Office of Planning
City Hall
Binghamton, New York 13901
607-772-7063
established: 1978
staff: 1

Brewster
Village of Brewster Historic Preservation Commission
Town Hall
Brewster, New York 10509

Brighton
Town of Brighton Board of Architectural Review
2300 Elmwood Avenue
Rochester, New York 14618

Brookhaven
Town of Brookhaven Historic District Advisory Committee
Planning Board
475 East Main Street
Patchogue, New York 11772
516-689-9166
established: 1979

Buffalo
Buffalo Preservation Board
428 City Hall
Buffalo, New York 14202
716-855-5071
established: 1975
staff: 2

Canajoharie
Village of Canajoharie Planning and Town Boards
Municipal Building
Canajoharie, New York 13311

Canandaigua
City of Canandaigua Planning Commission
205 Saltonstall Street
Canandaigua, New York 14424
716-394-7850
established: 1975
staff: 1

Canastota
Village of Canastota
205 South Peterboro Street
Canastota, New York 13032

Canton
Canton Preservation Advisory Board
Municipal Building
Canton, New York 13617

Castleton-on-Hudson
Village of Castleton-on-Hudson Historic District Review Commission
P.O. Box 126
Castleton, New York 12033
518-732-2211
established: 1983

Charlton
Town of Charlton
RD 3, Stage Road
Ballston Lake, New York 12019

Chester
Village of Chester
47 Main Street
Chester, New York 10918

Clarkson
Clarkson Architectural Review Board
Town Hall
Clarkson, New York 14430
716-637-3011
established: 1974

Clarkstown
Town of Clarkstown
10 Maple Avenue
New City, New York 10956

Cohoes
City of Cohoes Planning Commission
City Hall
Cohoes, New York 12047
518-237-5242
established: 1960

Cold Spring-on-Hudson
Cold Spring-on-Hudson Architectural Review Board
87 Main Street
Cold Spring, New York 10516
914-265-3611
established: 1972

Cooperstown
Cooperstown Planning Board
22 Main Street, P.O. Box 346
Cooperstown, New York 13326
607-547-3290
established: 1983

Cortland
City of Cortland
City Hall
Cortland, New York 13045

Coxsackie
Village of Coxsackie
38 Mansion Street
Coxsackie, New York 12051

Dobbs Ferry
Village of Dobbs Ferry
112 Main Street
Dobbs Ferry, New York 10522

East Aurora
Village of East Aurora Historic
Preservation Commission
Village Hall
571 Main Street
East Aurora, New York 14052
716-652-6000
established: 1987

East Hampton
Village of East Hampton Design
Review Board
27 Main Street
East Hampton, New York 11937
516-324-4150
established: 1983

Endicott
Endicott Historic Preservation
Commission
Municipal Building
Main Street
Endicott, New York 13760
607-757-2420
established: 1986
staff: 1

Fayetteville
Village of Fayetteville Historic
Review Commission
425 East Genesee Street
Fayetteville, New York 13066
315-637-9864
established: 1986
staff: 1

Freeport
Village of Freeport
46 North Ocean Avenue
Freeport, New York 11520

Garden City
Garden City Review Board
c/o Board of Trustees
Town Hall
Garden City, New York 11530

Geneva
Geneva Historic Zoning
Commission
543 South Main Street
Geneva, New York 14456
315-789-1751
established: 1969

Glens Falls
City of Glens Falls
42 Ridge Street
Glens Falls, New York 12801

Goshen
Village Hall
276 Main Street
Goshen, New York 10924

Great Neck
Great Neck Landmarks
Preservation Commission
c/o Board of Trustees
Village Hall
Great Neck, New York 11023

Head-of-the-Harbor
Head-of-the-Harbor Board of
Architectural Review
27 Bacon Road
St. James, New York 11780
516-584-5550
established: 1965

Hempstead
Town of Hempstead Landmarks
Preservation Commission
Public Information Office
350 Front Street
Hempstead, New York 11550

Henrietta
Henrietta Historic Site
Committee
475 Calkins Road
Henrietta, New York 14467
716-334-7700
established: 1977
staff: 1

Huntington
Town of Huntington Historic
Preservation Commission
228 Main Street
Huntington, New York 11743
516-421-5065
established: 1969

Hyde Park
Town of Hyde Park
P.O. Box 2002
Hyde Park, New York 12538

Irvington
Village of Irvington
85 Main Street
Irvington, New York 10533

Islip
Town of Islip Planned Landmark
Preservation Committee
655 Main Street
Islip, New York 11751
516-224-5450
established: 1977

Ithaca
Ithaca Landmarks Preservation
Commission
108 East Green Street
Ithaca, New York 14850
established: 1970
staff: 1

Johnson City
Johnson City Planning
Department
Municipal Building
Johnson City, New York 13790

Katonah
Katonah Historic District
Advisory Commission
Town House
321 Bedford Road
Bedford Hills, New York 10507

Kinderhook
Village of Kinderhook
Village Hall
Kinderhook, New York 12106

Kingston
City of Kingston Landmark
Preservation Commission
City Hall
One Garraghan Drive
Kingston, New York 12401
914-331-0560
established: 1966
staff: 2

Lake George
Village of Lake George
Architectural Review Board
Amherst Street
Lake George, New York 12845

Lake Placid
Village of Lake Placid
301 Main Street
Lake Placid, New York 12946

Lancaster
Village of Lancaster Historic
Preservation Commission
5423 Broadway
Lancaster, New York 14086

Larchmont
Village of Larchmont
Municipal Building
Larchmont, New York 10538

Lewisboro
Town of Lewisboro Landmarks
Advisory Committee
Town House
Main Street
South Salem, New York 10590

Lewiston
Village of Lewiston Historic
Preservation Commission
145 North Fourth Street
Lewiston, New York 14092
716-754-8271
established: 1978

Lloyd Harbor
Village of Lloyd Harbor
32 Middle Hollow Road
Huntington, New York 11743

Mamaroneck
Village of Mamaroneck
Landmarks Advisory Committee
169 Mount Pleasant Avenue,
P.O. Box 369
Mamaroneck, New York 10543
914-698-7434
established: 1982

McGraw
Village of McGraw
Planning Board
Cemetery Street, P.O. Box 537
McGraw, New York 13101
607-836-6294
established: 1981
staff: 1

New Hempstead
Village of New Hempstead
8 Old Schoolhouse Road
New City, New York 10956

New Hyde Park
Village of New Hyde Park
Historic Landmark Preservation
Commission
9 Baxter Avenue
New Hyde Park, New York
11040

New Paltz
Village of New Paltz
P.O. Box 877
New Paltz, New York 12561

New Rochelle
New Rochelle Department of
Development
City Hall
515 North Avenue
New Rochelle, New York 10801

New York City
New York Landmarks
Preservation Commission
225 Broadway
New York, New York 10007
212-553-1100
established: 1965
staff: 59

Newburgh
Village of Newburgh
Architectural Review
Commission
83 Broadway
Newburgh, New York 12550

Nissequogue
Village of Nissequogue
P.O. Box 352
St. James, New York 11780

North Castle
North Castle Landmarks
Preservation Committee
c/o Town Clerk
Town Hall
Armonk, New York 10504
914-273-3221
established: 1970

North Elba
Town of North Elba
301 Main Street
Lake Placid, New York 12946

North Hempstead
Town of North Hempstead
Historic Preservation
Commission
220 Plandome Road
Manhasset, New York 11030
516-627-0590
established: 1984
staff: 1

Northport
Village of Northport Board of
Architectural and Historic
Review
224 Main Street, P.O. Box 358
Northport, New York 11768
established: 1981

Nyack
Village of Nyack Historic
District and Landmarks
Preservation Commission
Nyack, New York 10960
914-358-0548
established: 1985

Orangetown
Town of Orangetown Historic
Areas Board of Review
Town Hall
Orangeburg, New York 10962
914-359-5100

Ossining
Village of Ossining Historic
Review Commission
Building Department
31 Water Street
Ossining, New York 10562
914-941-3199
established: 1975
staff: 1

Oswego
City of Oswego
City Hall
West Oneida Street
Oswego, New York 13126

Owego
Village of Owego Architectural
Review Board
90 Temple Street
Owego, New York 13827
607-687-3555
established: 1986

Oyster Bay
Town of Oyster Bay Landmarks
Preservation Commission
Town Hall
Audrey Avenue
Oyster Bay, New York 11771
516-922-5800
established: 1974
staff: 1

Patchogue
Patchogue Historic District
Advisory Committee
Town Hall
205 South Ocean Avenue
Patchogue, New York 11772

Peekskill
Peekskill Historic Preservation
Advisory Board
840 Main Street
Peekskill, New York 10566
914-737-3400
established: 1984

Penfield
Penfield Historic
Preservation Board
Town Hall
3100 Atlantic Avenue
Penfield, New York 14526
716-377-5500
established: 1973

Phoenix
Village of Phoenix/Town of
Schroeppel Preservation
Commission
Main Street
Phoenix, New York 13135
315-695-6082
established: 1986

Pittsford
Village of Pittsford Historic
Site Committee
98 Tall Oak Lane
Pittsford, New York 14534

Plandome
Village of Plandome Historic
Landmarks Preservation
Commission
44 Rockwood Road
Plandome, New York 11030

Pleasantville
Village of Pleasantville
P.O. Box 0236
Pleasantville, New York 10570

Port Washington North
Port Washington North
Landmarks Preservation
Commission
Village Hall
One Sound View
Port Washington North,
New York 11050

Potsdam
Village of Potsdam
Civic Center
Potsdam, New York 13676

Poughkeepsie
Poughkeepsie Historic District
and Landmarks Preservation
Commission
P.O. Box 300
Poughkeepsie, New York 12602
914-431-8415
established: 1979
staff: 2

Pound Ridge
Town of Pound Ridge Landmark
and Historic District
Commission
Town House
Westchester Avenue
Pound Ridge, New York 10576
914-764-5511
established: 1971

Putnam Valley
Town of Putnam Valley
Town Hall
Putnam Valley, New York 10579

Riverhead
Riverhead Town Landmarks
Preservation Commission
Town Hall
200 Howell Avenue
Riverhead, New York 11901
516-727-5126
established: 1976

Riverside
Village of Riverside
35 Stanton Street
Painted Post, New York 14870

Rochester
City of Rochester
Preservation Board
Zoning Bureau, City Hall
30 Church Street
Rochester, New York 14614
716-428-7063
established: 1969
staff: 1

Rochester
Town of Rochester
Box 155, RD 1
Accord, New York 12404

Rockville Centre
Village of Rockville Centre
Architectural Review Board
One College Place
Rockville Centre, New York
11571
516-766-0300 x 212
established: 1966

Rome
Rome Historic & Scenic
Preservation Commission
City Hall
Rome, New York 13440
315-336-6000 x 243
established: 1978

Roslyn
Village of Roslyn Historic
District Board
William M. Valentine House
One Paper Mill Road
Roslyn, New York 11576
516-625-0236
established: 1979

Rye
City of Rye Landmarks
Advisory Committee
City Hall
Rye, New York 10580
914-967-5400
established: 1977

Sackets Harbor
Village of Sacketts Harbor
Planning Board
112 North Broad Street
Sackets Harbor, New York
13685
315-782-5250
established: 1984

Sag Harbor
Village of Sag Harbor Historic
Preservation Commission
Main Street, P.O. Box 660
Sag Harbor, New York 11963
established: 1972

Saratoga Springs
City of Saratoga Springs Historic
Review Commission
City Hall
Broadway
Saratoga Springs, New York
12866
518-584-3550
established: 1977
staff: 2

Saugerties
Saugerties Historic District
Review Board
Partition Street, P.O. Box 96
Saugerties, New York 12477
914-246-2321
established: 1986

Schenectady
Schenectady Historic
District Commission
City Hall
Schenectady, New York 12305
518-382-5049
established: 1954

Schroeppel
Town of Phoenix / Town of
Schroeppel Preservation
Commission
Main Street
Phoenix, New York 13135
315-695-6082
established: 1986

Scottsville
Village of Scottsville, Rochester
Street Historic District
Review Commission
22 Main Street
Scottsville, New York 14546
716-889-4700
established: 1976

Sea Cliff
Village of Sea Cliff
Landmarks Commission
c/o Sea Cliff Landmarks
Association
Box 69
Sea Cliff, New York 11579

Seneca Falls
Seneca Falls Historic
District Commission
60 State Street
Seneca Falls, New York 13148
315-568-6894
established: 1980
staff: 1

Setauket
Setauket Landmarks Preservation
Commission
c/o Society for the Preservation
of Long Island Antiquities
93 North Country Road
Setauket, New York 11733

Skaneateles
Village of Skaneateles
Historical Landmarks
Preservation Commission
46 East Genesee Street
Skaneateles, New York 13152
315-685-3440
established: 1975
staff: 1

Smithtown
Village of Smithtown
P.O. Box 725
Smithtown, New York 11787

Somers
Town of Somers Planning Board
Somers, New York 10589
914-277-5366
established: 1978

South Salem
Village of South Salem
Landmarks Committee
c/o William Strauss
RFD
South Salem, New York 10590

Southampton
Village of Southampton
23 Main Street
Southampton, New York 11968

Southold
Southold Landmark Preservation
Commission
Town Hall
53095 Main Road,
P.O. Box 1179
Southold, New York 11971

Syracuse
Syracuse Landmark
Preservation Board
1100 Civic Center
421 Montgomery Street
Syracuse, New York 13202
315-425-2611
established: 1975
staff: 2

Tappan
Hamlet of Tappan Historic Area
Board of Review
62 Hickory Hill Road
Tappan, New York 10983

Tarrytown
Tarrytown Historic Architectural
Review Board
Village Hall
Tarrytown, New York 10591
914-631-1106
established: 1978

Troy
City of Troy Historic District
and Landmarks Review
Commission
Department of Planning and
Community Development
City Hall, Monument Square
Troy, New York 12180
518-270-4476
established: 1975
staff: 1

Tuxedo Park
Village of Tuxedo Park Board of
Architectural Review
Village Office
Tuxedo Park, New York 10987
914-351-4745
established: 1972

Utica
City of Utica
City Planning Board
One Kennedy Plaza
Utica, New York 13502
315-792-0181
established: 1970
staff: 1

Village of The Branch
Village of The Branch
P.O. Box 725
Smithtown, New York 11787

Wappinger
Town of Wappinger
P.O. Box 324
Wappingers Falls, New York
12590

Warwick
Village of Warwick
P.O. Box 369
Warwick, New York 10990

Waterford
Waterford Historical Commission
123 Fonda Road
Waterford, New York 12188
518-237-1416

Whitehall
Whitehall Historic Preservation
Commission
One Saunders Street
Whitehall, New York 12887
518-499-0871
established: 1985

Williamsville
Williamsville Historical
Preservation Commission
5565 Main Street,
P.O. Box 1557
Williamsville, New York 14221
716-632-4120
established: 1983

Yonkers
Yonkers Architectural
Board of Review
87 Nepperhan Avenue,
Room 311
Yonkers, New York 10701
914-964-3384
established: 1969

Yorktown
Town of Yorktown
Town Hall
363 Underhill Avenue
Yorktown Heights, New York
10598

Bibliography

General Information on Historic Districts

Beasley, Ellen. *Reviewing New Construction Projects in Historic Areas.* Boston, MA: Northeast Regional Office, National Trust for Historic Preservation, 1986.

Dennis, Stephen N., ed.; and Zizzi, Andrea, compiler. *Directory of American Preservation Commissions.* Washington, DC: The Preservation Press, National Trust for Historic Preservation, 1981.

Duerkson, Christopher J., ed. *A Handbook on Historic Preservation Law.* Washington, DC: The Conservation Foundation, 1983.

Historic Districts: Identification, Social Aspects, and Preservation. Washington, DC: National Trust for Historic Preservation for the American Committee of the International Centre, 1975.

Lynch, Kevin. *The Image of the City.* Cambridge, MA: The MIT Press, 1960.

Maddex, Diane, ed. *All About Old Buildings.* Washington, DC: The Preservation Press, National Trust for Historic Preservation, 1985.

Williams, Norman; Kellogg, Edmund; and Gilbert, Frank, eds. *Readings in Historic Preservation.* New Brunswick, NJ: Rutgers University Center for Urban Policy Research, 1983.

Administration

Freund, Charles, and Gilbert, Frank. *Preserving Historic Districts:* A Training Manual for Historic Preservation Commissions and Boards of Architectural Review. Washington, DC: National Trust for Historic Preservation, 1986.

Thoreson Group. *A Training Program for Local Historic District Commissions.* Durham, NH: New England Municipal Center, 1980.

Design Review

Brolin, Brent C. *Architecture in Context: Fitting New Buildings with the Old.* New York, NY: Van Nostrand Reinhold Co., 1980.

Colorado Historical Society. *Good Neighbors: Building Next to History: Design Guidelines Handbook.* Colorado Historical Society, 1980.

Old and New Architecture, Design Relationship. Washington, DC: The Preservation Press, National Trust for Historic Preservation, 1980.

Legal Aspects

Berle, Kass & Case. *A Primer on Preservation Law in the State of New York.* New York, NY: National Center for Preservation Law, 1985.

Dennis, Stephen N. *Do's and Don'ts in Drafting a Preservation Ordinance.* Washington, DC: National Trust for Historic Preservation, 1982.

Roddewig, Richard J. *Preparing a Historic Preservation Ordinance.* Chicago, IL: American Planning Association, 1983.

Stipe, Robert. *Local Preservation Legislation: Questions and Answers.* Technical Series No. 8. Albany, NY: Preservation League of New York State, 1982.

Thurber, Pamela, and Moyer, Robert. *State Enabling Legislation for Local Preservation Commissions.* Preservation Policy Research Series. Washington, DC: National Trust for Historic Preservation, 1984.

Wilburn, Gary, and Dennis, Stephen N. "Historic Preservation Case Law: 1895-1979." *Preservation Law Reporter*, Reference Materials, November 1982, pp. 12,003-12,127.

Easements, Tax Incentives, and Revolving Funds

Easements, Tax Incentives, and Revolving Funds

Easements

An easement is an interest in a property that is less than outright ownership. It is a legal agreement between a property owner and the holder of the easement which governs the treatment of the property, runs with the land in perpetuity, and is binding on subsequent owners. There are three general types of preservation and conservation easements. First, scenic or open-space easements may be used to protect historic and scenic views, the surroundings of historically significant structures, archeological sites, and ecologically important land. These easements generally prohibit property owners from building on the land. A second type of preservation easement is a facade easement, which protects the outer architectural features of the structure. These agreements usually control alterations to the exterior and may prohibit further development on the property. The third type of preservation easement is an interior easement, which protects the interior of a structure from alterations. This type of agreement, however, is not common because it is difficult to review interior spaces in privately used buildings.

Upon the donation of an easement to a government body or qualifying not-for-profit organization, the owner is eligible to receive a Federal income tax deduction. In order to receive the deduction, easements must be donated on certified historic structures or historically important land areas. This includes all properties and areas listed in the National Register of Historic Places or located in a registered historic district and certified by the Secretary of the Interior as being of historic significance to the district.

Through preservation easements the property owner relinquishes the right to alter a structure or open space in a manner inconsistent with the historic character of the property. However, the owner retains all other property rights.

Sources

Appraising Easements: Guidelines for Valuation of Historic Preservation and Land Conservation Easements. Washington, DC: National Trust for Historic Preservation and Land Trust Exchange, 1984.

Coughlin, Thomas. *Easements and Other Legal Techniques to Protect Historic Houses in Private Ownership.* Washington, DC: Historic House Program, 1981.

Diehl, Janet; Barrett, Thomas S; and others. *The Conservation Easement Handbook: Managing Land Conservation and Historic Preservation Easement Programs.* Washington, DC: Land Trust Exchange and Trust for Public Lands, 1988.

Fisher, Charles; MacRostie, William; and Sowick, Christopher. *Directory of Historic Preservation Easement Organizations.* Washington, DC: Technical Preservation Services, U.S. Department of the Interior, 1981.

Veeder-Montgomery, Marilyn. *Preservation Easements: A Legal Mechanism for Protecting Cultural Resources.* Denver, CO: Colorado Historical Society, 1984.

Preservation Easements. Annapolis, MD: Maryland Historical Trust, 1977.

Watson, A. Elizabeth. *Establishing an Easement Program to Protect Historic, Scenic, and Natural Resources.* Rev. ed. Information Series. National Trust for Historic Preservation. Washington, DC: Preservation Press, 1982.

Zick, Steven. *Preservation Easements: The Legislative Framework.* Preservation Policy Research Series. Washington, DC: National Trust for Historic Preservation, 1984.

Tax Incentives
Rehabilitation Tax Credit

By rehabilitating directly or investing in the rehabilitation of eligible buildings, taxpayers can take advantage of a two-tier tax credit. The federal income tax credit is equal to 20% of the cost of rehabilitating historic buildings or 10% of the cost of rehabilitating non-historic buildings constructed prior to 1936. These credits provide a dollar-for-dollar reduction of income tax owed. They are available for historic and non-historic buildings only if the buildings are used in trade or business, or held for the production of income. Buildings eligible for the 20% rehabilitation credit include those used for rental residential as well as non-residential purposes, while buildings eligible for the 10% credit must be non-residential, commercial, or industrial buildings.

To qualify for the 20% credit, a building must be a "certified historic structure" listed in the National Register of Historic Places, either individually or in a registered historic district, and certified by the Secretary of the Interior as being of historical significance to the district. A 10% rehabilitation credit is available only for non-residential, non-historic buildings built before 1936; it is not available for certified historic structures.

To receive a rehabilitation credit, a taxpayer must substantially rehabilitate a qualifying historic building. "Substantial" means that the expenditures must be equal to the purchase price of the building, and must be incurred during a 24-month period. To qualify for the 20% credit, the rehabilitation must also be consistent with the historic character of the building and, where applicable, with the district in which the building is located; this must be certified by the Department of the Interior. No certification of rehabilitation work is necessary to obtain the 10% credit.

Sources

Andrews, Gregory G., ed. *Tax Incentives for Historic Preservation.* Washington, DC: National Trust for Historic Preservation, 1981.

Preservation Tax Incentives for Historic Buildings. Washington, DC: National Park Service, 1987.

The Secretary of the Interior's Standards for Rehabilitation with Guidelines for Rehabilitating Historic Buildings. Washington, DC: National Park Service, 1983.

Spatz, Ian D., ed. *A Guide to Tax Advantaged Rehabilitation.* Washington, DC: National Trust for Historic Preservation, 1986.

Additional information on the tax credits can be obtained from the New York State Office of Parks, Recreation and Historic Preservation (see p.64) and the Mid-Atlantic Regional Office of the National Park Service (see p.41)

Revolving Funds

A revolving fund is a fund formed for the purpose of preserving the historic character of a community through the acquisition and restoration of historically or architecturally significant properties, and the subsequent disposition of those properties. In other words, funds are raised and used to buy and restore property; the restored property is then sold and the money from the sale put into the fund for reinvestment in another preservation project. A revolving fund gives an organization the ability to carry out consecutive preservation projects independent of a fluctuating financial environment. To operate a revolving fund, it is necessary to have some concrete objective or project, the money necessary to accomplish the goal, and an administrative body capable of planning and executing the activities necessary to achieve the goal.

Adequate financial assistance is essential to any preservation project. Conventional construction financing may be difficult to obtain when the project is the restoration of an old building. Often such structures are high-risk investments because they are located in less than desirable areas or may appear to be capable of yielding civic and historical, rather than monetary, returns. To fill this investment vacancy various devices have been developed, one of which is the revolving fund.

A revolving fund is started with seed money. Sources of seed money are varied and include loans, grants, and gifts. Seed money can be used as leverage to obtain additional money from civic-minded corporations, banks, or individuals. The seed money may represent only 10 to 20% of the total cost of a low-risk project, while in high-risk projects it may equal 70%. Obtaining a high degree of leverage depends on successful negotiation and a sympathetic financial environment. The resulting balance of seed money and additional funds creates a base for the revolving fund.

The legal form of a revolving fund should be a charitable corporation which then obtains exemption from federal income tax by qualifying under section 501 (c)(3) of the Internal Revenue Code. Such exemption makes gifts to the organization tax deductible and usually is a prerequisite for grants from foundations and certain federal government programs. Incorporation and application for the federal tax exemption of a new entity should be done as soon as possible. It may be, however, that an appropriate existing 501(c)(3) preservation organization is available to operate the revolving fund, which should expedite the approval of such operation by the Internal Revenue Service, or that an existing organization can be used to raise seed money under its tax exemption until the new entity to operate the revolving fund obtains its own exemption.

The final ingredient necessary for a successful revolving fund is an administrative staff capable of developing and carrying out an effective procedure for achieving the preservation goal with the money available. The size and sophistication of the administrative staff is based on the complexity of the project; small projects may require only two or three administrators in addition to an architect and contractor, whereas a large project may require as many as 20 staff members as well as a lawyer, real estate broker, architect, and others. Small groups may solicit assistance in these areas from civic-minded corporations, city agencies, or professional associations.

Not all projects require a revolving fund. A single structure may be preserved, for example, by soliciting funds to complete the work in a single phase. Revolving funds are of benefit when the preservation project is so large and financing so limited that several phases are required for completion. As one phase is completed, it generates enough capital to finance the next phase, and so on until the project is finished.

Sources

Brink, Peter. *Commercial Area Revolving Funds for Preservation.* Information Series, National Trust for Historic Preservation. Washington, DC: Preservation Press, 1976.

Coffey, Steven. *Revolving Funds for Neighborhood Preservation: Lafayette Square, St. Louis.* Information Series, National Trust for Historic Preservation. Washington, DC: Preservation Press, 1977.

The Revolving Fund Handbook: A Practical Guide to Establishing a Revolving Fund and the Development Through Adaptive Reuse of Historic Properties. Architectural Conservation Trust for Masschusetts and Architectural Heritage Foundation. Boston, MA: Architectural Conservation Trust, 1979.

"Revolving Funds: Recycling Resources for Neighborhoods." *Conserve Neighborhoods,* May/June, 1981. National Trust for Historic Preservation.

Ziegler, Arthur. *Revolving Funds for Historic Preservation: A Manual of Practice.* Pittsburgh, PA: Ober Park Associates, 1975.

Educational Programs

Educational Programs

Educational Programs

Degree Programs

As the historic preservation field has grown dramatically over the past decade, degree programs in the field have expanded accordingly. Those colleges and universities in New York State offering degree programs in historic preservation and preservation-related fields such as architecture and architectural history are listed in this section. Not only do these institutions provide training for individuals, but their programs often include projects that may be of benefit to a community and may offer opportunities for cooperative activities with local preservation organizations. Additions to this list are welcome. For lists of programs at institutions outside New York State, contact the Society of Architectural Historians (see p.29), the National Council for Preservation Education (see p.24), or the National Trust for Historic Preservation / Human Resources Office (see below).

City College of the City University of New York
School of Architecture and Environmental Studies
Convent Avenue and
138th Street
New York, New York 10031
212-690-4118
B. Architecture; B.S. Landscape Architecture

City University of New York
Graduate School of Art History
33 West 42nd Street
New York, New York 10036
212-790-4451
Ph.D. Art History

Columbia University
Department of Art History and Archaeology
Graduate School of Arts and Sciences
826 Schermerhorn Hall
New York, New York 10027
212-280-4505
M.A.; M.Phil.; Ph.D. Art History

Columbia University
Graduate School of Architecture and Planning
Avery Hall
New York, New York 10027
212-280-3504
M. Architecture; M.S. Historic Preservation

> Preservation Alumni, Inc.
> P.O. Box 669
> New York, New York 10272
> 212-280-3504

Cooper Union
School of Architecture
New York, New York 10003
212-254-6397
B. Architecture

Cornell University
College of Architecture, Art, and Planning
106 West Sibley Hall
Ithaca, New York 14853
607-255-7439
B. Architecture; M. Architecture; M.A. and Ph.D. History of Architecture and Urbanism; M.A. Preservation Planning; Ph.D. Planning, Urban History and Historic Preservation

> Historic Preservation Planning Alumni
> P.O Box 4362
> Ithaca, New York 14852
> 607-255-6848

Cornell University
Landscape Architecture Program
230 East Roberts Hall
Ithaca, New York 14853
607-255-4487
B.S. Landscape Architecture; M. Landscape Architecture

Fashion Institute of Technology
Interior Design Department
227 West 27th Street
New York, New York 10001
212-760-7800
courses offered in the history of interiors

New York School of Interior Design
155 East 56th Street
New York, New York 10022
212-753-5365
courses offered in the history of interiors

New York University
Institute of Fine Arts
One East 78th Street
New York, New York 10021
212-772-5800
M.A.; Ph.D. Art History

New York University
Urban Planning Program
4 Washington Square North
New York, New York 10003
212-998-7430
M. Urban Planning; M.A. History; workshops offered in historic preservation, environment, and the arts

Pratt Institute
School of Architecture
200 Willoughby Avenue
Brooklyn, New York 11205
718-636-3407
B. Architecture; M. Architecture

Rensselaer Polytechnic Institute
Department of Anthropology and Sociology
Troy, New York 12180
518-276-6574
M.S. Public Archaeology— emphasis on historic preservation

Rensselaer Polytechnic Institute
School of Architecture
Troy, New York 12180
518-276-6460
B. Architecture; M. Architecture

State University of New York at Binghamton
Department of Art History
Binghamton, New York 13901
607-777-2111
M.A.; Ph.D. Art History

State University of New York at Binghamton
Department of Anthropology
Public Archaeology Facility
Binghamton, New York 13901
607-777-4786
M.S. Public Archaeology

**State University of
New York at Buffalo**
School of Architecture and
Environmental Design
139 Hayes Hall
34-35 Main Street
Buffalo, New York 14214
716-831-3485
B.A. Environmental Design; M.
Architecture; M. Urban Planning

Friends of the School
of Architecture and
Environmental Design
SUNY at Buffalo
Hayes Hall
34-35 Main Street
Buffalo, New York 14214
716-831-3543

**State University of New York
College at Buffalo**
Art History Department
Buffalo, New York 14215
716-878-6108
courses offered in architectural
history

**State University of New York
College of Environmental Science
and Forestry**
Faculty of Landscape
Architecture
Syracuse, New York 13210
315-470-6541
B. Landscape Architecture;
M. Landscape Architecture

**State University of New York
College at Oneonta**
Cooperstown Graduate Program
Cooperstown, New York 13326
607-547-2533
M.A. American Folk Culture;
M.A. Conservation of Historic
and Artistic Works; M.A.
History Museum Studies

Syracuse University
Department of Fine Arts in
cooperation with the School of
Architecture
441 Hall of Languages
Syracuse, New York 13244-1170
315-423-4069 / 4184
M.A. Art History; Ph.D.
Humanities

Syracuse University
School of Architecture
Syracuse, New York 13210
315-423-2256
B. Architecture; M. Architecture

Summer Programs

Within New York State, summer
institutes related to historic
preservation are sponsored annually by the New York State
Historical Association and
Rensselaer Polytechnic Institute.
Listed below are the addresses of
these and other summer internships and educational programs
in historic preservation and
related fields. The Human Resources Office of the National
Trust maintains a file on such
programs around the country.

Archaeological Field School
Department of Archaeology
Rensselaer Polytechnic Institute
Troy, New York 12180
518-276-6574
six weeks

Attingham Summer School
The American Friends of
Attingham Summer School, Inc.
285 Central Park West
New York, New York 10024
212-362-0701
three weeks

Christie's
Personnel Office
502 Park Avenue
New York, New York 10022
212-546-1111
ten-fourteen weeks

Eastfield Village
RD, Box 143
East Nassau, New York 12062
518-766-2422
one-five days

**Environmental Intern
Program / Northeast**
68 Harrison Avenue
Boston, Massachusetts 02111
617-426-4783
twelve weeks

**Historic American
Buildings Survey**
National Park Service
U.S. Department of the Interior
Washington, D.C. 20402
202-343-9625
six-eight weeks

**Historic American
Engineering Record**
National Park Service
U.S. Department of the Interior
Washington, D.C. 20402
202-343-9625
six-eight weeks

**National Trust
Summer Intern Program**
Human Resources Office
National Trust
for Historic Preservation
1785 Massachusetts
Avenue, N.W.
Washington, D.C. 20036
202-673-4120

Seminars on American Culture
New York State
Historical Association
Cooperstown, New York 13326
607-547-2533
one-two weeks

Sotheby's
Personnel Department
1334 York Avenue
New York, New York 10022
212-606-7202
six weeks

Summer Institute
University of Vermont
322 South Prospect Street
Burlington, Vermont 05401-3505
802-656-2085
two days-one week

Victorian Society Summer School
The Victorian Society in America
219 South Sixth Street
Philadelphia, Pennsylvania
19106
215-627-4252
three weeks

Yankee Intern Program
National Trust
for Historic Preservation
Northeast Regional Office
45 School Street, 4th Floor
Boston, Massachusetts 02108
617-523-0885
twelve weeks

Special Preservation Training Programs

Architectural Artisanry Program
Southeastern Massachusetts
University
1213 Purchase Street
New Bedford, Massachusetts
02740
508-999-8605

This program offers classroom
and studio instruction and
supervised appropriate work
experience at the college level to
train architectural artisans,
defined as professionals who
have "the academic, technical
and aesthetic abilities required to
work as an artist/craftsperson
on the design, construction
and/or preservation of architectural ornament, decorative
building elements, and works of
art within an architectural context."

Campbell Center
P.O. Box 66
Mount Carroll, Illinois 61053
815-244-1173

During the year, approximately
20 summer workshops and a
number of three- to five-day
workshops are held focusing on
the conservation of buildings,
furniture, decorative arts, and
museum collections.

Ironbridge Institute
Ironbridge Gorge Museum
Ironbridge
Telford, Shropshire
ENGLAND TF8 7AW
(0952 45) 2751

The Ironbridge Institute is a
center for research and professional training in industrial
archeology and heritage studies—management, interpretation,
and education—based in Coal-
brookdale, England, and administered jointly by the University of Birmingham and the Ironbridge Gorge Museum. The Institute offers a graduate program, special short course programs, and conferences and
seminars focusing on industrial
history, social history, and
archeology. Field work takes
place both within the Ironbridge
Gorge—a UNESCO World Heritage Site—and at other archeological sites, historic houses,
towns, and gardens throughout
England.

National Preservation Institute
National Building Museum
Judiciary Building, N.W.
Washington, D.C. 20001
202-393-0038

Short courses on historic
buildings and districts, cultural
landscapes, archeology, and the
history and practice of preservation.

**Pre-Conference
Training Workshops**
Association for
Preservation Technology
Box 2487
Station D
Ottawa, Ontario K1P 5W6
CANADA
613-238-1972

Offered at Association for
Preservation Technology annual
conferences, these two- to three-
day workshops on materials conservation, maintenance and
historical technologies are open
to contractors and tradesmen,
although primarily attended by
design professionals and administrators.

Preservation Carpentry Program
North Bennet Street School
39 North Bennet Street
Boston, Massachusetts 02113
617-227-0155

Now in its second year, this program offers a nine-month training program in restoration
carpentry for experienced
carpenters.

**Preservation Institute for the
Building Crafts**
Main Street
P.O. Box 1777
Windsor, Vermont 05089
802-674-6752

Professional advancement in
preservation building skills is em-
phasized through short courses
in plaster and wood conservation, masonry repointing, and
architectural history. Classes are
often held on weekends.

**Repair and Remodeling
Estimating**
R.S. Means Company
100 Construction Plaza
Kingston, Massachusetts 02364
617-585-7880

Offers two-day seminars at
varied locations for "discussion
of practical solutions to the difficult and varied cost estimating
problems associated with the
reuse and conversion of existing
structures."

Restore Skills Training Program
RESTORE
160 South Street
New York, New York 10038
212-766-0210

Nine-month evening course or
five-day workshop series designed to upgrade restoration
and preservation skills of craftsmen, contractors, architects,
engineers, and others in the
building trades; focus is on
analysis and resolution of
maintenance problems.

The Stoneyard Institute
1047 Amsterdam Avenue
New York, New York 10025
212-316-7400

Founded in 1979 to complete the
Cathedral of St. John the Divine,
the Institute teaches traditional
artisanry skills and stone
masonry construction. A two-
week summer program in stone-
cutting, carving and construction
techniques is offered to students
and design professionals.

Technical Assistance Programs

Sands Point Lighthouse (1809), Sands Point. John McComb, Jr. architect. Drawing by Herb Kashian.

Technical Assistance Programs

Technical Assistance Programs

Technical assistance programs in New York State have emerged during the last decade to service the increasingly sophisticated strategies developed by preservation organizations to save and manage historic properties. Each of the programs in New York State was established and has evolved to meet specific local needs. Technical assistance activities include in-house services, outside consulting or outreach, and public education through research and dissemination vehicles. In-house services are those activities requiring limited professional participation in one or more of the organization's advocacy initiatives, financial or legal services programs, and/or in management of a property system.

Outside consulting or outreach activities are those services provided to the organization's membership as a benefit and/or to the public at large to help fulfill the organization's general mission, for example, "to promote the appropriate preservation of historic buildings." In the latter case, the role of technical assistance activities is similar to that of trade organizations and manufacturer's product support systems, intended to provide accurate information and engender goodwill.

Another kind of outreach service is building inspection or "walk-throughs" conducted on a site visit. On one level, these serve a purpose similar to "energy audits" conducted by utilities and other organizations, in this case to assess a building's general maintenance and rehabilitation needs and potential. Some programs provide follow-up letters or conditions reports which organize the field data, recommend priorities, and in some cases, outline a preliminary

budget. Such documents are used by owners to help focus their efforts and, in the case of not-for-profits, as backup in funding proposals.

Assisting clients through the regulatory framework of the Tax Act and Environmental Quality Bond Act is another important outreach activity practiced by technical assistance programs. Workshops are a vehicle used to bring knowledgeable speakers from within and outside the community to examine a preservation issue. Some technical assistance programs provide construction administration services.

Technical Preservation Services Center
New York Landmarks Conservancy
141 Fifth Avenue
New York, New York 10010
212-995-5260

The New York Landmarks Conservancy established its Technical Preservation Services Center (TPSC) in 1979 to participate in Conservancy projects and to provide technical assistance to owners of landmark properties in New York City (all boroughs). TPSC provides major project review for the Conservancy's grant program, the Sacred Sites and Properties Fund, and a revolving loan fund for owners of landmark properties. TPSC has also mobilized to participate in advocacy initiatives for endangered landmark buildings in roles ranging from project review to project management.

TPSC promotes the appropriate rehabilitation and maintenance of landmark properties by directing research studies on local,

primarily urban, preservation issues and disseminating results to general and target audiences through publications, workshops, slide-tapes, and community sponsored presentations. Research is conducted by consultants at the direction of TPSC. TPSC has developed particular expertise in sandstone conservation, window rehabilitation, maintenance methods, and preservation of armories and religious properties. TPSC publishes *The Restoration Directory, Historic Building Facades: A Manual for Inspection and Rehabilitation*, and *The Maintenance and Repair of Architectural Sandstone*.

TPSC directly assists owners of landmark properties by acting as a preservation consultant in planning and implementing restoration and rehabilitation projects. Services include telephone consultation to all owners of landmark-quality buildings. Site visits and often follow-up letters that prioritize needs, identify options, and develop preliminary budgets are provided primarily to not-for-profit owners of designated properties. TPSC also provides project administration services on a fee basis, including assistance with Environmental Quality Bond Act applications, contract administration, and restoration project management.

Technical Assistance Program
Historic Ithaca and Tompkins County
120 North Cayuga Street
Ithaca, New York 14850
607-273-6633

Historic Ithaca's Technical Assistance Program provides the expertise of an architectural conservator to the owners of older and historic properties. Through site visits and consultation, the conservator examines and assesses a building's problems so as to recommend corrective and preventive measures. In addition, the architectural conservator works with homeowners to select interior and exterior treatments appropriate to the historic building. The program also provides advice on Environmental Quality Bond Act applications and National Register nominations.

The opportunity to augment technical assistance was provided in 1984 when Historic Ithaca became a Rural Preservation Company (RPC). Funded by the State Division of Housing and Community Renewal, the RPC provides free technical assistance to homeowners in rural Tompkins County, particularly those of low- to moderate-income. Surveys of housing conditions, specifications for rehabilitation, and individual consultations are offered under this program. In addition, the RPC renovates housing for sale to low- to moderate-income families.

Preservation Services
Society for the Preservation of Long Island Antiquities
93 North Country Road
Setauket, New York 11733
516-941-9444

The Society for the Preservation of Long Island Antiquities provides technical advice through a staff preservation services coordinator trained in architectural conservation. Services are available in Kings, Nassau, Queens, and Suffolk counties.

Preservation Services Division
Landmark Society of Western New York
130 Spring Street
Rochester, New York 14608
716-546-7029

The Landmark Society of Western New York (LSWNY) established its Preservation Services Division (PSD) in 1984. Much of PSD's activities are centered on the planning and administration of maintenance and rehabilitation projects at LSWNY's own historic properties, four of which are operated as house museums. This situation has allowed PSD to develop a strong core of professional staff with extensive hands-on experience. PSD focuses primarily on Monroe County, with services offered also in Genesee, Livingston, Ontario, Orleans, Wayne, Wyoming, and Yates counties.

Technical Services Unit
New York State Office of Parks, Recreation, and Historic Preservation
Agency Building 1
Empire State Plaza
Albany, New York 12238
518-474-7750

The Technical Services Unit provides inter- and intra-agency project review for compliance with state and federal regulations including Sec. 14.09 of the State Historic Preservation Act, Sec. 106 of the National Historic Preservation Act, the State Environmental Quality Bond Act, and investment tax credits.

The Unit provides technical assistance to property owners, design professionals, and other state agencies whose projects are subject to their review. Pre-application assistance and site visits are limited.

Design and Technical Services
Historic Albany Foundation
44 Central Avenue
Albany, New York 12206
518-463-0622

Historic Albany Foundation has provided technical assistance through a staff position since 1981. Services include assistance by telephone and site visits to buildings of members and non-members in the greater Albany area. The program maintains a source file of preservation craftspeople, services, and products for historic buildings available locally, regionally, and nationally.

Fee-based consulting services provided to developers engaged in investment tax credit rehabilitation projects include building research, photography, building survey, design assistance, and completion of application forms. Additionally, the office consults with developers on historic buildings prior to purchase concerning re-use strategies, integrity of existing fabric, and cost estimation.

The program is responsible for development and management of revolving loan fund projects and special housing rehabilitation projects; exhibitor solicitation for the annual Rehab Fair Northeast; initiates advocacy issues; and monitors city-wide architectural review.

**Westchester County
Department of Planning**
Division of Housing and Community Development
416 Michaelian Office Building
148 Martine Avenue
White Plains, New York 10601
914-285-2412

The Westchester County Department of Planning includes a position of Associate Planner: Historic Preservation, which was established to provide internal review of low- and moderate-income housing grants and loans, capital improvement projects in consortium communities, and general county projects impacting resources listed on or eligible for the State and National Registers for compliance with state and federal preservation regulations. The position also provides technical assistance to local governments, not-for-profit organizations, and other owners of listed, eligible, or locally designated properties through telephone consultation and public programming initiatives such as slide shows, workshops, and exhibits.

**Preservation League
Assistance Center**
Preservation League of
New York State
307 Hamilton Street
Albany, New York 12210
518-462-5658

The Preservation League of New York State established the Preservation League Technical Assistance Center (PLAC) in 1987 to serve owners and others involved in the preservation of architectural resources in New York State.

Preservation services, provided by the League's staff and a statewide network of professionals on a fee basis, include: survey of architectural resources; historic structures reports; building inspections and conditions reports; preparation of reports on stabilization, restoration, and rehabilitation options and priorities; training of local historic preservation commissions; telephone consultation on appropriate restoration design; and applied research.

PLAC gives priority to not-for-profit organizations, local preservation commissions, public agencies, concerned individuals in areas of New York State where technical assistance is not available, and members of the Preservation League.

Beebe Windmill (1821), Bridgehampton. Samuel Schellinger, builder. Drawing by Herb Kashian.

Regional and Local Organizations

Regional and Local Organizations

This section was compiled from information collected from a survey completed by the Preservation League in 1988. Entries are arranged alphabetically by county. The first four entries in each county are the county arts council, county historian, county historical society, and county planning office. The remaining entries are arranged alphabetically by community, then by the organizations in that community. Wherever possible, regional organizations whose jurisdictions extend beyond the county in which they are headquartered are cross-referenced in the other counties at the end of the county organizational listings.

A full listing contains the name of the organization; address; telephone number; mailing address (if different from organization address); name of director, president, or contact person; number of members; founding date; and major programs. Those organizations that did not respond to the questionnaire mailings are also listed, but the amount of information about the organization is considerably less than that of those that responded.

Albany County

County Arts Council

Albany League of Arts
19 Clinton Avenue
Albany, New York 12203
518-449-5380
Jacqueline Cavalier, Executive Director
members: 800
founded: 1946
staff: 4 full-time, 8 part-time, 50 volunteer
major programs: workshops, publications, periodical, grants, awards

County Historian

Robert W. Arnold III
250 South Pearl Street
Albany, New York 12202
518-434-3527

County Historical Society

Albany County Historical Association
9 Ten Broeck Place
Albany, New York 12210
518-436-9826
Jeane N. Miller, Executive Director
members: 120
founded: 1941
staff: 1 part-time, 10 volunteer
major programs: historic site, periodical, tours, lectures

County Planning Office

Albany County Planning Board
Stedman House
One Lodge Street
Albany, New York 12207
518-445-7964

see also Capital District Regional Planning Commission, Schenectady, Schenectady County; Federation of Historical Services, Troy, Rensselaer County

Albany

Albany County Hall of Records
250 South Pearl Street
Albany, New York 12202
518-434-3527
Robert W. Arnold III, Executive Director
founded: 1980
staff: 21 full-time, 7 part-time, 6 volunteer
major programs: archives, photo collection, periodical, research, school programs, tours, lectures, workshops, exhibits, publications, surveys

Albany Housing Coalition
95 Livingston Street
Albany, New York 12210

Albany Institute of History and Art
125 Washington Avenue
Albany, New York 12210
518-463-4478
Christine M. Miles, Director
members: 2,000
founded: 1791
staff: 35 full-time, 2 part-time
major programs: library, archives, museum, photo collection, research, school programs, tours, lectures, workshops, exhibits, periodical, publications, technical preservation services

Albany Public Library
161 Washington Avenue
Albany, New York 12210

Albany South End Historical Society
20 Second Avenue
Albany, New York 12202
518-463-0249
William J. Smith, President
members: 104
founded: 1984
staff: 4 volunteer
major programs: library, photo collection, lectures, markers program, periodical

Albany Urban Cultural Park
25 Quackenbush Square
Albany, New York 12207
518-434-5131
Elizabeth Spencer-Ralph, Director

Arbor Hill Development Corporation
92 Clinton Avenue
Albany, New York 12210
518-463-9993
Joseph P. Sluszka, Executive Director

Capital Region Center Institute
for Arts in Education
State University of New York
at Albany
Performing Arts Center,
Room 146
Albany, New York 12222
518-442-4240
Sandra Ray, Director
founded: 1984
staff: 3 full-time, 3 part-time
major programs: school
programs, tours, lectures,
workshops, archeology

Capitol Hill Improvement
Corporation
260 Lark Street
Albany, New York 12210
518-462-9696
Kathleen Dorgan, Executive
Director
founded: 1975
staff: 10 full-time, 2 part-time,
many volunteer
major programs: library,
lectures, workshops, periodical,
publications, awards, historic
preservation, rural preservation,
affordable housing, technical
preservation services

Dutch Settlers Society of Albany
23 Dresden Court
Albany, New York 12203
518-456-7202
John G. Wemple, Jr., President
members: 300
founded: 1924
staff: 4 volunteer
major programs: historic
preservation, periodical

Historic Albany Foundation
44 Central Avenue
Albany, New York 12206
518-463-0622
members: 700
founded: 1984
staff: 6 full-time, 5 part-time
major programs: school
programs, tours, lectures,
workshops, periodical, awards,
historic preservation, markers
program, technical preservation
services, grants, revolving fund,
easements

Historic Cherry Hill
523½ South Pearl Street
Albany, New York 12202
518-434-4791
Anne W. Ackerson, Director
members: 256
founded: 1964
staff: 4 full-time, 1 part-time,
30 volunteer
major programs: museum,
research, school programs, tours,
lectures, periodical, publications

Museum of the Historical Society
of Early American Decoration
19 Dove Street
Albany, New York 12210
518-462-1676
William Jenney, Museum
Director
members: 850
founded: 1946
staff: 1 full-time, 25 volunteer
major programs: museum,
research, tours, workshops,
exhibits, periodical, publications

South End Improvement
Corporation
34 Catherine Street
Albany, New York 12202

St. Joseph's Housing
Corporation
301 Clinton Avenue
Albany, New York 12210

West Hill Improvement
Corporation
340 First Street
Albany, New York 12206
518-462-6469
founded: 1976
staff: 4 full-time, 3 part-time
major programs: tool library,
historic preservation, easements,
grants, technical preservation
services, housing rehabilitation

Altamont

Albany-Schenectady-Greene
Counties Agricultural and
Historical Societies
Box 506, Altamont Fairgrounds
Altamont, New York 12009

Berne

Berne Historical Society
Berne Town Hall, P.O. Box 22
Berne, New York 12023

Coeymans

Historic Coeymans Preservation
Society
P.O. Box 1673
Coeymans, New York 12045

Coeymans Hollow

Little Red Schoolhouse
Historical Society
P.O. Box 25
Coeymans Hollow, New York
12046
Mrs. Arthur Gurney, Secretary
members: 50
founded: 1963
staff: all volunteer
major programs: museum,
research, school programs,
exhibits

Cohoes

Historical and Cultural
Society of Cohoes
P.O. Box 544
Cohoes, New York 12047

Hudson-Mohawk Urban
Cultural Park Commission
97 Mohawk Street
Cohoes, New York 12047
518-237-7999
Lawrence Callander, Executive
Director
founded: 1977
staff: 1 full-time, 1 part-time
major programs: historic sites,
photo collection, tours, periodical, publications, historic
preservation

Colonie

Shaker Heritage Society
Shaker Meeting House
Albany Shaker Road
Albany, New York 12211
518-456-7890
members: 100
founded: 1977
staff: 2 part-time, 20 volunteer
major programs: historic sites,
school programs, tours, workshops, periodical, publications,
surveys, historic preservation,
rural preservation

Delmar

Bethlehem Archaeology Group
P.O. Box 93
Delmar, New York 12054
518-439-4863
Floyd I. Brewster, Field Director
members: 20
founded: 1982
staff: 10 volunteer
major programs: library, historic
sites, photo collection, research,
school programs, tours, lectures,
exhibits, publications, historic
preservation, technical preservation services, archeology

Feura Bush

Onesquethaw Creek
Historic District
RD, Box 88
Feura Bush, New York 12067

Guilderland Center

Guilderland Historical Society
P.O. Box 76
Guilderland Center, New York
12085
Mark John Hesler, President

Guilderland League of Arts
P.O. Box 305
Guilderland Center, New York
12086
518-456-2913

Knox

Knox Historical Society
State Route 156, P.O. Box 11
Knox, New York 12107
518-872-2137
Mary Feeley Daniels, President
members: 23
founded: 1973
staff: 23 volunteer
major programs: museum,
periodical, rural preservation

Loudonville

Fort Orange Garden Club
26 Cherry Tree Road
Loudonville, New York 12211
518-434-0370

New Scotland

Town of New Scotland Historical
Association
P.O. Box 72
New Scotland, New York 12127
Lee Flanders, President
members: 60
founded: 1971
staff: 10 volunteer
major programs: museum, photo
collection

Newtonville

Friends of Pruyn House
207 Old Niskayuna Road
Newtonville, New York 12128
518-783-1435
mail to: Memorial Town Hall,
Newtonville, New York 12128
Jean S. Olton, Trustee
members: 375
founded: 1983
staff: 30 volunteer
major programs: historic site,
school programs, tours, exhibits,
surveys, historic preservation

Historical Society of the
Town of Colonie
Memorial Town Hall
Newtonville, New York 12128
518-783-1435
Jean S. Olton, Advisor
members: 250
founded: 1972
staff: 2 part-time, 20 volunteer
major programs: library,
archives, historic sites, school
programs, tours, exhibits,
surveys, historic preservation,
markers program

Rensselaerville

Rensselaerville Historical Society
P.O. Box 8
Rensselaerville, New York 12147
Robert Scardamalia, President

Selkirk

Bethlehem Historical Association
Rt. 144 at Clapper Road
Selkirk, New York 12158
Evelyn Alford, President

Voorheesville

Albany County Rural
Housing Alliance
Martin Road, P.O. Box 131
Voorheesville, New York 12186
518-765-3535
Maureen Costello, Assistant
Director
founded: 1982
staff: 4 full-time
major programs: lectures,
workshops, surveys, rural
preservation, technical
preservation referral services

Watervliet

Watervliet Arsenal Museum
U.S. Department of the Army
Watervliet, New York 12189
518-266-5805
William Bradford, Curator

Watervliet Historical Society
P.O. Box 123
Watervliet, New York 12189
Eugene Burns, Treasurer
founded: 1974
major programs: photo
collection

Westerlo

Westerlo Historical Society
P.O. Box 148
Westerlo, New York 12193

Allegany County

County Arts Council

Allegany Arts Association
Allegany County Courthouse,
Room 207
Belmont, New York 14813

County Historian

see County Historical Society

County Historical Society

Allegany County Museum
Court Street
Belmont, New York 14813
716-268-9293
Craig R. Braack, County
Historian
founded: 1972

staff: 1 full-time, 3 volunteer
major programs: library, archives, museum, photo collection, school programs, tours, lectures, technical preservation services

County Planning Office

Allegany County Planning Board
County Court House
Belmont, New York 14813
716-268-7612

see also Southern Tier West Regional Planning and Development Board, Salamanca, Cattaraugus County; Western New York Association of Historical Agencies, Avon, Livingston County

Alfred

Alfred Historical Society
P.O. Box 1137
Alfred, New York 14802
607-587-8886
Dr. Warren M. Bouck, President
members: 78
staff: 22 volunteer
major programs: museum, exhibits, periodical, publications, historic preservation, easements

Alfred Housing Committee
Village Hall
Alfred, New York 14802
607-587-8010
Susan B. Szczerbacki, Executive Director
founded: 1979
staff: 2 full-time
major programs: surveys, historic preservation, rural preservation, affordable housing, revolving fund, easements, grants, matching grants

Alfred Station

Baker's Bridge Historical Association
Alfred Station, New York 14803
Lyle W. Palmatier, President

Almond

Almond Historical Society
11 North Main Street
P.O. Box 98
Almond, New York 14804
607-276-6166

Linn L. Phelan, Curator
members: 386
founded: 1965
staff: 40 volunteer
major programs: library, archives, museum, photo collection, school programs, lectures, exhibits, periodical, publications, surveys

Hagadorn Historical House
11 North Main Street
Almond, New York 14804

Andover

Andover Historic Preservation Corporation
4 Main Street, P.O. Box 713
Andover, New York 14806
607-478-8009
Frank Evangelisti, Executive Director
founded: 1980
staff: 1 full-time, 4 part-time, 8 volunteer
major programs: awards, surveys, rural preservation, affordable housing, periodical, grants, matching grants

Andover Historical Society
Andover, New York 14806

Angelica

Angelica Library Association
Angelica, New York 14709
716-466-3347

Belfast

Belfast Historical Society
Belfast, New York 14711

Belmont

Belmont Literary and Historical Society
Belmont, New York 14813

Housing Action Corporation
84 Schuyler Street
Belmont, New York 14813
716-268-7605
Charles T. Kalthoff, Jr., Executive Director
founded: 1972
staff: 12 full-time
major programs: rural preservation, grants

Bolivar

Pioneer Oil Museum of New York
Main Street
Bolivar, New York 14715
716-928-1433
Thomas Manning, Trustee
founded: 1969
staff: 1 part-time
major programs: museum, photo collection

Cuba

Cuba Community Development Corporation
17½ West Main Street
P.O. Box 33
Cuba, New York 14727
716-968-3131
Ruth Miller, Executive Director
founded: 1981
staff: 1 full-time, 3 part-time
major programs: historic preservation, rural preservation, affordable housing, periodical, revolving fund, grants, matching grants

Cuba Historical Society
P.O. Box 71
Cuba, New York 14727

Friendship

Friendship Landmark Society
Main Street
Friendship, New York 14739

Rushford

Rushford Historical Society
Rushford, New York 14777
716-437-2474
Mildred Worthington Falsion, Chair
members: 22
founded: 1958
staff: 20 volunteer
major programs: museum, historic sites, exhibits, historic preservation, rural preservation

Wellsville

The Mather Homestead Museum, Library and Memorial Park
343 North Main Street

Wellsville, New York 14895
716-593-1636
Mrs. Glenn Williams, Director
founded: 1981
staff: 2 part-time
major programs: museum,
research, tours, exhibits,
periodical, publications, historic
preservation, services and
displays for blind and poorly
sighted

Rogers Genealogical and
Historical Society
Wellsville, New York 14895

Bronx County

County Arts Council

Bronx Council on the Arts
1738 Hone Avenue
Bronx, New York 10461
212-931-9500
William Aguado, Executive
Director

County Historian

The Rev. William Tieck
3930 Bailey Avenue
Bronx, New York 10463

County Historical Society

Bronx County Historical Society
3309 Bainbridge Avenue
Bronx, New York 10467
212-881-8900
Dr. Gary D. Hermalyn,
Executive Director
members: 850
founded: 1955
staff: 12 full-time, 6 part-time,
10 volunteers
major programs: library,
archives, museum, historic sites,
photo collection, research,
school programs, tours, lectures,
exhibits, periodical, publications,
awards, historic preservation,
archeology

County Planning Office

Bronx Office, Department of
City Planning
One Fordham Plaza
Bronx, New York 10458
212-220-8500
see also New York County
listings

Bronx

Alpha Housing Coalition
1183 Franklin Avenue
Bronx, New York 10456

Banana Kelly Community
Improvement Corporation
965 Longwood Avenue,
Room 313
Bronx, New York 10459

Bartow-Pell Landmark Fund
Pelham Bay Park
Bronx, New York 10464

Bartow-Pell Mansion Museum
Pelham Bay Park
Bronx, New York 10464
212-885-1461
Joanne V. Kottke, Trustee
members: 400
founded: 1914
staff: 2 full-time, 200 volunteer
major programs: museum,
school programs, tours, historic
preservation

Bronx Heights Neighborhood
Community Corporation
99 Featherbed Lane
Bronx, New York 10453

Bronx Museum of the Arts
1040 Grand Concourse
Bronx, New York 10456
212-681-6000
Dee Barbato, Public Relations
Director

Bronx River Restoration Project
375 East Fordham Road
Bronx, New York 10458
212-933-4079
Nancy Wallace, Executive
Director
founded: 1974
staff: 4 full-time, 5 part-time,
300 volunteer
major programs: research, school
programs, lectures, workshops,
exhibits, periodical, publications,
surveys, technical preservation
services

Bronx Shepherds Restoration
Corporation
1309 Boston Road
Bronx, New York 10456

Bronx Task Force
c/o Robert Nolan
Borough President's Office
85 Grand Concourse
Bronx, New York 10451

City Island Historical Society
190 Fordham Street
City Island, New York 10464
212-885-1616
founded: 1964
staff: 1 full-time, 1 part-time,
17 volunteer
major programs: library,
archives, museum, historic sites,
periodical, photo collection,
research, school programs, tours,
lectures, exhibits, historic
preservation, affordable housing,
archeology

Coalition for Housing
Improvement in Bathgate
538 Claremont Parkway
Bronx, New York 10456

Edgehill Church at
Spuyten Duyvil
2570 Independence Avenue
Bronx, New York 10463
212-549-7324
William A. Tieck, Pastor
major programs: historic
preservation

Fordham Bedford Housing
Corporation
2656 Decatur Avenue
Bronx, New York 10458

Friends of the Riverdale
Historic District
5286 Sycamore Avenue
Riverdale, The Bronx, New York
10471
212-549-6643
Robert Cornfeld, Chair

Kingsbridge Historical Society
144 West 288th Street
Bronx, New York 10463

Kingsbridge-Riverdale-Van
Cortlandt Development
Corporation
5760 Broadway
Bronx, New York 10463
212-543-7100
Floyd Lapp, Executive Director
members: 75
founded: 1981

staff: 2 full-time, 1 part-time,
25 volunteer
major programs: research,
lectures, workshops, periodical,
publications, awards, surveys,
affordable housing, revolving
fund, grants, matching grants

Longwood Historic District
Community Association
947 East 156th Street
Bronx, New York 10455
212-374-5812

Marble Hill Neighborhood
Improvement Corporation
135 Terrace View Avenue
Bronx, New York 10463

Mid-Bronx Desperados
Community Housing
Corporation
1690 Vyse Avenue
Bronx, New York 10460

Morrisiana Revitalization
Association
1028 Cauldwell Avenue
Bronx, New York 10456

Neighborhood Housing
Services/WOW
3550 White Plains Road
P.O. Box 774
Bronx, New York 10467
212-881-6801
James M. Oliver, Director
founded: 1981
staff: 3 full-time, 2 part-time,
1 volunteer
major programs: tours, lectures,
workshops, surveys

Neighborhood Initiatives
Development Corporation
2541 Olinville Avenue
Bronx, New York 10467
212-231-9800
Kristine Haag, Executive
Director
founded: 1982
staff: 4 full-time, 1 part-time,
1 volunteer
major programs: affordable
housing, periodical

Neighborhood Housing Services
of Soundview
912 Soundview Avenue
Bronx, New York 10473

North Bronx Neighborhood
Restoration Association
25 Westchester Square
Bronx, New York 10461
Thomas J. Sudano, Executive
Director

People's Development
Corporation
1162 Washington Avenue
Bronx, New York 10456

SEBCO Development
Corporation
923 Simpson Street
Bronx, New York 10459

Van Cortlandt Mansion Museum
North 242nd Street and
Broadway
Bronx, New York 10471
Robert Porter, Director

Wave Hill
675 West 252nd Street
Bronx, New York 10471
212-549-3200
Peter H. Sauer, Executive
Director
major programs: horticulture,
exhibits, lectures, research,
school programs, workshops,
archeology, historic site

West Bronx Housing and
Neighborhood Resources Center
2641 Grand Concourse
Bronx, New York 10468

West Bronx Restoration
Committee
c/o Hunter College, CUNY
790 Madison Avenue
New York, New York 10021
212-360-5594

Westbro Community
Development Corporation
66 West Tremont Avenue
P.O. Box 90
Bronx, New York 10453
212-299-8582
James L. Wilson, Chair
major programs: neighborhood
preservation

163rd Street Improvement
Council
1180 Rev. James A. Polite
Avenue
Bronx, New York 10459

212-589-5080
Mrs. Reeves Dixon, Executive
Director
founded: 1963
staff: 5 full-time
major programs: historic
preservation, affordable housing

Broome County

County Arts Council

Broome County Arts Council
69 Main Street
Binghamton, New York 13905
607-723-4620

County Historian

Lawrence L. Bothwell
Nanticoke Road, Box 23
Maine, New York 13802

County Historical Society

Broome County
Historical Society
30 Front Street
Binghamton, New York 13905
607-772-0660
Wesley G. Balla, Curator
members: 225
founded: 1939
staff: all volunteer
major programs: library,
archives, lectures, exhibits,
periodical, publications

County Planning Office

Broome County Department of
Planning and Economic
Development
County Office Building
Box 1766
Binghamton, New York 13902
607-772-2114

see also Regional Council of
Historical Agencies, Syracuse,
Onondaga County

Binghamton

Broome County Public Library
78 Exchange Street
Binghamton, New York 13901
607-723-6457
Carlton A. Sears, Library
Director
founded: 1902
staff: 41 full-time, 37 part-time
major programs: library,
archives, periodical

City of Binghamton Office of
Planning, Housing and
Community Development
City Hall, Governmental Plaza
Binghamton, New York 13901
Denise Balkas, Director

Merton-Eaton Historical Society
1137 Front Street
Binghamton, New York 13905
607-723-6599
Robert L. Bridges, Historian

Preservation Association of
the Southern Tier
10 New Street
Binghamton, New York 13903
607-862-9255
Richard I. Barons, Executive
Director
members: 157
founded: 1976
staff: 1 full-time, 2 volunteer
major programs: research, school
programs, tours, lectures,
workshops, periodical, publications, awards, surveys, historic
preservation, rural preservation,
technical preservation services

Public Archaeology Facility
State University of New York
Binghamton, New York 13901
607-798-4786
Albert A. Dekin, Jr., Director

Roberson Center for the Arts
and Sciences
30 Front Street
Binghamton, New York 13905
607-772-0660
Robert W. Aber, Executive
Director
members: 1,100
founded: 1954
staff: 30 full-time, 14 part-time,
200 volunteer
major programs: library,
archives, museum, historic sites,
school programs, tours, lectures,
workshops, exhibits, periodical,
publications, archeology

Southern Tier East Regional
Planning Development Board
84 Hawley Street
Binghamton, New York 13901
607-724-1327
Robert Augenstern, Director

Susquehanna Urban Cultural
Park Program
Lackawanna Station, P.O. Box 5
45 Lewis Street
Binghamton, New York 13902
607-724-7537

Valley Development Foundation
212 Security Mutual Building
Binghamton, New York 13901
607-722-4215

Deposit

Deposit-Sanford Rural Housing
Council
172 Front Street
Deposit, New York 13754
607-467-4760
Andrea M. Santacroce,
Executive Director
staff: 2 full-time, 2 part-time
major programs: photo
collection, research, tours,
lectures, workshops,
publications, surveys, historic
preservation, rural preservation,
affordable housing

Deposit, New York Community
Historical Society
145 Second Street
Deposit, New York 13754
607-467-4422
Ruth V. Axtell, President
members: 200
founded: 1971
staff: 10 volunteer
major programs: museum,
periodical

Endicott

Endicott Historical and
Preservation Society
P.O. Box 52
Endicott, New York 13760
607-785-8373
James V. Fioni, President
members: 19
founded: 1968
staff: 5 volunteer
major programs: photo
collection, research, exhibits,
periodical

Endwell

Amos Patterson
Memorial Museum
3300 East Main Street
P.O. Box 3
Endwell, New York 13760

Claudia Baker, Director
founded: 1984
staff: 20 volunteer
major programs: museum, tours,
lectures, markers program

Harpursville

Old Onaquaga Historical Society
St. Luke's Museum
Harpursville, New York 13787

Kirkwood

Kirkwood Historical Society
Town Hall, P.O. Box 2000
Kirkwood, New York 13795

Maine

Nanticoke Valley Historical
Society
Nanticoke Road, P.O. Box 75
Maine, New York 13802
Janet Bothwell, Curator
members: 210
founded: 1973
staff: 1 part-time
major programs: museum,
historic sites, photo collection,
exhibits, periodical, historic
preservation

Vestal

Vestal Museum
Vestal Town Hall
Vestal, New York 13850
members: 129
founded: 1954
major programs: museum,
lectures, exhibits, historic
preservation, technical
preservation services

Windsor

Old Stone House Museum
10 Chestnut Street
Windsor, New York 13865
607-655-1443

Cattaraugus County

County Arts Council

see Chautauqua County Arts
Council for decentralization
information

County Historian

Kenneth Kysor
Little Valley, New York 14755

County Historical Society

Cattaraugus County Memorial
Museum
Court Street
Little Valley, New York 14755
716-938-9111 x440
Lorna Spencer, Curator
founded: 1914
staff: 2 part-time, 2 volunteer
major programs: library,
museum

County Planning Office

Cattaraugus County Department
of Development and Planning
303 Court Street
Little Valley, New York 14755
716-938-9111

see also Western New York
Association of Historical
Agencies, Avon, Livingston
County

Cattaraugus

Allegany Area Historical Society
23 Main Street
Cattaraugus, New York 14719
716-257-9012
mail to: Lovers Lane Road
Cattaraugus, New York 14719
Kenneth Kysor, President
members: 40
founded: 1955
staff: 8 volunteer
major programs: archives, photo
collection, school programs,
exhibits, periodical

Dayton

Town of Dayton Historical
Society
P.O. Box 15
Dayton, New York 14041

Ellicottville

Cattaraugus County
Neighborhood Preservation
Corporation
One Washington Street
P.O. Box 806
Ellicottville, New York 14731
716-699-2075
Blair W. Sebastian, Executive
Director
founded: 1980

staff: 4 full-time
major programs: rural
preservation, affordable housing,
grants

Ellicottville Historical Society
Ellicottville, New York 14731

Franklinville

Ischua Valley Historical Society
24 Howard Street
Franklinville, New York 14737
716-676-3128
Gene A. Gena, Treasurer
members: 200
founded: 1966
staff: 9 volunteer
major programs: archives,
museum, research, periodical

Gowanda

Gowanda Area Historical Society
P.O. Box 372
Gowanda, New York 14070
Louise R. Gleason, President
members: 80
founded: 1968
staff: 3 volunteer
major programs: library,
archives, school programs

Leon

Leon Historical Society
Route 62, Box 61
Leon, New York 14751
716-296-5217
Bertha Milspaw, Town Historian
members: 18
founded: 1977
staff: 3 volunteer
major programs: museum

Olean

Eastside Neighborhood
Organization for Development
National Bank Building
602 Exchange Street
Olean, New York 14760

Olean Historical Society
119 Bradley Drive
Olean, New York 14760

Portville

Portville Historical and
Preservation Society
One North Main Street,
Drawer M

Portville, New York 14770
716-933-8917
Ronda S. Pollock, President
members: 110
founded: 1985
staff: 4 volunteer
major programs: archives, photo
collection, tours, lectures,
periodical, publications, awards

Salamanca

Rural Revitalization Corporation
41 Main Street
Salamanca, New York 14779

Salamanca Landmark
Association
464 Fair Oak Street
Salamanca, New York 14779
716-945-1225
Rosalyn Hoag, President
members: 25
founded: 1980
staff: 25 volunteer
major programs: library,
archives, historic sites, photo
collection, research, tours,
lectures, workshops, exhibits,
historic preservation, markers
program

Salamanca Rail Museum
225 Wildwood Avenue
Salamanca, New York 14779
716-945-4688

Seneca-Iroquois
National Museum
Allegany Indian Reservation
P.O. Box 442
Salamanca, New York 14779
716-945-1738
Dr. Martha I. Symes, Assistant
Director
members: 20
founded: 1985
staff: 20 volunteer
major programs: historic sites,
photo collection, research, tours,
exhibits, historic preservation,
markers program

Southern Tier West Regional
Planning and Development
Board
445 Broad Street
Salamanca, New York 14779
716-945-5301
Roy B. Campbell, Executive
Director

West Valley

Ashford Historical Society
660 Main Street
West Valley, New York 14171
Earline E. Scharf, President

Cayuga County

County Arts Council

Cayuga County Arts Council
City Hall
24 South Street
Auburn, New York 13021
315-252-9531 x19
Karen Bove, Executive Director

County Historian

Tom Eldred
Cayuga County Office Building,
6th Floor
160 Genesee Street
Auburn, New York 13021

County Historical Society

Cayuga Museum of
History and Art
203 Genesee Street
Auburn, New York 13021
315-253-8051
Marion E. Balyszak, Director
members: 530
founded: 1936
staff: 3 full-time, 4 part-time
major programs: library, archives, periodical, museum,
photo collection, school programs, tours, lectures, exhibits

County Planning Office

Cayuga County Planning Office
160 Genesee Street
Auburn, New York 13021
315-253-1276

see also Central New York
Regional Planning and Develop-
ment Board, Syracuse, Onon-
daga County; Regional Council
of Historical Agencies, Syracuse,
Onondaga County; Preservation
Association of Central New
York, Syracuse, Onondaga
County

Auburn

Cayuga County Agricultural
Museum

Emerson Park
Auburn, New York 13021

Cayuga County Homesite
Development Corporation
60 Clark Street
Auburn, New York 13021
315-253-8451
Barbara Lamphere, Executive
Director
founded: 1972
staff: 10 full-time, 5 part-time
major programs: rural
preservation, affordable housing,
revolving fund

Community Preservation
Committee of Cayuga County
P.O. Box 1021
Auburn, New York 13021
315-253-1276
Michael Long, Chair
members: 30
founded: 1983
staff: 10 volunteer
major programs: photo
collection, research, lectures,
exhibits, periodical, awards

Foundation Historical
Association
33 South Street
Auburn, New York 13021
315-252-1283
Betty Mae Lewis, Curator

Schweinfurth Art Center
205 Genesee Street
Auburn, New York 13021
315-255-1553
James Dungey, Director
founded: 1981
staff: 3 full-time, 1 part-time,
20 volunteer
major programs: museum,
exhibits, publications

Moravia

Cayuga-Owasco Lakes
Historical Society
15 Main Street, P.O. Box 241
Moravia, New York 13118
Dwain Francis, President
members: 75
founded: 1966
major programs: library,
archives, museum, photo
collection

Port Byron

Lock Fifty-two Historical
Society of Port Byron
Municipal Building
Utica Street
Port Byron, New York 13140

Sterling Center

Sterling Historical Society
Sterling Center, New York 13156

Union Springs

Frontenac Historical Society
One Factory Street
Union Springs, New York 13160
315-253-4658
Ward O'Hara, President

Weedsport

Old Brutus Historical Society
8943 North Seneca Street
Weedsport, New York 13166
315-834-6779
Howard J. Finley, Historian

Chautauqua County

County Arts Council

Arts Council for Chautauqua
County
116 East Third Street
Jamestown, New York 14701
716-664-2465
Philip Morris, Executive Director

County Historian

Elizabeth L. Crocker
131 Center Street
Fredonia, New York 14063

County Historical Society

Chautauqua County Historical
Society
P.O. Box 7
Westfield, New York 14787
716-326-2977
Roderick A. Nixon, President
members: 525
founded: 1883
staff: 1 full-time, 3 part-time

major programs: library, archives, museum, photo collection, research, school programs, tours, exhibits, periodical, publications, historic preservation, rural preservation

County Planning Office

Chautauqua County Planning and Development
County Office Building
Mayville, New York 14757
716-753-4296

see also Southern Tier West Regional Planning and Development Board, Salamanca, Cattaraugus, County; Western New York Association of Historical Agencies, Avon, Livingston County

Busti

Busti Historical Society
RD 3, Box 398A
Jamestown, New York 14701

Chautauqua

Chautauqua Institution
Box 28, Colonnade Building
Chautauqua, New York 14722
716-357-5635

Dunkirk

Historical Society of Dunkirk
513 Washington Avenue
Dunkirk, New York 14048
716-366-3797
Robert J. Harris, President
members: 250
founded: 1973
staff: 1 part-time, 10 volunteer
major programs: museum, photo collection, school programs, exhibits, periodical, historic preservation

Ellington

Ellington Historical Society
P.O. Box 1824
Ellington, New York 14732

Fredonia

Fredonia Preservation Society
P.O. Box 422
Fredonia, New York 14063
Winifred Shepard, President

members: 310
founded: 1985
staff: 11 volunteer
major programs: historic sites, historic preservation

Historical Museum of the D.R. Barker Library
20 East Main Street
Fredonia, New York 14063
716-672-2114
mail to: 7 Day Street
Fredonia, New York 14063
Donna N. Carlson, Curator
founded: 1884
staff: 2 part-time, 13 volunteer
major programs: library, archives, museum, photo collection, research, school programs, lectures, exhibits, historic preservation

French Creek

French Creek Historical Society
RD 2
Clymer, New York 14724

Jamestown

Chautauqua Opportunities
204 Lafayette Street
Jamestown, New York 14701
Barbara Boon

Fenton Historical Society
67 Washington Street
Jamestown, New York 14701
716-483-7521
Candace Larson, Director
members: 800
founded: 1964
staff: 2 full-time, 16 part-time, 40 volunteer
major programs: library, archives, museum, photo collection, research, school programs, tours, exhibits, periodical

Mayville

Chautauqua Home Rehabilitation and Improvement Corporation
149 Gerace Office Building
Mayville, New York 14757

Peacock Landmark Society
Morris Road
Mayville, New York 14757

Panama

Harmony Historical Society
P.O. Box 32
Panama, New York 14767
Willis B. Waite, President
members: 51
founded: 1972
staff: 4 volunteer
major programs: archives, museum, historic sites, photo collection, exhibits, historic preservation

Silver Creek

Hanover Historical Society
239 Central Avenue
Silver Creek, New York 14136

Sinclairville

Valley Historical Society
Sinclairville, New York 14782
716-962-8520
Ruth I. Smith, President
members: 60
founded: 1976
staff: 10 volunteer
major programs: archives, museum, historic sites, photo collection, school programs, tours

Chemung County

County Arts Council

see Chemung Valley Arts Council, Corning, Steuben County for decentralization information; *see also* Arnot Art Museum, Elmira

County Historian

Thomas Byrne
415 East Water Street
Elmira, New York 14901

County Historical Society

Chemung County Historical Society
415 East Water Street
Elmira, New York 14901
607-734-4167
Constance B. Barone, Director
members: 1,200
founded: 1923
staff: 4 full-time, 4 part-time 50 volunteer

major programs: archives, museum, school programs, tours, exhibits, publications

County Planning Office

Chemung County Planning Department
425-427 Pennsylvania Avenue
Elmira, New York 14904
607-737-5510

see also Regional Council of Historical Agencies, Syracuse, Onondaga County; Southern Tier Central Regional Planning and Development Board, Corning, Steuben County

Big Flats

Big Flats Historical Society
P.O. Box 262
Big Flats, New York 14814
607-562-8527
Arthur Devenport, Chair
members: 140
founded: 1970
staff: 15 volunteer
major programs: school programs, tours, lectures, periodical, historic preservation

Elmira

Arnot Art Museum
235 Lake Street
Elmira, New York 14901
607-734-3697
Kenneth H. Lindquist, Director
members: 1,000
founded: 1911
staff: 7 full-time, 7 part-time, 40 volunteer
major programs: museum, school programs, tours, lectures, workshops, exhibits, periodical, publications

Chemung County Historic Preservation League
P.O. Box 828
Elmira, New York 14902
607-739-0858
Claudia Radin, Chair

Eastside Neighborhood Action Committee
320 Lake Street
Elmira, New York 14901

Historic 1897 Fire House Preservation Committee
120 Country Club Drive
Elmira, New York 14905
607-734-2897
Jeffrey C. Burger, Chair
members: 20
founded: 1986
staff: all volunteer
major programs: museum

Near Westside Neighborhood Association
Church and Davis streets
Elmira, New York 14905
607-733-4924
Carol Wells Shepard, Executive Director
members: 150
founded: 1978
staff: 2 full-time, 30 volunteer
major programs: library, historic sites, research, school programs, tours, workshops, periodical, historic preservation, technical preservation services, grants

Regional Housing Council of Southern Tier
355 College Avenue
Elmira, New York 14901
607-734-5266
T.A. Langstine, Executive Director
founded: 1975
major programs: rural preservation

Underwater Archeology Association
Box 964, Elmira College
Elmira, New York 14901
607-734-3911 x325
Ronald W. Hynes, President

Elmira Heights

Elmira Heights Historical Society
266 East 14th Street
Elmira Heights, New York 14903
607-732-7638
James W. Bensley, Village Historian

Horseheads

Erin Historical Society
1264 Main Street
Horseheads, New York 14845

Horseheads Historical Society
Grand Central and Broad Street
Horseheads, New York 14845
607-739-3938
Nadine Ferraioli, President
members: 425
founded: 1972
staff: 1 part-time, 35 volunteer
major programs: museum, historic sites, photo collection, school programs, tours, exhibits, periodical, publications

Pine City

Southport Historical Society
P.O. Box 146
Pine City, New York 14871

Chenango County

County Arts Council

Chenango County Council of the Arts
27 West Main Street
P.O. Box 483
Norwich, New York 13815
607-336-5227
Lucy Funke, Executive Director
members: 600
founded: 1975
staff: 3 full-time, 60 volunteer
major programs: school programs, exhibits, periodical, grants

County Historian

Mabel Smith
RD 3, Woods Corners
Norwich, New York 13815

County Historical Society

Chenango County Historical Society
45 Rexford Street
Norwich, New York 13815
607-334-9227
E.J. Frink, President
members: 350
founded: 1936
staff: 10 volunteer
major programs: archives, museum, photo collection, school programs, tours, lectures, exhibits, publications, markers program, archeology

County Planning Office

Chenango County Department of
Planning and Development
5 Maple Street
Norwich, New York 13815
607-335-4620

see also Preservation Association
of the Southern Tier,
Binghamton, Broome County;
Regional Council of Historical
Agencies, Syracuse, Onondaga
County; Southern Tier East
Regional Planning Development
Board, Binghamton, Broome
County

Afton

Afton Historical Society
116 Main Street, P.O. Box 28
Afton, New York 13730

Jericho Historical Society
169 Main Street
Afton, New York 13630

Earlville

Earlville Opera House
P.O. Box 111
Earlville, New York 13332
315-691-3550
John Grossman, Co-Chair
members: 40
founded: 1970
staff: 1 part-time
major programs: arts
presentation, periodical

Greene

Greene Revitalization Project
49 Genesee Street
Greene, New York 13778
607-656-4500
Kimber Madara, Chair
founded: 1985
staff: 7 volunteer
major programs: lectures,
exhibits, historic preservation,
revolving fund

Moore Memorial Library
59 Genesee Street
Greene, New York 13778
607-656-9349
Scott Clark, Librarian
founded: 1903
staff: 1 full-time, 4 part-time,
4 volunteer
major programs: library,
museum

Mount Upton

Unadilla Valley
Historical Society
Route 8
Mount Upton, New York 13809

New Berlin

New Berlin Housing and
Preservation Company
20 South Main Street
P.O. Box 359
New Berlin, New York 13411

New Berlin Library and Museum
South Main Street
New Berlin, New York 13411
607-847-8564
Susan Ackerman, Library
Director
founded: 1903
staff: 2 part-time, 1 volunteer
major programs: library

Norwich

Chenango Housing
Improvement Program
99 North Broad Street
Norwich, New York 13815

Guernsey Memorial Library
Court Street
Norwich, New York 13815
607-334-4034
Margaret Finch, Director

Oxford

Historic Oxford Preservation
P.O. Box 527
Oxford, New York 13830
607-843-9287

Oxford Historical Society
Fort Hill Park
Oxford, New York 13830
607-843-9531
Charlotte Stafford, President

Oxford Revitalization Project
P.O. Box 651
Oxford, New York 13830
Barbara Marotta, Executive
Director
members: 300
founded: 1980

staff: 8 volunteer
major programs: historic
preservation, rural preservation,
annual arts and crafts festival

Plymouth

Town of Plymouth
Historical Society
Plymouth, New York 13832

Smithville Flats

Smithville Historical Society
P.O. Box 2
Smithville Flats, New York
13841

Clinton County

County Arts Council

Council on the Arts
for Clinton County
P.O. Box 451
Plattsburgh, New York 12901
518-563-5222
Lola Johnson, Executive Director

County Historian

Addie Shields
Clinton County Government
Center
Plattsburgh, New York 12901
518-565-4749

County Historical Society

Clinton County Historical
Association
City Hall
P.O. Box 332
Plattsburgh, New York 12901
518-561-0340
Helen W. Allan,
Director/Curator
members: 400
founded: 1945
staff: 1 full-time, 1 part-time
6 volunteer
major programs: museum, photo
collection, school programs,
tours, lectures, exhibits,
periodical, publications

County Planning Office

Clinton County Planning Office
County Government Center
137 Margaret Street
Plattsburgh, New York 12901
518-565-4711

see also Federation of Historical Services, Troy, Rensselaer County

Plattsburgh

Kent-Delord House Museum
17 Cumberland Avenue
Plattsburgh, New York 12901
518-561-1035
Joann F. Perry, Director
members: 400
founded: 1926
staff: 2 full-time, 1 part-time
35 volunteer
major programs: museum, research, school programs, lectures, workshops, exhibits, periodical

Saranac

Rural Preservation Company of Clinton County
P.O. Box 798
Saranac, New York 12981
518-293-7569
Daniel Malone, Director
founded: 1985
staff: 1 full-time, 2 part-time
major programs: rural preservation, affordable housing, grants, matching grants

Columbia County

County Arts Council

Columbia County Council on the Arts
729 Columbia Street
Hudson, New York 12534
518-828-4731

County Historian

Florence C. Mossman
P.O. Box 8
Philmont, New York 12665

County Historical Society

Columbia County Historical Society
5 Albany Avenue, P.O. Box 341
Kinderhook, New York 12106
518-758-9265
Sally A. Bottiggi, Executive Director
members: 750
founded: 1916
staff: 2 full-time, 3 part-time,
50 volunteer
major programs: archives, museum, historic sites, research, school programs, tours, lectures, exhibits, periodical, historic preservation

County Planning Office

Columbia County Development and Planning Department
414 Union Street
Hudson, New York 12534
518-828-1527
see also Federation of Historical Services, Troy, Rensselaer County

Ancram

Ancram Historical Society
P.O. Box 125
Ancram, New York 12502

Canaan

Canaan Historical Society
Warner Crossing Road
Canaan, New York 12029
518-781-4868
Stephen J. Munno, President
members: 350
founded: 1963
staff: 10 volunteer
major programs: library, archives, museum, historic sites, photo collection, research, tours, lectures, exhibits, periodical, publications, historic preservation, rural preservation

Claverack

Esselstyn Museum
Star Route, P.O. Box 88
Claverack, New York 12513
518-851-2411
Lillian Esselstyn, Executive Director
founded: 1986
staff: 1 full-time
major programs: library, archives, photo collection, exhibits

Copake

Roeliff Jansen Historical Society
P.O. Box 313
Copake, New York 12516
518-329-7292
mail to: East Ancram Road, Ancramdale, New York 12503

Dorothy V. Lampman, President
members: 200
founded: 1975
major programs: library, museum, rural preservation

East Chatham

Red Rock Historical Society
East Chatham, New York 12060

Germantown

Friends of Clermont
P.O. Box 217
Germantown, New York 12526
518-537-4240
Janet Graham, President
members: 350
founded: 1977
staff: 25 volunteer
major programs: library, historic site, school programs, tours, lectures, exhibits, periodical, publications

Hudson

Columbia Preservation Corporation
557 Warren Street
Hudson, New York 12534
518-828-0066
Rufus S. Overby, Executive Director
founded: 1982
staff: 2 full-time, 1 volunteer
major programs: periodical, workshops, surveys, rural preservation, affordable housing, technical preservation services, revolving fund

Hendrick Hudson Chapter, Daughters of the American Revolution
113 Warren Street
Hudson, New York 12534
518-828-9764
mail to: RD 2, Knollwood Drive, Valatie, New York 12184
Dana Berntson, Curator
members: 100
founded: 1896
major programs: library, museum, photo collection, research, school programs, tours, lectures, exhibits, awards

Friends of Olana
P.O. Box 199
Hudson, New York 12534
Edwina Thorn, President

Hudson Athens Lighthouse
Preservation Committee
725 Warren Street
Hudson, New York 12534

Hudson Housing Services
Corporation
4461 Warren Street
Hudson, New York 12534

New Lebanon

Lebanon Valley Historical
Society
New Lebanon, New York 12125

Mount Lebanon Shaker Village
Shaker Road, P.O. Box 628
New Lebanon, New York 12125
518-794-9500
Charles L. Flint, Director
members: 200
founded: 1984
staff: 1 part-time, 6 volunteer
major programs: museum,
school programs, tours, lectures,
exhibits, archeology, periodical

Old Chatham

Shaker Museum
Shaker Museum Road
Old Chatham, New York 12136
Viki Sand, Director

Shaker Museum Foundation
Shaker Museum Road
Old Chatham, New York 12136

Riders Mills

Rider's Mills Historical
Association
Rider's Mills Road
Brainard, New York 12024
518-794-9105

Spencertown

Spencertown Academy Society
P.O. Box 80
Spencertown, New York 12165
Mary Zander, President

Cortland County

County Arts Council

Council on the Arts for
Cortland County

23 Main Street
Cortland, New York 13045
607-753-0722

County Historian

Shirley G. Heppell
Courthouse
P.O. Box 5590
Cortland, New York 13045
607-753-5360

County Historical Society

Cortland County Historical
Society
25 Homer Avenue
Cortland, New York 13045
607-756-6071
Rachel Dickinson Savage,
Director
members: 725
founded: 1925
staff: 2 full-time, 1 part-time
major programs: library,
archives, museum, research,
periodical, publications

County Planning Office

Cortland County Planning Office
County Office Building
60 Central Avenue
P.O. Box 5590
Cortland, New York 13045
607-753-5043

see also Regional Council of
Historical Agencies, Syracuse,
Onondaga County; Southern
Tier East Regional Planning
Development Board,
Binghamton, Broome County

Cincinnatus

Cincinnatus Area Heritage
Society
Main Street
Cincinnatus, New York 13040

Cortland

Cortland Arts Council
19 Main Street
Cortland, New York 13045
Janet Steck, Executive Director

Cortland County Residential
Resource Corporation
23 Main Street
McNeil Building
Cortland, New York 13045
607-753-6781

James Bennett, Executive
Director
staff: 2 full-time
major programs: rural
preservation, affordable housing,
grants

Cortland Housing Assistance
Council
10½ Main Street
Cortland, New York 13045
607-753-8271
Gary L. Thomas, Executive
Director
founded: 1973
staff: 3 full-time, many volunteer
major programs: surveys, rural
preservation, affordable housing,
technical preservation services

The 1890 House
37 Tompkins Street
Cortland, New York 13045
607-756-7551
John Nozynski, Director
members: 500
founded: 1974
staff: 3 full-time, 8 part-time,
60 volunteer
major programs: library,
archives, museum, historic sites,
photo collection, research,
school programs, tours, lectures,
workshops, exhibits, periodical,
historic preservation

Cortlandville

Cortlandville Historical Society
15 Terrace Road
Cortlandville, New York 13045

Cuyler

Cuyler Historical Society
Cuyler, New York 13050

Homer

Glen Haven Historical Society
733 East Lake Road, RD 1
Homer, New York 13077

Landmark Society of
Cortland County
Town Hall
31 North Main Street
Homer, New York 13077
607-749-4801
Harry Bellardini, President
members: 150
founded: 1973

staff: all volunteer
major programs: photo
collection, lectures, periodical,
grants, historic preservation,
markers programs, technical
preservation

McGraw

McGraw Historical Museum
P.O. Box 467
McGraw, New York 13101
Mrs. S. Kullman, Secretary

Virgil

Virgil Historical Society
RD 2
Cortland, New York 13028

Delaware County

County Arts Council

see The Erpf Catskill Cultural
Center, Arkville; see Roxbury
Arts Group, Roxbury, for
decentralization information

County Historian

John E. Raitt
41 Clinton Street
Delhi, New York 13753

County Historical Society

Delaware County Historical
Association
RD 2, Box 201C
Delhi, New York 13753

County Planning Office

Delaware County Planning
Board
P.O. Box 367
Delhi, New York 13753
607-746-2944

see also Preservation Association
of the Southern Tier,
Binghamton, Broome County;
Regional Council of Historical
Agencies, Syracuse, Onondaga
County; Southern Tier East
Regional Planning Development
Board, Binghamton, Broome
County

Andes

Andes Society for History and
Culture
Route 28
Andes, New York 13731
914-676-4446
Anne Geiger, Chair
members: 200
founded: 1975
staff: all volunteer
major programs: archives,
museum, photo collection,
school programs, lectures,
exhibits, periodical, historic
preservation

Arkville

Catskill Center for Conservation
and Development
Arkville, New York 12406
914-586-2611
Thomas H. Miner, Executive
Director
members: 2,000
founded: 1969
staff: 4 full-time, 2 part-time
major programs: library,
lectures, workshops, periodical,
publications, awards, surveys,
historic preservation, rural
preservation, easements

The Erpf Catskill
Cultural Center
Route 28
Arkville, New York 12406
914-586-3326
Whitty Sanford, Executive
Director
members: 623
founded: 1974
staff: 3 full-time, 3 part-time,
20 volunteer
major programs: library,
archives, historic sites, photo
collection, exhibits, periodical,
publications, historic
preservation, rural preservation

Bovina

Bovina Historical Society
Bovina, New York 13740

Colchester

Colchester Historical Society
P.O. Box Q
Colchester, New York 13755

Davenport Center

Davenport Historical Society
P.O. Box 88
Davenport Center, New York
13751

Delhi

Delaware Opportunities
119 Main Street
Delhi, New York 13753

Downsville

Delaware Heritage
P.O. Box 442
Downsville, New York 13755
Robert Terry, President

East Meredith

Hanford Mills Museum
P.O. Box 99
East Meredith, New York 13757
607-278-5744
Keith Bott, Director
members: 250
founded: 1973
staff: 7 full-time, 5 part-time,
40 volunteer
major programs: library,
archives, museum, historic sites,
photo collection, research,
periodical, school programs,
tours, lectures, workshops,
exhibits

Franklin

Oulehoudt Valley Historical
Society
P.O. Box 931
Franklin, New York 13775
607-829-6771
R.H. Simmons, President
members: 23
founded: 1965
staff: 23 volunteer
major programs: archives,
museum, historic sites, photo
collection, exhibits, historic
preservation, markers program

Roxbury

Roxbury Arts Group
P.O. Box 93
Roxbury, New York 12474
607-326-7908
Nancy Harding, Executive
Director

Roxbury Burroughs Club
Roxbury, New York 12474
607-326-3611

Woodchuck Lodge
P.O. Box 184
Roxbury, New York 12474
mail to: 72 Country Club Road,
Oneonta, New York 13820
John E. Lutz, President
staff: 1 part-time
major programs: museum,
historic sites, school programs,
workshops, periodical, easements

Sidney

Sidney Historical Association
P.O. Box 217
Sidney, New York 13838
607-563-2134
Grace Terwilliger, President
members: 80
founded: 1945
staff: 6 volunteer
major programs: archives,
museum, photo collection,
research, school programs,
periodical

Stamford

Western Catskills Community
Revitalization Corporation
P.O. Box 123
Stamford, New York 12167

Walton

William B. Ogden Free Library
42 Gardiner Place
Walton, New York 13856
607-865-5929
Anne R. Turner, Librarian
founded: 1894
staff: 1 full-time, 7 part-time
major programs: library

Walton Historical Society
129 Prospect Avenue
Walton, New York 13856

Walton Restoration Committee
39 Gardiner Place
Walton, New York 13856
Andrea R. Paternoster, Chair

Dutchess County

County Arts Council

Dutchess County Arts Council
39 Market Street
Poughkeepsie, New York 12601
Judith Levine, Executive Director
914-454-3222

County Historian

Joyce Ghee
11 Rogers Place
Hyde Park, New York 12538

County Historical Society

Dutchess County Historical
Society
549 Main Street, P.O. Box 88
Poughkeepsie, New York 12602
914-471-1630
Susan Jensen Brown, Director
members: 650
founded: 1914
staff: 2 full-time, 2 part-time,
20 volunteer
major programs: library,
archives, museum (collections),
publications

County Planning Office

Dutchess County Department of
Planning and Transportation
47 Cannon Street
Poughkeepsie, New York 12601
914-431-2480

see also Lower Hudson
Conference, Elmsford,
Westchester County

Amenia

Amenia Historical Society
Amenia, New York 12501

Annandale-on-Hudson

Bard College
Annandale-on-Hudson,
New York 12504
914-758-6822 x108
Ann Gourlay Gabler,
Special Programs

Montgomery Place
(*see* Historic Hudson Valley,
Tarrytown, Westchester County)
River Road, P.O. Box 32
Annandale-on-Hudson,
New York 12504
914-758-5461

Beacon

Beacon Historical Society
P.O. Box 89
Beacon, New York 12508

Howland Center
477 Main Street, P.O. Box 606
Beacon, New York 12508
914-831-4988
Craig Wolf, President
members: 165
founded: 1977
staff: 1 full-time, 21 volunteer
major programs: historic sites,
workshops, exhibits, periodical,
historic preservation, easements

Mount Gulian Society
145 Sterling Street
Beacon, New York 12508
914-831-8172
Barbara E. Peters, Director
members: 156
founded: 1966
staff: 1 full-time, 1 part-time,
5 volunteer
major programs: museum,
historic sites, tours, lectures,
workshops, exhibits, periodical

Dover Plains

Dover Historical Society
North Nellie Hill Road
Dover Plains, New York 12522

Fishkill

Fishkill Historical Society
P.O. Box 133
Van Wyck Homestead Museum
Fishkill, New York 12524
914-896-9560
Willa Skinner, Town Historian

Hopewell Junction

East Fishkill Historical Society
P.O. Box 245
Hopewell Junction, New York
12533
M.C. Kulschinsky, Trustee

Hyde Park

Hyde Park Historical Society
P.O. Box 182
Hyde Park, New York 12538

Hyde Park Visual Environment
Committee
P.O. Box 125
Hyde Park, New York 12538

Lagrangeville

La Grange Historical Society
P.O. Box 412
Lagrangeville, New York 12540

Millbrook

Rural Preservation Company of
Dutchess County
RD 2, Box 30
South Road
Millbrook, New York 12545
914-677-5324
Joan Moriarty-Cafiero,
Executive Director
founded: 1984
staff: 2 full-time
major programs: rural
preservation, affordable housing,
revolving fund

Town of Washington Historical
Society
P.O. Box 592
Millbrook, New York 12545

Millerton

North East Historical Society
Downey Road, Box 54
Millerton, New York 12545

Pawling

Historical Society of Quaker Hill
and Pawling
East Main Street, P.O. Box 99
Pawling, New York 12564
914-855-9316
Mrs. N. Edward Mitchell,
President
members: 300
founded: 1910
staff: 20 volunteer
major programs: museum,
historic sites, tours, lectures,
exhibits, historic preservation

Pine Plains

Little Nine Partners
Historical Society
P.O. Box 243
Pine Plains, New York 12567

Pleasant Valley

Pleasant Valley Historical Society
P.O. Box 766
Pleasant Valley, New York 12569
Alson Van Wagner, President
members: 72
founded: 1976

staff: all volunteer
major programs: historic sites,
markers program, periodical

Poughkeepsie

City of Poughkeepsie
Department of Community
Development
Memorial Square
Poughkeepsie, New York 12601
914-485-4710

Cuneen-Hackett Cultural Center
9 Vassar Street
Poughkeepsie, New York 12601
914-471-1221
Nancy Maddocks, Executive
Director

Dutchess County Department
of History
22 Market Street
Poughkeepsie, New York 12601
914-431-2065
Joyce C. Ghee, Historian
staff: 1 full-time, 2 part-time
major programs: archives, photo
collection, research, school
programs, tours, lectures,
workshops, exhibits, periodical,
publications, surveys, historic
preservation, markers program

Dutchess County Landmarks
Association
P.O. Box 944
Poughkeepsie, New York 12602
914-471-8777

Hudson River Sloop Clearwater
112 Market Street
Poughkeepsie, New York 12601
914-454-7673
John Mylod, Director

Hudson Valley Regional Council
61 Livingston Street
P.O. Box 1900
Poughkeepsie, New York 12601
914-452-4864
William J.D. Boyd, Executive
Director

Marist College
North Road, P.O. Box 729
Poughkeepsie, New York 12601
914-471-3240 x314
Wilma J. Burke, Director,
Regional Historical Program

Scenic Hudson, Inc.
9 Vassar Street
Poughkeepsie, New York 12601
914-473-4440
Klara B. Sauer, Executive
Director
founded: 1963
staff: 7 full-time, 3 part-time,
5 volunteer
major programs: tours, lectures,
workshops, exhibits, periodical,
publications, surveys, historic
preservation, rural preservation,
easements

Vassar College Art Gallery
Raymond Avenue
Poughkeepsie, New York 12601
Sandra Phillips, Curator

Young-Morse Historic Site
370 South Road, P.O. Box 103
Poughkeepsie, New York 12601
914-454-4500
Kenneth E. Hasbrouck, President
founded: 1979
staff: 7 full-time, 10 part-time
major programs: historic site,
tours, exhibits

Poughquag

Beekman Historical Society
P.O. Box 165
Poughquag, New York 12570

Red Hook

Egbert Benson Historical Society
P.O. Box 1812
Red Hook, New York 12571
914-758-8279
mail to: RD 3, Box 472,
Red Hook, New York 12571
Linda Keeling, President
members: 107
founded: 1978
staff: 9 volunteer
major programs: archives,
awards, historic preservation

Friends of Elmendorph
P.O. Box 1776
Red Hook, New York 12571

Rhinebeck

Hudson River Heritage
P.O. Box 287
Rhinebeck, New York 12572
914-758-5264

Patricia W. Weber, President
members: 200
founded: 1972
major programs: photo
collection, lectures, periodical,
publications, historic
preservation, grants, easements

Rhinebeck Historical Society
P.O. Box 291
Rhinebeck, New York 12572
914-876-6031
Kenneth J. Mule, President
members: 288
founded: 1967
staff: 12 volunteer
major programs: archives,
historic sites, photo collection,
school programs, lectures,
periodical, publications, awards,
historic preservation, archeology,
easements

Wilderstein Preservation
P.O. Box 383
Rhinebeck, New York 12572
Elise M. Barry, Executive
Director
members: 128
founded: 1980
staff: 1 part-time
major programs: historic sites,
historic preservation, periodical

Stanfordville

Stanford Historical Society
Stanfordville, New York 12581
members: 25
founded: 1969
staff: 5 volunteer

Verbank

Union Vale Historical Society
P.O. Box 100
Verbank, New York 12585

Wappingers Falls

Bowdoin Park Cultural
Heritage Center
Dutchess County Department of
Parks
85 Sheafe Road
Wappingers Falls, New York
12590
914-297-1224
Glenn Dochtermann, Program
Supervisor

founded: 1978
staff: all volunteer
major programs: school
programs, exhibits, archeology

Center for the
Hudson River Valley
Route 9D, Stony Kill
Wappingers Falls, New York
12590
914-831-8190

Wappingers Falls
Historical Society
Wappingers Falls, New York
12590

Erie County

County Arts Council

Arts Council in Buffalo
and Erie County
700 Main Street
Buffalo, New York 14202
716-856-7520

County Historian

see County Historical Society

County Historical Society

Buffalo and Erie County
Historical Society
25 Nottingham Court
Buffalo, New York 14216
716-873-9644
William Siener, Executive
Director
members: 1,200
founded: 1852
staff: 20 full-time, 2 part-time,
45 volunteer
major programs: library,
archives, museum, historic sites,
photo collection, research,
school programs, tours,
workshops, exhibits, periodical,
publications, markers program

County Planning Office

Erie County Planning
Department
Rath Building
95 Franklin Street
Buffalo, New York 14202
716-866-8390

see also Western New York
Association of Historical
Agencies, Avon, Livingston
County

Akron

Newstead Historical Society
P.O. Box 222
Akron, New York 14001
David Wakeman, President
members: 380
founded: 1958
staff: all volunteer
major programs: historic sites,
historic preservation, periodical

Alden

Alden Historical Society
13213 Broadway
Alden, New York 14004
716-937-7606
mail to: 299 Exchange Street
Alden, New York 14004
Nathan E. Sweet, President
members: 35
founded: 1965
staff: all volunteer
major programs: school
programs

Amherst

Erie and Niagara Counties
Regional Planning Board
3103 Sheridan Drive
Amherst, New York 14226
716-837-2035
David J. Evans, Director
founded: 1966
staff: 8 full-time
major programs: research,
periodical, publications,
technical preservation services,
grants

Boston

Boston Historical Society
9410 State Road
Boston, New York 14025

Southtowns Rural
Preservation Company
8500 Boston State Road
P.O. Box 153
Boston, New York 14025
716-941-5787
Karen M. Diemunsca, Executive
Director

founded: 1986
staff: 3 full-time
major programs: rural preservation, affordable housing, revolving fund

Brant

Brant Cemetery Association
Brant North Collins Road
Brant, New York 14027
716-549-0513
J. Carlton Winters, President
staff: 12 volunteer
major programs: periodical, historic preservation, markers program

Buffalo

Allentown Association
234 Allen Street
Buffalo, New York 14201
716-881-1024
Louise McMillan, Historic Preservation Specialist

Black Rock/Riverside
Neighborhood Housing Services
380 Ontario Street
Buffalo, New York 14207

Broadway-Fillmore
Neighborhood Housing Services
1129 Broadway
Buffalo, New York 14212
716-896-3030
Robert J. Sienkiewicz, Executive Director
founded: 1979
staff: 8 full-time, 1 part-time
major programs: photo collection, research, workshops, periodical, publications, awards, surveys, affordable housing, technical preservation services, revolving fund

Buffalo Community
Development Organization
1490 Jefferson Avenue
Buffalo, New York 14208

Buffalo Fire Historical Society
195 Court Street
Buffalo, New York 14202

Buffalo Friends of Olmsted Parks
Buffalo, New York 14075
716-649-5476
mail to: P.O. Box 509
Buffalo, New York 14205

Gretchen S. Toles, President
members: 100
founded: 1979
staff: all volunteer
major programs: historic sites, photo collection, research, lectures, exhibits, periodical, publications, historic preservation

Buffalo Preservation Board
428 City Hall
Buffalo, New York 14202
716-855-5071
James P. Mandell, Executive Secretary
founded: 1975
staff: 2 full-time, 2 volunteer
major programs: library, archives, historic sites, photo collection, research, surveys, historic preservation, technical preservation services

Buffalo Urban Cultural
Park Program
Office of Community
Development
City Hall
Buffalo, New York 14202
716-851-5016
Mark Tytka, Project Coordinator

Community Planning Assistance
Center of Western New York
25 High Street
Buffalo, New York 14203
716-886-1400

Darwin D. Martin House
(SUNY/Buffalo)
125 Jewett Parkway
Buffalo, New York 14214
716-831-2406
John D. O'Hern, Curator
members: 100
founded: 1986
staff: 1 full-time, 1 part-time, 15 volunteer
major programs: historic sites, research, tours, lectures, exhibits, historic preservation

Ellicott District
Community Development
644 William Street
Buffalo, New York 14206

Erie County Preservation Board
Department of Environmental
Planning

County Hall
95 Franklin Street
Buffalo, New York 14202
716-689-1440
Andrea Shaw, Chair

Fillmore-Leroy Area Residents
307 Leroy Avenue
Buffalo, New York 14214
716-838-6740
Stephen Karnath, Executive Director
members: 300
founded: 1975
staff: 12 full-time, 5 part-time, 19 volunteer
major programs: workshops, affordable housing, periodical, revolving fund, grants

Friends of the School of
Architecture and Environmental
Design
SUNY at Buffalo
Hayes Hall
3435 Main Street
Buffalo, New York 14214
716-831-3543
Suzanne Murray, Coordinator
members: 300
founded: 1977
major programs: school programs, tours, lectures, periodical, publications, awards

Fruitbelt Redevelopment, Inc.
326 High Street
Buffalo, New York 14204
716-882-2222
David C. Bell, Director
staff: 4 full-time, 1 volunteer
major programs: workshops, surveys, rural preservation, affordable housing, periodical, grants, matching grants

Greater East Side Community
Development Corporation
551 East Utica Street
Buffalo, New York 14208

Housing Assistance Center of
Niagara Frontier
1233 Main Street
Buffalo, New York 14209
716-881-2200
Denis J. Woods, Executive Director

founded: 1973
staff: 17 full-time, 1 part-time,
1 volunteer
major programs: affordable
housing, periodical

Housing Council of the
Niagara Frontier
470 Franklin Street
Buffalo, New York 14202

Junior League of Buffalo
45 Elmwood Avenue
Buffalo, New York 14201

Kensington Bailey Neighborhood
Housing Services
1048 Kensington Avenue
Buffalo, New York 14215

Landmark Society of the
Niagara Frontier
25 Nottingham Court
Buffalo, New York 14216
716-873-9644
John Conlin, President
members: 300
founded: 1969
staff: 1 part-time
major programs: tours, lectures,
exhibits, awards, historic
preservation, markers program,
periodical, easements

Linwood Oxford
Association Inc.
681 Linwood Avenue
Buffalo, New York 14209
716-881-0150
Rolessie Harwell Kirkland,
Executive Director
members: 265
founded: 1975
staff: 8 full-time
major programs: school
programs, workshops, awards,
surveys, historic preservation,
affordable housing, technical
preservation services, periodical,
grants, matching grants

Lower West Side Resource
Development Corporation
266 West Tupper Street
Buffalo, New York 14201
716-847-1171
Michael M. Edwards, Executive
Director

members: 190
founded: 1976
staff: 4 full-time, 1 part-time,
20 volunteer
major programs: library, school
programs, workshops,
periodical, publications, surveys,
historic preservation, affordable
housing, technical preservation
services, revolving fund, grants,
matching grants

Masten Neighborhood
Housing Services
568 Riley Street
Buffalo, New York 14208

Neighborhood Housing Services
of South Buffalo
2118 Seneca Street
Buffalo, New York 14210

Parkside Community Association
10 West Oakwood Place
Buffalo, New York 14222
716-838-1240
Derek Bateman, Program
Director
founded: 1963
staff: 2 full-time, 3 part-time,
200 volunteer
major programs: affordable
housing, periodical

Preservation Coalition
of Erie County
20 Angle Street
Buffalo, New York 14214
716-837-8858
A. Scott Field, Counsel
members: 500
founded: 1980
staff: 1 part-time, 25 volunteer
major programs: tours, lectures,
periodical, publications, historic
preservation

Seventy-eight Restoration
Corporation
1716 Main Street
Buffalo, New York 14209
716-883-7623
Jesse E. Nash, Jr., President,
Board of Directors
founded: 1977
staff: 2 full-time, 1 part-time
major programs: historic
preservation, affordable housing

West Side Neighborhood
Housing Services
359 Connecticut Street
Buffalo, New York 14213
716-885-2344
Fred G. Williams, Executive
Director
members: 225
founded: 1980
staff: 5 full-time
major programs: tours, historic
preservation, affordable housing,
technical preservation services,
periodical, revolving fund, grants

Cambria

Cambria Historical Society
4159 Lower Mountain Road
Lockport, New York 14094

Chaffee

Sardinia Historical Society
3829 Creek Road
Chaffee, New York 14030

Cheektowaga

Erie County Historical
Federation
11 Danforth Street
Cheektowaga, New York 14227
716-941-3475
Julia B. Reinstein, President
members: 100
founded: 1953
staff: all volunteer
major programs: historic sites,
lectures, periodical, workshops,
rural preservation, markers
program

Clarence

Historical Society of the
Town of Clarence
P.O. Box 86
Clarence, New York 14031

Asa Ransom House
10529 Main Street
Clarence, New York 14031
716-759-2315

East Amherst

Amherst Museum
Old Colony Park
3755 Tonawanda Creek Road
East Amherst, New York 14051
716-689-1440
Andrea Shaw, Executive Director

East Aurora

Aurora Historical Society
5 South Grove Street
East Aurora, New York 14052
716-652-3280
members: 240
founded: 1951
staff: 150 volunteer
major programs: library,
archives, museums, historic sites,
photo collection, tours, exhibits,
markers program, periodical

Eden

Eden Historical Society
8584 South Main Street
Eden, New York 14057
716-992-3488
Nathalie Leonard, Town
Historian
members: 217
founded: 1963
staff: 15 volunteer
major programs: library,
archives, museum, photo
collection, research, tours,
workshops, exhibits, historic
preservation, rural preservation,
markers program

Elma

Elma Historical Society
P.O. Box 84
Elma, New York 14059
716-652-6310
Mae C. Yacobush, Curator
members: 40
founded: 1957
major programs: museum,
workshops, exhibits

Grand Island

Grand Island Historical Society
2255 Baseline Road
Grand Island, New York 14072
716-773-3001
Marion E. Klingel, Town
Historian
founded: 1962
major programs: library,
museum, tours, exhibits,
markers program

Hamburg

Hamburg Historical Society
4237 Glenwillow Drive
P.O. Box 400
Hamburg, New York 14075

Holland

Holland Historical Society
Olean Road
Holland, New York 14080

Lackawanna

Lackawanna Community
Development Corporation
2558 Hamburg Turnpike
Lackawanna, New York 14218

Lancaster

Lancaster New York
Historical Society
40 Clark Street
Lancaster, New York 14086
mail to: 39 Glendale Avenue
Lancaster, New York 14086
Jan Pecqueur, President
major programs: historic sites,
school programs, tours,
periodical

Lancaster New York Opera
House
21 Central Avenue
Lancaster, New York 14086
716-683-1776
Karen I. Kosman, Executive
Director
members: 500
founded: 1980
staff: 1 full-time, 9 part-time,
175 volunteer
major programs: school
programs, tours, public
performances, periodical

North Collins

North Collins Historical Society
Shirley Road
North Collins, New York 14111

Orchard Park

Orchard Park Historical Society
East Quaker Street
Orchard Park, New York 14127
716-662-3285
mail to: 5800 Armor Road,
Orchard Park, New York 14127
John N. Printy, Historian
members: 50
founded: 1950
staff: 3 volunteer
major programs: museum, photo
collection, tours, exhibits,
surveys, markers program

South Wales

Wales Historical Society
Emery Road, P.O. Box 65
South Wales, New York 14139
Molly B. Gavin Hauck, President
members: 5
founded: 1978
staff: 2 volunteer
major programs: museum,
research, school programs

Springville

Concord Historical Society
98 East Main Street
Springville, New York 14141
716-592-2342
Alan V. Manchester, President
members: 10
founded: 1941
staff: 10 volunteer
major programs: library,
museum, photo collection,
school programs, lectures,
exhibits, publications, markers
program

Tonawanda

Historical Society of
the Tonawandas
113 Main Street
Tonawanda, New York 14150
716-694-7406
Willard B. Dittmar, Executive
Director
members: 380
founded: 1961
staff: 1 full-time, 75 volunteer
major programs: library,
archives, museum, historic sites,
photo collection, research,
school programs, exhibits,
periodical, publications, historic
preservation, markers program

Tonawanda-Kenmore
Historical Society
100 Knoche Road
Tonawanda, New York 14150
716-873-5774
Marilyn Brown, President
members: 280
founded: 1929
staff: 1 part-time, 4 volunteer
major programs: archives,
museum, photo collection,
research, school programs, tours,
lectures, workshops, exhibits,
periodical, publications, surveys,
historic preservation

West Seneca

West Seneca Historical Society
919 Mill Road
West Seneca, New York 14224
James J. Ciesla, Town Historian
members: 100
founded: 1946
staff: 1 full-time, 1 part-time
major programs: library, photo
collection, research, exhibits

Williamsville

Amherst Historical and
Genealogical Society
175 North Long Street
Williamsville, New York 14221

Village of Williamsville Historical
Society
5658 Main Street
Williamsville, New York 14221

Woodlawn

Woodlawn Community
Revitalization Corporation
3291 Lake Shore Road
Woodlawn, New York 14219
716-826-1288
Stanley J. Figiel, Executive
Director
members: 55
founded: 1984
staff: 1 full-time, 2 part-time
major programs: awards,
surveys, technical preservation
services, periodical, revolving
fund

Essex County

County Arts Council

Essex County Arts Council
Church Street, P.O. Box 805
Elizabethtown, New York 12932
518-873-6301
Caroline Rubino, Executive
Director
members: 150
founded: 1983
staff: 1 part-time
major programs: workshops,
periodical, publications

County Historian

Charlotte J. McCormick
Elizabethtown, New York 12932

County Historical Society

Essex County
Historical Society
Court Street
Elizabethtown, New York 12932
518-873-6466
James A. Kinley, Director
members: 325
founded: 1954
staff: 2 full-time, 3 part-time,
4 volunteer
major programs: library,
archives, museum, photo
collection, research, school
programs, lectures, workshops,
exhibits, periodical, publications

County Planning Office

Essex County
Planning Office
Church Street
Elizabethtown, New York 12932
518-873-6301 x375

see also Federation of Historical
Services, Troy, Rensselaer
County

Crown Point

Crown Point Foundation
P.O. Box 427
Elizabethtown, New York 12932

Penfield Museum and
Foundation
RD 1, Box 117
Crown Point, New York 12928
518-597-3963
Douglas Brooks, Caretaker
members: 100
founded: 1962
staff: 2 full-time, 15 volunteer
major programs: library,
museum, historic sites, photo
collection, research, tours,
exhibits, historic preservation

Elizabethtown

Adirondack Council
P.O. Box D-2
Elizabethtown, New York 12932
518-873-2240
members: 4,000
major programs: land
conservation, periodical

Adirondack Land Trust
P.O. Box D-2
Elizabethtown, New York 12932
518-873-9239

major programs: land
conservation, publications,
easements

Housing Assistance Program
of Essex County
2 Church Street, P.O. Box 157
Elizabethtown, New York 12932
518-873-6888
Alan S. Hips, Executive Director
founded: 1976
staff: 11 full-time, 2 part-time
major programs: library, historic
sites, research, surveys, historic
preservation, rural preservation,
affordable housing, archeology,
grants, matching grants

Essex

Essex Community Heritage
Organization
P.O. Box 260
Essex, New York 12936
518-963-7088
Robert J. Hammerslag,
Executive Director
members: 225
founded 1969
staff: 2 full-time, 1 part-time
major prgrams: photo collection,
research, school programs,
lectures, workshops, periodical,
publications, surveys, historic
preservation, rural preservation,
affordable housing, technical
preservation services, revolving
fund, easements

Keeseville

Friends of Keeseville
Civic Center
Main Street, P.O. Box 446
Keeseville, New York 12944
518-834-9606
Ann Ruzow Holland, Executive
Director
founded: 1981
staff: 7 full-time
major programs: historic
preservation, rural preservation,
affordable housing

Keeseville Historical Society
Keeseville, New York 12944

Lake Placid

Adirondack North Country
Association
P.O. Box 148
93 Saranac Avenue

Lake Placid, New York 12946
major programs: rural
preservation, affordable housing,
economic development,
periodical

Lake Placid-North Elba
Historical Society
Averyville Road
Lake Placid, New York 12946
518-523-1608

Olmstedville

Minerva Historical Society
P.O. Box 81
Olmstedville, New York 12851
518-251-2229

Schroon Lake

Schroon-North Hudson
Historical Society
Main Street
Schroon Lake, New York 12870
518-532-7798
Jack Richards, President
members: 260
founded: 1970
staff: 30 volunteer
major programs: library,
archives, museum, photo
collection, research, lectures,
exhibits, surveys, historic
preservation, markers program,
periodical

Ticonderoga

PRIDE of Ticonderoga
146 Montcalm Street
Ticonderoga, New York 12883
518-585-6366
Susan D. Rathbun, Executive
Director
members: 115
founded: 1984
staff: 2 full-time, 3 part-time,
15 volunteer
major programs: museum,
historic preservation, rural
preservation, affordable housing,
periodical, grants, matching
grants

Ticonderoga Historical Society
Moses Circle
Ticonderoga, New York 12883

Westport

Westport Historical Society
P.O. Box 414
Westport, New York 12993

Willsboro

Willsborough Historical Society
Willsboro, New York 12996

Franklin County

County Arts Council

see Malone Arts Council,
Malone; Ballard Mill Center for
the Arts, Malone

County Historian

Office of the Franklin County
Historian
Franklin County Historical
Society (see next entry)

County Historical Society

Franklin County Historical and
Museum Society
51 Milwaukee Street
Malone, New York 12953
518-483-2750
Wendell C. Denny, President
members: 300
founded: 1903
staff: 1 part-time, 60 volunteer
major programs: library,
museum, photo collection,
research, school programs, tours,
lectures, workshops, exhibits,
periodical, publications, historic
preservation

County Planning Office

Franklin County
63 West Main Street
Malone, New York 12953
518-483-6767

see also Regional Council of
Historical Agencies, Syracuse,
Onondaga County

Malone

Ballard Mill Center for the Arts
South William Street
Malone, New York 12953
518-483-5863
Gladys L. Chetney, Chair
founded: 1972
staff: 1 part-time, 15 volunteer
major programs: museum,
historic sites, school programs,
tours, workshops, rural
preservation

Franklin County Community
Housing Council
345 Elm Street
Malone, New York 12953

Malone Arts Council
South William Street
Malone, New York 12953
Jane Otis, Executive Director

Malone Office of Community
Development
One Elm Street
Malone, New York 12953
Pat Murtagh, Jr., Director

Almanzo and Laura Ingalls
Wilder Association
P.O. Box 283
Malone, New York 12953
518-483-5595
Dorthy B. Smith, President
founded: 1986
staff: 20 volunteer
major programs: exhibits,
periodical, publications, historic
preservation

Onchiota

Six Nations Indian Museum
Onchiota, New York 12968

Paul Smiths

Paul Smiths Historical Museum
Paul Smiths, New York 12970
518-327-6313

Saranac Lake

Historic Saranac Lake
North Elba Town House
132 River Street, P.O. Box 1030
Saranac Lake, New York 12983
518-891-0971
Mary B. Hotaling, Executive
Director
members: 125
founded: 1980
staff: 13 volunteer
major programs: publications,
surveys, historic preservation,
affordable housing

Northern Adirondack
Historical Association
P.O. Box 463
Saranac Lake, New York 12983

Fulton County

County Arts Council

Fulton County Arts Council
86 North Main Street
Gloversville, New York 12078

County Historian

Lewis Decker
187 Bleeker Street
Gloversville, New York 12078

County Historical Society

Fulton County Historical
Society and Museum
239 Kingsborough Avenue
P.O. Box 711
Gloversville, New York 12078
518-725-2203
Elwood A. Stowell, President
members: 162
founded: 1897
staff: 1 part-time, 2 volunteer
major programs: library,
museum, school programs,
lectures, historic preservation

County Planning Office

Fulton County Planning Office
Fort Johnston Building
One East Montgomery Street
Johnstown, New York 12095
518-762-5832

see also Federation of Historical
Services, Troy, Rennssealer
County; Mohawk Valley
Museums Consortium,
Amsterdam, Montgomery
County

Caroga Lake

Caroga Historical Association
and Museum
London Bridge Road
P.O. Box 434
Caroga Lake, New York 12032
518-835-4400
Emma B. Krause, President
members: 106
founded: 1977
staff: 2 part-time, 30 volunteer
major programs: museum,
school programs, tours, lectures,
workshops, exhibits, periodical

Ephratah

Ephratah Historical Society
Ephratah, New York 13452

Gloversville

Community Heritage Company
86 North Main Street
Gloversville, New York 12078
518-725-2114
David Henderson, Director
founded: 1986
staff: 1 full-time, 1 part-time
major programs: historic
preservation, rural preservation,
affordable housing, technical
preservation services, revolving
fund

Johnstown

Friends of Johnson Hall
Hall Avenue
Johnstown, New York 12095

Johnstown Historical Society
17 North William Street
Johnstown, New York 12095

Mayfield

Mayfield Historical Society
Church Hall
Mayfield, New York 12117

Perth

Perth Historical Society
Perth, New York 12010

Genesee County

County Arts Council

Genesee Arts Council
10 West Main Street
Batavia, New York 14020
716-343-9313

County Historian

see County Historical Society

County Historical Society

Genesee County History
Department
Holland Land Office Museum
131 West Main Street
Batavia, New York 14020
716-344-2550 x275
Susan L. Conklin, County
Historian

founded: 1950
staff: 2 part-time
major programs: library,
research, lectures

County Planning Office

Genesee County Planning
Department
3837 West Main Street Road
Batavia, New York 14020
716-344-2480

see also Genesee-Finger Lakes
Regional Planning Council,
Rochester, Monroe County;
Landmark Society of Western
New York, Rochester, Monroe
County; Western New York
Association of Historical
Agencies, Avon, Livingston
County

Alabama

Alabama Historical Society
2237 Lewiston Road
Oakfield, New York 14125

Alexander

Alexander Historical Society
Alexander, New York 14005

Batavia

Holland Land Office Museum
131 West Main Street
Batavia, New York 14020
716-343-4727
Kathleen Armstrong, Curator
staff: 2 part-time, 12 volunteer
major programs: museum, tours

Holland Purchase
Historical Society
131 West Main Street
Batavia, New York 14020

Landmark Society of
Genesee County
P.O. Box 342
Batavia, New York 14020
716-343-3833
Anthony Kutter, President
members: 105
founded: 1964
staff: 3 volunteer
major programs: library, photo
collection, school programs,
tours, lectures, workshops,
periodical, publications, awards,
historic preservation

Bergen

Bergen Historical Society
6833 Pocock Road
Bergen, New York 14416

Byron-Bergen Public Library
13 South Lake Street
P.O. Box 417
Bergen, New York 14416
716-494-1120
F. Eileen Almquist, Director
staff: 1 full-time
major programs: library, historic
sites, research, historic
preservation, grants

Village of Bergen
16 North Lake Street
Bergen, New York 14416
716-494-1513
Ralph Garnish, Mayor
major programs: historic
preservation

Byron

Byron Historical Museum
East Main Street
Byron, New York 14422

Corfu

Pembroke Historical Association
Town Hall
Routes 5 and 77
Corfu, New York 14036

Le Roy

Le Roy Historical Society
23 East Main Street
Le Roy, New York 14482
716-768-7433
Edward G. Cornwell, Jr.
Director
members: 200
founded: 1940
staff: 1 part-time, 4 volunteer
major programs: library,
archives, museum, photo
collection, research, tours,
lectures, exhibits

Pavilion

Pavilion Historical Society
11134 East Park Street
P.O. Box 94
Pavilion, New York 14525

Stafford

Stafford Historical Society
6018 Main Road
Stafford, New York 14143
Gary Churchill, President
members: 40
founded: 1982
major programs: historic
preservation

Greene County

County Arts Council

Greene County Council
on the Arts
398 Main Street, P.O. Box 463
Catskill, New York 12414
518-943-3400
Kay Stamer, Executive Director
founded: 1976
staff: 2 full-time, 3 part-time,
many volunteer
major programs: school
programs, workshops, exhibits,
periodical, publications, grants

County Historian

Mabel Parker Smith
251 Main Street
Catskill, New York 12414

County Historical Society

Greene County Historical Society
RD, Route 9W
Coxsackie, New York 12501
518-731-6490
Edwin G. Grossmann, President
members: 960
founded: 1936
staff: 2 part-time, 40 volunteer
major programs: library,
museum, historic sites,
periodical, historic preservation

County Planning Office

Greene County Planning
Department
Route 3, Box 909
Cairo, New York 12413
518-622-3251

see also Albany-Schenectady-
Greene Counties Agricultural
and Historical Societies,
Altamont, Albany County;
Federation of Historical Services,

Troy, Rensselaer County;
Catskill Center for Conservation
and Development, Arkville,
Delaware County

Athens

Athens Museum
4 Mile Point
Athens, New York 12015
Richard Talay, Curator

Catskill

Catskill Mountain Housing
329 Main Street
Catskill, New York 12414
518-943-6700
Glenn Gidaly, Executive Director
founded: 1981
staff: 2 full-time, 1 part-time,
3 volunteer
major programs: rural
preservation, affordable housing,
periodical, revolving fund,
grants, matching grants

East Durham

Catskill Valley Historical Society
East Durham, New York 12426

Haines Falls

Mountain Top Historical Society
of Greene County
P.O. Box 263
Haines Falls, New York 12436
518-589-6191
Justine L. Hommel, President
members: 281
founded: 1973
staff: all volunteer
major programs: photo
collection, school programs,
lectures, periodical, rural
preservation

Jewett

Music and Art Center of
Greene County
Division of Architecture and
Historic Preservation
P.O. Box 20
Jewett, New York 12444
518-734-3890
Ihor Sonevytsky, President
major programs: surveys, rural
preservation

Prattsville

Zadock Pratt Museum
P.O. Box 333
Prattsville, New York 12468
518-299-3395
James Erdman, Curator/Director
members: 150
founded: 1963
staff: 1 full-time, 1 part-time,
5 volunteer
major programs: museum, tours,
historic preservation

Hamilton County

County Arts Council

see Adirondack Lakes Center for
the Arts, Blue Mountain Lake

County Historian

Frederick C. Aber, Jr.
P.O. Box 3
Indian Lake, New York 12842

County Historical Society

Hamilton County Historical
Society
Hamilton County Court House
Lake Pleasant, New York 12108

County Planning Office

Hamilton County Planning
Office
County Office Building
Lake Pleasant, New York 12108
518-548-7191

see also Regional Council of
Historical Agencies, Syracuse,
Onondaga County

Blue Mountain Lake

Adirondack Historical Society
Adirondack Museum Library
Blue Mountain Lake, New York
12812

Adirondack Lakes Center for the
Arts
Route 28, P.O. Box 101
Blue Mountain Lake, New York
12812
518-352-7715
Betsy Folwell, Director

The Adirondack Museum
Routes 28N and 30
Blue Mountain Lake, New York
12812
518-352-7311
Craig Gilborn, Director
members: 1,040
founded: 1957
staff: 22 full-time, 33 part-time
major programs: museum,
periodical,publications, exhibits,
school programs

Indian Lake

Warren-Hamilton Housing
Corporation
Town Hall
Indian Lake, New York 12842
518-648-5947
Nancy Berkowitz, Executive
Director
founded: 1984
staff: 3 full-time
major programs: rural
preservation, affordable housing

Raquette Lake

Sagamore Institute
Sagamore Road
Raquette Lake, New York 13436
315-354-5311
Howard Kirschenbaum,
Executive Director
members: 400
founded: 1973
staff: 12 full-time, 10 part-time,
100 volunteer
major programs: museum,
historic sites, school programs,
tours, workshops, historic
preservation, periodical

Wells

Wells Historical Society
Algonquin Drive
Wells, New York 12190

Herkimer County

County Arts Council

see Central New York
Community Arts Council, Utica,
Oneida County for
decentralization information

County Historian

H. Paul Draheim
705 Bellinger Street
Herkimer, New York 13350

County Historical Society

Herkimer County Historical
Society
400 North Main Street
Herkimer, New York 13350
315-866-6413
Jane S. Spellman, Director
members: 910
founded: 1896
staff: 2 full-time, 3 part-time,
54 volunteer
major programs: library,
archives, museum, photo
collection, research, school
programs, tours, exhibits,
periodical, publications, historic
preservation

County Planning Office

Herkimer County
Planning Board
RD 1, Box 125
Utica, New York 13502

see also Regional Council of
Historical Agencies, Syracuse,
Onondaga County; Oneida
County Planning Department

Dolgeville

Dolgeville-Manheim Historical
Society
41 North Main Street
Dolgeville, New York 13329

Herkimer

Herkimer Arts Council
P.O. Box 25
Herkimer, New York 13350

Ilion

Remington Gun Museum
Catherine Street
Ilion, New York 13357

Jordanville

Town of Warren Historical
Society
Main Street, P.O. Box 103
Jordanville, New York 13361
315-858-0365
John Pronko, President

Little Falls

Little Falls Historical Society
77 Petrie Street
Little Falls, New York 13365
315-823-2441

Little Falls Public Library
10 Waverly Place
Little Falls, New York 13365
315-823-1542

Middleville

Kuyahoora Valley Historical
Society
P.O. Box 336
Middleville, New York 13406

Ohio

Ohio Historical Society
RD, Cold Brook
Ohio, New York 13324

Old Forge

Arts Guild of Old Forge
Arts Center, Route 28
Old Forge, New York 13420
315-369-6411
Beatrice D. Foley, Executive
Coordinator
members: 300
founded: 1968
staff: 1 full-time, 3 part-time,
many volunteer
major programs: lectures,
workshops, exhibits

Town of Webb Historical
Association
Crosby Boulevard
Old Forge, New York 13420
315-369-3838
Marion G. Holmes, President
founded: 1977
staff: 2 part-time, 3 volunteer
major programs: photo
collection, research, school
programs, tours, lectures,
exhibits

Salisbury

Salisbury Historical Group
RD 1
Dolgeville, New York 13329
315-429-7793

Salisbury Center

Salisbury Historical Society
P.O. Box 185
Salisbury Center, New York
13454

Jefferson County

County Arts Council

see North Country Library
System, Watertown, for
decentralization information

County Historian

Charles Dunham
P.O. Box 86
Chaumont, New York 13622

County Historical Society

Jefferson County
Historical Society
228 Washington Street
Watertown, New York 13601
315-782-3491
Margaret Shaeffer, Director

County Planning Office

Jefferson County Department
of Planning
163 Arsenal Street
Watertown, New York 13601
315-785-3144

see also Regional Council of
Historical Agencies, Syracuse,
Onondaga County

Adams

Historical Association of
South Jefferson
9 East Church Street
Adams, New York 13605

Alexandria Bay

A. Graham Thomson
Memorial Museum
James and Market streets
Alexandria Bay, New York
13607
315-482-3110
Kimberly A. Keinz,
Director/Curator

Alexandria Town Historical
Society
Alexandria Bay, New York
13607

Brownville

General Jacob Brown
Historical Society
216 Brown Boulevard
Brownville, New York 13615

Railway Historical Society of
Northern New York
P.O. Box 97
Brownville, New York 13615

Cape Vincent

Cape Vincent Historical Museum
Market and Joseph streets,
P.O. Box 223
Cape Vincent, New York 13618
315-654-3126
Dorothy B. Allen, Village
Historian
founded: 1968
staff: 20 volunteer
major programs: archives,
museum, photo collection,
research, tours, lectures,
exhibits, historic preservation,
rural preservation

Carthage

Four River Valleys
Historical Society
P.O. Box 504
Carthage, New York 13619
Nelson F. Eddy, President
members: 550
founded: 1977
staff: 25 volunteer
major programs: historic sites,
research, tours, exhibits,
periodical, publications, rural
preservation, markers program

Clayton

Clayton Improvement
Association
P.O. Box 312
Clayton, New York 13624
315-686-3212
Robert Bastian, Executive
Director
founded: 1977
staff: 3 full-time
major programs: library,
research, lectures, workshops,
surveys, rural preservation,
affordable housing, revolving
fund, grants

Thousand Island Craft School
and Textile Museum
314 John Street
Clayton, New York 13624
315-686-4123
Margret Rood, Director
members: 250
founded: 1966
staff: 5 part-time, 30 volunteer
major programs: library,
archives, museum, school
programs, workshops, exhibits,
periodical

Thousand Islands
Shipyard Museum
750 Mary Street
Clayton, New York 13624
315-686-4104
F.I. Collins, Jr., Director
members: 900
founded: 1964
staff: 5 full-time, 1 part-time
major programs: library,
archives, museum, historic sites,
photo collection, research,
school programs, tours, exhibits,
periodical, publications

Dexter

Frontier Housing Corporation
P.O. Box 56
Dexter, New York 13634

LaFargeville

Northern New York Agricultural
Historical Society
Agricultural Museum at
Stone Mills
LaFargeville, New York 13656
315-658-2582
Rose P. Cullen, Curator
members: 100
founded: 1968
staff: 1 full-time, 2 part-time,
many volunteer
major programs: museum,
school programs, tours, exhibits,
historic preservation

Mannsville

Mannsville Museum
Lilac Park Drive, P.O. Box 34
Mannsville, New York 13661
315-465-6375
Henry Colby, Chair

members: 50
founded: 1950
staff: 6 volunteer
major programs: museum

Oxbow

Oxbow Historical Association
P.O. Box 182
Oxbow, New York 13671
315-287-2972
Eleanor M. Jones, President
members: 30
founded: 1974
staff: all volunteer
major programs: photo
collection, exhibits, historic
preservation

Sackets Harbor

North Shore Preservation
Company
P.O. Box 55
Sackets Harbor, New York
13685
315-646-2337
Richard S. Hersey, Secretary
founded: 1986
major programs: historic
preservation, rural preservation,
affordable housing

Pickering Beach Museum
501 West Main Street
Sackets Harbor, New York
13685

Sackets Harbor
Historical Society
100 West Main Street
P.O. Box 78
Sackets Harbor, New York
13685
John Burdick, President
members: 35
founded: 1976
staff: all volunteer
major programs: historic
preservation, periodical

Sackets Harbor Urban Cultural
Park Program
Sackets Harbor Municipal
Building
Sackets Harbor, New York
13685
315-782-5250
Norman Hunneyman, Director

Thousand Island Park

Thousand Island Park
Landmark Society
Thousand Island Park,
New York 13692
315-482-3071
mail to: 745 Harvard Street
Rochester, New York 14610
Trude Brown Fitelson, Director
members: 100
founded: 1978
staff: 6 volunteer
major programs: library, photo
collection, tours, lectures,
workshops, exhibits, awards,
periodical, surveys

Watertown

Black River Housing Council
216 Washington Street
Watertown, New York 13601

Burr Mills Historical Museum
Star Route
Watertown, New York 13601

Neighbors of Watertown
116 Franklin Street
Watertown, New York 13601

Office of City Historian
City of Watertown
Municipal Building, Room 201
Watertown, New York 13601
Junia Fitch Stanton, City
Historian

Kings County

County Arts Council

Brooklyn Arts Council
200 Eastern Parkway
Brooklyn, New York 11238
718-783-4469

County Historian

Elliot Willensky
Brooklyn Borough Hall
Office of Brooklyn Borough
Preservation
16 Court Street
Brooklyn, New York 11241

County Historical Society

Brooklyn Historical Society
128 Pierrepont Street
Brooklyn, New York 11201
718-624-0890

David M. Kahn, Executive
Director
founded: 1863
staff: 16 full-time, 8 part-time
major programs: library,
archives, museum, photo
collection, school programs,
tours, lectures, exhibits,
periodical

County Planning Office

Brooklyn Office, Department of
City Planning
16 Court Street
Brooklyn, New York 11241
718-643-7550

see also New York County
listings ; Society for the
Preservation of Long Island
Antiquities, Setauket, Suffolk
County

Brooklyn

Amersfort Flatlands
Development Corporation
2076 Flatbush Avenue
Brooklyn, New York 11234
718-253-1117
Ben DuBose, Executive Director
founded: 1979
staff: 1 full-time, 6 part-time,
10 volunteer
major programs: periodical,
surveys, affordable housing

Astella Development
Corporation
1520 Mermaid Avenue
Brooklyn, New York 11216
718-266-4653
Gregory Dormani, Executive
Director
founded: 1978
staff: 4 full-time
major programs: tours,
workshops, periodical, surveys,
affordable housing

Bay Ridge Historical Society
P.O. Box 483, Fort Hamilton
Station
Brooklyn, New York 11209

Bedford Stuyvesant Restoration
1368 Fulton Street
Brooklyn, New York 11216
Theodore Gunns, Director

Borough Hall Restoration
Foundation
209 Joralemon Street
Brooklyn, New York 11201
Marion Scotto, Treasurer

Brighton Neighborhood
Association
1002 Brighton Beach Avenue
Brooklyn, New York 11235
718-891-0800
Pat Singer, Joel Samuels, Co-
Executive Directors
members: 2,000
founded: 1977
staff: 6 full-time, 2 part-time,
3 volunteer
major programs: school
programs, lectures, workshops,
periodical, awards, rural
preservation, affordable housing,
technical preservation services

Brooklyn Heights Association
55 Pierrepont Street
Brooklyn, New York 11201
718-858-9193
Denise Clayton, President
members: 1,200
founded: 1910
staff: 1 full-time, 2 part-time,
50 volunteer
major programs: research,
periodical, publications, awards,
historic preservation

Brooklyn Hispanic Community
Organization
116 Smith Street
Brooklyn, New York 11217

Brooklyn Historical Railway
Association
599 East Seventh Street
Brooklyn, New York 11218
718-941-3160
Robert Diamond, President

Brooklyn Neighborhood
Improvement Association
648 Washington Avenue
Brooklyn, New York 11238
718-622-6026
Carlyle McKetty, Executive
Director
staff: 8 full-time, 5 part-time
major programs: periodical,
affordable housing

Brooklyn Public Library
Grand Army Plaza
Brooklyn, New York 11238
718-780-7781
Marguerite A. Dodson,
Cordinator, Programming
Services

Canarsie Historical Society
9501 Schenck Street
Brooklyn, New York 11236

Carroll Gardens Association
515 Court Street
Brooklyn, New York 11231
718-858-0557
Joseph L. Maniscalco, Executive
Director
staff: 3 full-time, 1 part-time
major programs: affordable
housing

Cobble Hill Association
P.O. Box 376
Brooklyn, New York 11201
718-855-8841
Richard C. Hayes, President
members: 750
founded 1959
major programs: historic
preservation, periodical

Council of Neighborhood
Organizations
3918 Fort Hamilton Parkway
Brooklyn, New York 11218
718-853-0100
Jeanne DiLascio, Executive
Director
members: 100
founded: 1978
staff: 3 full-time, 3 part-time,
3 volunteer
major programs: photo
collection, research, school
programs, lectures, workshops,
exhibits, periodical, publications,
awards, surveys, affordable
housing, technical preservation
services, grants

Crown Heights Neighborhood
Improvement Association
728 Nostrand Avenue
Brooklyn, New York 11216

Cypress Hills Local Development
Corportation
3152 Fulton Street
Brooklyn, New York 11208
718-647-8100

Michelle Neugebauer, Executive
Director
members: 50
founded: 1983
staff: 5 full-time, 4 part-time,
40 volunteer
major programs: workshops,
periodical, publications, surveys,
historic preservation, affordable
housing, matching grants

Charles Drew Local
Development Corporation
1285A St. Marks Avenue
Brooklyn, New York 11213

East New York
Development Corporation
2644 Atlantic Avenue
Brooklyn, New York 11207
718-495-3232
Sybil Dodson Lucas, Executive
Director
founded: 1968
staff: 56 full-time
major programs: affordable
housing, periodical

Erasmus Neighborhod
Federation
1565 Nostrand Avenue, #1E
Brooklyn, New York 11226

Fifth Avenue Committee
375 Fifth Avenue
Brooklyn, New York 11215
718-965-2777
Wendy Fleischer, Executive
Director
founded: 1977
staff: 4 full-time, 1 part-time,
12 volunteer
major programs: lectures,
workshops, periodical,
affordable housing

Flatbush Development
Corporation
1418 Cortelyou Road
Brooklyn, New York 11226

Flatbush East Development
Corporation
559 East 43rd Street
Brooklyn, New York 11203

Flatbush Historical Society
2255 Church Avenue
Brooklyn, New York 11226
Irving Choban, President

Flatlands Historical Foundation
3846 Flatlands Avenue
Brooklyn, New York 11234

Fort Greene Landmarks
Preservation Committee
P.O. Box 401198
Brooklyn, New York 11240
718-789-8559
Eric Allison, Chair

Fort Hamilton Historical Society
Fort Hamilton
Brooklyn, New York 11252
718-630-4349
Joseph Tedeschi, President
members: 480
founded: 1980
staff: 8 volunteer
major programs: museum, photo
collection, research, school
programs, tours, lectures,
periodical, publications

Gowanus Canal Community
Development Corporation
515 Court Street
Brooklyn, New York 11231
718-858-0558
Joseph L. Maniscalco, Executive
Director
staff: 2 full-time, 3 part-time
major programs: affordable
housing

Gravesend Historical Society
P.O. Box 1643,
Gravesend Station
Brooklyn, New York 11223

Greater Sheepshead Bay
Development Corporation
2930 Avenue X
Brooklyn, New York 11235
718-332-0582
Michael Crawford, Executive
Director
members: 210
founded: 1978
staff: 3 full-time, 100 part-time,
20 volunteer
major programs: research, school
programs, workshops, periodical, publications, surveys,
affordable housing, markers
programs

James A. Kelly Institute for
Local Historical Studies
180 Remsen Street
Brooklyn, New York 11201

Junction College Development
Corporation
1569 Flatbush Avenue
Brooklyn, New York 11210
Barbara Sheeran, President

Kingborough Historical Society
2001 Oriental Boulevard
Brooklyn, New York 11235

Lefferts Homestead
95 Prospect Park West
Brooklyn, New York 11215
718-965-6505
Evan Kingsley, Director
founded: 1918
staff: 2 full-time, 1 part-time,
many volunteer
major programs: museum

Litchfield Villa
95 Prospect Park West
Brooklyn, New York 11215
Tupper Thomas, Admisistrator

Los Sures Community
Development
213 South Fourth Street
Brooklyn, New York 11211

Midwood Development
Corporation
1416 Avenue M
Brooklyn, New York 11230
718-376-0999
David Greenbaum, Executive
Director
founded: 1976
staff: 5 full-time, 45 part-time,
20 volunteer
major programs: school
programs, workshops,
periodical, publications,
affordable housing, revolving
fund

Neighborhood Housing Services
of East Flatbush
3009 Glenwood Road
Brooklyn, New York 11210

North Brooklyn Development
Corporation
894 Manhattan Avenue
Brooklyn, New York 11222

Northeast Brooklyn Housing
Development Corporation
1746 Broadway
Brooklyn, New York 11207
718-453-9490

Joseph E. Holley, Sr., Director
staff: 2 full-time, 3 volunteer
major programs: affordable
housing, grants, matching grants

Ocean Parkway Community
Development Corporation
4520 18th Avenue
Brooklyn, New York 11204

Opportunity Development
Association Corporation
12 Heyward Street
Brooklyn, New York 11211

Park Slope Civic Council
550 Second Street
Brooklyn, New York 11215
718-768-4699

Parkway Stuyvesant Community
and Housing Corporation
77 New York Avenue
Brooklyn, New York 11216
718-604-1948
Lionel L. Daniels, Chair
founded: 1957
staff: 4 full-time, 8 volunteer
major programs: workshops,
surveys, affordable housing,
grants, matching grants

People's Firehouse
113 Berry Street
Brooklyn, New York 11211
718-388-4696
Adam Veneski, President
founded: 1977
staff: 40 full-time
major programs: affordable
housing, periodical, grants

Prospect Lefferts Gardens
Neighborhood Association
575 Flatbush Avenue
Brooklyn, New York 11222
718-693-7777
Sharman Blake, Executive
Director
members: 300
founded: 1967
staff: 4 full-time, 4 part-time
major programs: affordable
housing, technical preservation
services, periodical, matching
grants

Prospect Park
Administrator's Office
95 Prospect Park West
Brooklyn, New York 11215
718-965-8451

Tupper Thomas, Administrator
staff: 10 full-time, many
volunteer
major programs: museum, photo
collection, exhibits, periodical,
historic preservation

Prospect Park
Environmental Center
The Tennis House,
Prospect Park
Brooklyn, New York 11215
718-788-8500
John C. Muir, Executive
Director
members: 800
founded: 1978
staff: 9 full-time, 8 part-time,
3 volunteer
major programs: museum,
school programs, tours, lectures,
workshops, exhibits, periodical,
publications

Prospect Park South Association
196 Marlborough Road
Brooklyn, New York 11226
718-282-3141
Mary Kay Gallagher, Director,
Landmarks
members: 170
founded: 1900
staff: 17 volunteer
major programs: archives, photo
collection, tours, periodical,
publications, historic
preservation

Renaissance Development
Corporation
489 Rockaway Avenue
Brooklyn, New York 11212

Society for the Preservation of
Weeksville and Bedford-
Stuyvesant History
1698 Bergen Street, P.O. Box
120, St. Johns Station
Brooklyn, New York 11213
718-756-5250
Joan Maynard, Executive
Director
members: 250
founded: 1971
staff: 6 full-time
major programs: museum,
historic preservation, archeology,
periodical

St. Ann Center for Restoration
and the Arts
157 Montague Street
Brooklyn, New York 11201
718-834-8794
Susan Feldman, Artistic Director
founded: 1983
staff: 6 full-time, 2 part-time
major programs: historic
preservation, performing arts

St. Nicholas Neighborhood
Preservation Corporation
11-29 Catherine Street
Brooklyn, New York 11211
718-388-5454
Gary Hattem, Executive Director
founded: 1975
staff: 75 full-time
major programs: affordable
housing, periodical

Sunset Park Redevelopment
Committee
1501 Fourth Avenue
Brooklyn, New York 11220

Vanguard Urban Improvement
Association
556 Nostrand Avenue
Brooklyn, New York 11216

Wyckoff House
5816 Clarendon Road
Brooklyn, New York 11203
718-629-5400
mail to: P.O. Box 7743, FDR
Station, New York, New York
10150
Donald L. Wyckoff, Executive
Director
members: 2,400
founded: 1937
staff: 3 full-time, 4 part-time, 36
volunteer
major programs: museum, photo
collection, school programs,
tours, lectures, workshops,
exhibits, publications, historic
preservation, periodical

17th Street Brooklyn Association
1663 Eighth Avenue
Brooklyn, New York 11215

Lewis County

County Arts Council

see North Country Library System, Watertown, Jefferson County, for decentralization information

County Historian

Barbara A. Evans
P.O. Box 306
Lyons Falls, New York 13368

County Historical Society

Lewis County Historical Society
High Street, P.O. Box 306
Lyons Falls, New York 13368
315-348-8089
Barbara A. Evans, Director
members: 400
founded: 1928
staff: 1 full-time, 20 volunteer
major programs: library, museum, tours, exhibits, publications, historic preservation, rural preservation, periodical

County Planning Office

Lewis County Planning Board
County Court House
Lowville, New York 13367
315-376-5333

see also Regional Council of Historical Agencies, Syracuse, Onondaga County

Constableville

Constable Hall Association
John Street, P.O. Box 36
Constableville, New York 13325
315-397-2323
Robert H. McNeilly, Director
members: 1,100
founded: 1949
staff: 4 part-time, 100 volunteer
major programs: museum, historic sites, tours, periodical

Highmarket Restoration Society
Constableville, New York 13325

Croghan

American Maple Museum
P.O. Box 81
Croghan, New York 13327

Port Leyden

Port Leyden Historical Club
West Main Street
Port Leyden, New York 13433
315-348-6047
Florence W. Burnap, Secretary

Livingston County

County Arts Council

Genesee Valley Council
on the Arts
2 North Street
Geneseo, New York 14454
716-243-1522
Nancy O'Dea, Executive Director
members: 650
founded: 1967
staff: 3 part-time, 200 volunteer
major programs: school programs, workshops, exhibits, periodical

County Historian

Mary Patricia Schaap
History Research Center
30 Center Street
Geneseo, New York 14454

County Historical Society

Livingston County
Historical Society
30 Center Street
Geneseo, New York 14454
Kenneth Blakely, President
members: 250
founded: 1879
staff: all volunteer
major programs: exhibits, periodical

County Planning Office

Livingston County Planning
County Campus, Building 2
Mount Morris, New York 14510
716-658-2851

see also Genesee-Finger Lakes Regional Planning Council, Rochester, Monroe County; Landmark Society of Western New York, Rochester, Monroe County

Avon

Avon Preservation and Historical Society
Erie Depot Museum
Avon, New York 14414
716-226-8118
Robert C. Hoffman, President
major programs: library, museum, historic sites, surveys, historic preservation, rural preservation, affordable housing, markers program

Western New York Association of Historical Agencies
230 Rochester Street
P.O. Box 207
Avon, New York 14414
716-226-6330
Hans-J. Finke, Executive Director
members: 320
founded: 1985
staff: 1 full-time, 1 part-time, 25 volunteer
major programs: school programs, workshops, publications, technical preservation services, periodical

Caledonia

Big Springs Historical Society Museum
Main Street
Caledonia, New York 14423
716-538-4473
mail to: 1067 Main Street
Mumford, New York 14511
Ella K. McGinnis, Curator
members: 80
founded 1936
staff: all volunteer
major programs: museum, photo collection, school programs, lectures, exhibits

Dansville

Dansville Area Historical Society
P.O. Box 481
Dansville, New York 14437

Geneseo

Association for the Preservation
of Geneseo
P.O. Box 294
Geneseo, New York 14454
716-243-2376
Margaret Vangalio, President
members: 228
founded: 1973
major programs: school
programs, lectures, historic
preservation, periodical

Lima

Lima Historial Society
1850 Rochester Street
P.O. Box 532
Lima, New York 14485
Frances Gotcsik, President
members: 125
founded: 1973
staff: all volunteer
major programs: museum, tours,
surveys, historic preservation,
periodical

Livonia

Town of Livonia
10 Commercial Street
Livonia, New York 14487
716-346-5580
Maurice Sweeney, Town
Historian
staff: 3 full-time, 3 volunteer
major programs: library, archives, museum, photo collection

Mount Morris

Genesee Valley Rural
Preservation Company
P.O. Box 271
Mount Morris, New York 14510

Mount Morris Historical Society
14 Main Street, P.O. Box 94
Mount Morris, New York 14510
716-658-3548/3292
Dolores D. Scura, President
members: 250
founded: 1976
staff; 1 part-time, 75 volunteer
major programs: museum,
historic sites, school programs,
tours, lectures, exhibits

Nunda

Nunda Historical Society
Nunda, New York 14517

Madison County

County Arts Council

see Central New York
Community Arts Council, Utica,
Oneida County, for
decentralization information

County Historian

Isabel Bracy
616 McDonal Street
Chittenango, New York 13037

County Historical Society

Madison County Historical
Society
435 Main Street, P.O. Box 415
Oneida, New York 13421
315-363-4136
Donald Ekola, Director
members: 475
founded: 1900
staff: 2 full-time, 4 volunteer
major programs: library,
archives, museum, exhibits,
publications, periodical

County Planning Office

Madison County Planning Office
County Office Building
Wampsville, New York 13163
315-366-2376

see also Central New York
Regional Planning and
Development Board, Syracuse,
Onondaga County; Regional
Council of Historical Agencies,
Syracues, Onondaga County;
Preservation Association of
Central New York, Syracuse,
Onondaga County

Brookfield

Brookfield Township
Historical Society
Main Street
Brookfield, New York 13314
Gwendolyn Wittes, Treasurer
members: 25
founded: 1971
major programs: museum, photo
collection, exhibits, periodical

Canastota

Canastota Canal Town
Corporation
122 Canal Street

Canastota, New York 13032
315-697-3451
Charles Rock, Director
members: 90
founded: 1968
staff: 2 full-time, 1 part-time
major programs: museum, rural
preservation, affordable housing,
grants

Stoneleigh Housing Corporation
120 East Center Street
Canastota, New York 13032

Cazenovia

Cazenovia Preservation
Foundation
P.O. Box 266
Cazenovia, New York 13035
J. Rush Marshall, President
members: 400
founded: 1967
staff: 1 full-time, 1 part-time,
1 volunteer
major programs: photo
collection, tours, lectures,
publications, historic
preservation, rural preservation,
markers program, easements,
periodical

Cazenovia Public Library
100 Albany Street
Cazenovia, New York 13035
315-655-9322
Elizabeth K. Michael, Director
founded: 1886
staff: 2 full-time, 2 part-time,
12 volunteer
major programs: library, historic
sites, research

De Ruyter

Tromptown Historical Society
715 Division Street
De Ruyter, New York 13052

Hamilton

Hamilton Historical Commission
Public Library Building
Broad Street
Hamilton, New York 13346
315-824-1111
staff: 5 volunteer
major programs: museum,
exhibits, markers program

Morrisville

Morrisville Public Library
87 East Main Street
P.O. Box 37
Morrisville, New York 13408
315-684-9130
Patricia Congdon, Librarian

Munnsville

Fryer Memorial Library/
Museum
West Peterboro Road
P.O. Box 177
Munnsville, New York 13409
315-495-5395
Olive S. Boylan, Museum
Director
founded: 1976
staff: 10 volunteer
major programs: library,
archives, museum, photo
collection, research, school
programs, tours, lectures,
exhibits, publications,
archeology

New Woodstock

New Woodstock
Historical Society
New Woodstock, New York
13122

Monroe County

County Arts Council

Arts for Greater Rochester
335 East Main Street
Suite 200
Rochester, New York 14604
716-546-5602
Judith W. Kaplan, Executive
Director
members: 773
founded: 1981
staff: 7 full-time, 1 part-time,
530 volunteer
major programs: research, school
programs, workshops, exhibits,
publications, awards, surveys,
periodical, grants

County Historian

Shirley Cox Husted
115 South Avenue
Rochester, New York 14604

County Historical Society

no listing

County Planning Office

Monroe County Department of
Planning
47 South Fitzhugh Street,
Suite 200
Rochester, New York 14614
716-428-5461

see also Western New York
Association of Historical
Agencies, Avon, Livingston
County

Brighton

Brighton Historical Society
1775 East Avenue
Rochester, New York 14610
716-381-6202
mail to: 52 Kimbark Road
Rochester, New York 14610
Roberta LaChiusa, President
members: 600
founded: 1946
staff: all volunteer
major programs: periodical

Brockport

Brockport Museum
49 State Street
Brockport, New York 14420
716-637-5342
Mrs. Willis Knapp, Chair,
Museum Committee
founded: 1946
staff: 14 volunteer
major programs: museum,
historic sites, photo collection,
research, school programs, tours,
markers program

Western Monroe
Historical Society
151 Main Street
Brockport, New York 14420
716-637-3645
Susanna P. Hickerson, Business
Manager
founded: 1965
staff: 2 part-time
major programs: museum, tours

Fairport

Perinton Historical Society
Fairport Historical Museum
18 Perrin Street
Fairport, New York 14450

Gates

Gates-Northampton
Heritage Society
293 Youngs Avenue
Gates, New York 14606

Greece

Historical Society of Greece, NY
1077 English Road
P.O. Box 16249
Rochester, New York 14616
716-225-0293
Walter Goulding, President
members: 180
founded: 1969
staff: 50 volunteer
major programs: museum, photo
collection, research, lectures,
exhibits, historic preservation,
periodical

Hamlin

North Star History Center
and Museum
864 Walker-Lake Ontario Road
Hamlin, New York 14464
716-964-7385
mail to: 731 Walker-Lake
Ontario Road, Hilton, New York
14468
Mary E. Smith, Town of Hamlin
Historian
staff: 1 full-time
major programs: library,
museum, photo collection,
research, lectures, exhibits,
publications

Henrietta

Henrietta New York
Historic Site Committee
Henrietta Town Hall
475 Calkins Road
Henrietta, New York 14467
716-334-7700
mail to: 98 Tall Oak Lane
Pittsford, New York 14534
Helen Elam, Chair
founded: 1977
staff: 1 part-time, 6 volunteer
major programs: archives,
historic sites, photo collection,
research, school programs, tours,
lectures, exhibits, publications,
awards, surveys, historic
preservation, rural preservation,
markers program, technical
preservation services, archeology

Hilton

Parma Meeting House Museum
460 Parma Center Road
Hilton, New York 14468
716-428-7375
mail to: 1300 Hilton-Parma
Road, Hilton, New York 14468
Shirley Cox Husted, Curator
founded: 1977
staff: 1 part-time, 14 volunteer
major programs: museum, tours,
exhibits, surveys, crafts

Town of Parma Museum
1300 Hilton-Parma Road
Hilton, New York 14468
716-392-9461
Shirley Cox Husted, Historian
founded: 1976
staff: 1 full-time, 12 volunteer
major programs: library,
archives, museum, historic sites,
photo collection, research,
school programs, tours, lectures,
exhibits, publications, historic
preservation

Honeoye Falls

Honeoye Falls/Town of Mendon
Historical Society
50 East Street
Honeoye Falls, New York 14472
716-624-3810
Robert R. Borsching, Sr.,
President
members: 60
founded: 1968
staff: 60 volunteer
major programs: library,
archives, museum, photo
collection, school programs,
workshops

Irondequoit

Irondequoit Historical Society
877 Helendale Road
Rochester, New York 14609
716-288-1121
members: 130
founded: 1964
staff: 1 volunteer
major programs: archives,
historic sites, research, awards,
historic preservation, markers
program

Mumford

Genesee Country Museum
Flint Hill Road
Mumford, New York 14511
716-538-6822
Stuart Bolger, Director
members: 1,800
founded: 1966
major programs: historic village
reconstruction, museum,
exhibits, periodical, publications,
research

North Chili

Chili Cobblestone School
Museum
160 King Road
North Chili, New York 14468

Chili Historical Society
3883 Union Street
North Chili, New York 14514
716-889-2823
mail to: 1365 Paul Road
Churchville, New York 14428
Edward G. Cornwell, Jr.,
President
members: 149
founded: 1964
staff: all volunteer
major programs: library,
museum, archives, research,
tours, lectures, workshops,
exhibits, awards, surveys

Pittsford

Historic Pittsford
18 Monroe Avenue
P.O. Box 38
Pittsford, New York 14534
716-381-2941
Mary K. Menzie, President
founded: 1966
staff: 1 part-time,
many volunteer
major programs: museum,
lectures, surveys, historic
preservation, markers program,
technical preservation services,
periodical

Rochester

Susan B. Anthony Memorial
17 Madison Street
Rochester, New York 14608
716-235-6124
Roberta LaChiusa, President

members: 400
founded: 1946
staff: 25 volunteer
major programs: museum,
historic sites, tours, historic
preservation, periodical

Bishop Sheen Ecumenical
Housing Foundation
1150 Buffalo Road
Rochester, New York 14624
716-436-7260
mail to: 935 East Avenue,
Rochester, New York 14607
Allynn Smith, Executive Director
founded: 1968
staff: 3 full-time, 4 part-time,
25 volunteer
major programs: historic
preservation, rural preservation,
affordable housing, revolving
fund, grants, matching grants

Charlotte-Genesee Lighthouse
Historical Society
70 Lighthouse Street
Rochester, New York 14612
716-621-6179
Felipe de Chauteauvieux,
President
members: 275
founded: 1982
staff: 75 volunteer
major programs: museum,
research, tours, lectures,
exhibits, publications, historic
preservation, archeology,
periodical

Chocolate City Neighborhood
Association, Inc.
446 West Main Street
Rochester, New York 14611
716-436-4037

Genesee Street Corporation
713 Monroe Avenue
Rochester, New York 14607

Genesee/Finger Lakes Regional
Planning Council
33 South Washington Street
Rochester, New York 14608
Glenn R. Cooke,
Executive Director

Group 14621 Community
Association
945 Joseph Avenue
Rochester, New York 14621

International Museum of
Photography
900 East Avenue
Rochester, New York 14607
716-271-5211
Marion Simon, Director of
Development

Irondequoit Chapter
Daughters of the American
Revolution
11 Livingston Park
Rochester, New York 14608
716-232-4509
Margaret Carnahan, Irondequoit
Regent
members: 145
founded: 1893
staff: 1 part-time, 10 volunteer
major programs: library,
museum, historic sites, tours,
workshops, awards, historic
preservation

Junior League of Rochester
444 East Main Street
Rochester, New York 14604
716-232-7040
members: 800
founded: 1933
staff: 2 part-time
major programs: periodical,
grants

Landmark Society of
Western New York
130 Spring Street
Rochester, New York 14608
716-546-7029
Henry A. McCartney,
Executive Director
members: 3,400
founded: 1937
staff: 11 full-time, 5 part-time,
500 volunteer
major programs: library,
museum, historic sites, photo
collection, school programs,
tours, workshops, awards,
surveys, historic preservation,
rural preservation, technical
preservation services, periodical,
revolving fund

Marketview Heights Association
95 Davis Street
Rochester, New York 14605

Memorial Art Gallery
University of Rochester
490 University Avenue
Rochester, New York 14607
716-275-3081

North East Area Development
1564 East Main Street
Rochester, New York 14609

Photographic Historical Society
P.O. Box 39563
Rochester, New York 14604

Rochester Community for
Better Architecture
383 Park Avenue
Rochester, New York 14607
716-271-8612

Rochester Historical Society
485 East Avenue
Rochester, New York 14607
716-271-2705
Elizabeth G. Holahan, President
members: 723
founded: 1861
staff: 2 full-time, 2 part-time,
10 volunteer
major programs: library,
archives, museum, photo
collection, research, lectures,
exhibits, publications, periodical

Rochester Museum
and Science Center
657 East Avenue
P.O. Box 1480
Rochester, New York 14603
716-271-4320
Richard C. Shult, President
members: 9,300
founded: 1912
staff: 100 full-time
major programs: library,
archives, museum, research,
school programs, lectures,
exhibits, publications,
archeology

Rochester Preservation Board
Zoning Bureau, City Hall
30 Church Street
Rochester, New York 14614
716-428-7063
Pat Mackey, Director of
Library Promotions

Rochester Public Library
115 South Avenue
Rochester, New York 14604
716-428-7355
Pat Mackey, Director of
Library Promotions

Rochester Urban Cultural
Park Program
Recreation/Community Services
City Hall
Rochester, New York 14614
716-428-6502

Rural Opportunities
339 East Avenue, Suite 305
Rochester, New York 14604

South Wedge Historical Office
697 South Avenue
Rochester, New York 14620

South Wedge Planning
Committee
68 Ashland Street
Rochester, New York 14620
716-325-4950
Rev. Judy Lee Hay,
Executive Director
staff: 3 full-time, 11 part-time,
20 volunteer
major programs: workshops,
historic preservation, affordable
housing, periodical, grants,
matching grants

The Margaret Woodbury
Strong Museum
One Manhattan Square
Rochester, New York 14607
716-263-2700 x269
G. Rollie Adams, President
members: 850
founded: 1982
staff: 85 full-time, 10 part-time,
180 volunteer
major programs: library,
archives, museum, photo
collection, research, school
programs, tours, lectures,
workshops, exhibits,
publications, periodical

Rush

National Railway Historical
Society, Rochester Chapter
282 Rush-Scottsville Road
Rush, New York 14543
716-533-1431

mail to: P.O. Box 664,
Rochester, New York 14603
David Shields, Vice President
members: 150
founded: 1937
staff: 150 volunteer
major programs: library,
museum, photo collection, tours,
publications, historic
preservation, periodical

New York Museum of
Transportation
6393 East River Road
Rush, New York 14543
716-533-1113
mail to: P.O. Box 136,
West Henrietta, New York 14586
Theodore H. Strang, Jr.,
President
members: 55
founded: 1972
staff: 5 volunteer
major programs: archives,
museum, photo collection,
exhibits, periodical

Scottsville

Wheatland Historical Association
69 Main Street, P.O. Box 137
Scottsville, New York 14546
Beverley F. Reeves, President
members: 120
founded: 1972
staff: 9 volunteer
major programs: library,
archives, museum, research,
school programs, tours, lectures,
exhibits, historic preservation,
markers program, periodical

Spencerport

Ogden Historical Society
568 Colby Street
Spencerport, New York 14559
mail to: 2437 South Main Street,
Spencerport, New York 14559
Mrs. James Case, President
members: 25
founded: 1965
staff: 10 volunteer
major programs: museum, photo
collection, school programs,
tours, exhibits

Webster

Webster Historical Society
151 Basket Road
Webster, New York 14580

Montgomery County

County Arts Council

Montgomery County
Arts Council
Room 136L, Fulton-
Montgomery Community
College
Johnstown, New York 12095

County Historian

Violet D. Fallone
Old Court House
Fonda, New York 12068

County Historical Society

Montgomery County
Historical Society
Routes 5 and 6
Fort Johnson, New York 12070
Katherine Strobeck, President
518-762-7769

County Planning Office

Montgomery County
Planning Department
County Office Building Annex
Park Street
Fonda, New York 12068
518-853-4355

see also Federation of Historical
Services, Troy, Rensselaer
County

Amsterdam

City of Amsterdam
4 McClellan Avenue
Amsterdam, New York 12010
Gerry K. Schultz, Chair,
Planning Commission

Walter Elwood Museum
300 Guy Park Avenue
Amsterdam, New York 12010
518-843-3180 x445
Mary Margaret Gage, Director
members: 400
founded: 1940
staff: 1 full-time, 3 part-time,
15 volunteer
major programs: library, archives
museum, photo collection,
school programs, tours, lectures,
workshops, exhibits, periodical

Mohawk Valley
Museums Consortium
366 West Main Street
Amsterdam, New York 12010
Helene Farrell, President
518-842-7550

Charleston

Charleston Historical Society
Polin Road, off route 30A
Town of Charleston, New York
12066
518-875-6533
mail to: RD 1, Box 713
Esperance, New York 12066
Edythe J. Meserand, Chair
members: 215
founded: 1978
staff: all volunteer
major programs: library,
archives, museum, research,
exhibits, historic preservation

Fonda

Heritage Genealogical Society
of Montgomery County
Old Court House
Fonda, New York 12068
518-853-3431
Violet D. Fallone, County
Historian
major programs: library,
archives, research

Mohawk Valley Historic
Association
8 South Center Street
Fonda, New York 12068

Montgomery County
Department of History and
Archives
Old Court House
Fonda, New York 12068
518-853-3431
Violet D. Fallone, County
Historian
founded: 1934
staff: 2 full-time, 1 part-time,
5 volunteer
major programs: library,
archives, research, tours, exhibits

Preserve It Now
P.O. Box 325
Fonda, New York 12068

Fort Hunter

Fort Hunter Canal Society
P.O. Box 82
Fort Hunter, New York 12069

Fort Plain

Fort Plain Museum
Upper Canal Street
P.O. Box 324
Fort Plain, New York 13339
518-993-2527
Kingston Larner, Chair
members: 100
founded: 1963
staff: 6 volunteer
major programs: museum,
historic sites, school programs,
exhibits, historic preservation

St. Johnsville

Fort Klock Historic Restoration
RD 3, P.O. Box 42
St. Johnsville, New York 13452
518-568-7779
Charlotte Therrien, Curator
members: 60
founded: 1956
staff: 2 part-time, 25 volunteer
major programs: historic sites,
school programs, tours,
workshops, historic preservation,
rural preservation

Palatine Settlement Society
76 West Main Street
St. Johnsville, New York 13452
518-568-2738
Milford A. Decker, President
members: 115
founded: 1982
staff: 20 volunteer
major programs: historic sites,
research, tours, lectures,
workshops, exhibits, historic
preservation, periodical

Salt Springville

Salt Springville Community
Restoration
RD 1, Box 272
Cherry Valley, New York 13320

Nassau County

County Arts Council

see Nassau County Office of
Cultural Affairs, Roslyn, for
decentralization information

County Historian

Edward J. Smits
1864 Muttontown Road
Syosset, New York 11791

County Historical Society

Nassau County
Historical Society
P.O. Box 207
Garden City, New York 11530

County Planning Office

Nassau County Planning
Department
222 Willis Avenue
Mineola, New York 11501
516-535-5844

see also Society for the
Preservation of Long Island
Antiquities, Setauket, Suffolk
County; Long Island Regional
Planning Board, Happauge,
Suffolk County

Baldwin

Baldwin Historical
Society and Museum
1980 Grand Avenue
Baldwin, New York 11510
516-223-6900
Glenn F. Sitterly, Curator
members: 200
founded: 1971
staff: 1 full-time
major programs: archives,
museum, photo collection,
school programs, exhibits,
publications, markers program,
periodical

Bayville

Bayville Historical Museum
School Street
Bayville, New York 11709

Bellmore

Historical Society of the
Bellmores
2717 Grand Avenue
Bellmore, New York 11710

Bellerose

Colonial Farmhouse Restoration
Society of Bellerose
73-50 Little Neck parkway
Floral Park, New York 11004

Cedar Swamp

Cedar Swamp Historical Society
Cedar Swamp, Long Island,
New York 11545
516-671-6156
John G. Peterkin, President
members: 500
founded: 1977
staff: all volunteer
major programs: historic sites,
photo collection, research,
school programs, tours, lectures,
exhibits, awards, surveys,
historic preservation, rural
preservation, markers program,
periodical

East Rockaway

Old Grist Mill Historical Society
160 Main Street
East Rockaway, New York
11518

Farmingdale

Farmingdale Bethpage
Historical Society
P.O. Box 500
Farmingdale, New York 11735

Floral Park

Floral Park Council of
Cultural Affairs
One Floral Boulevard
Floral Park, New York 11001
516-437-9198
Diane M. Percoco, Chair

Franklin Square

Franklin Square
Historical Society
P.O. Box 45
Franklin Square, New York
11010

Freeport

Arts Council at Freeport
130 East Merrick Road
P.O. Box 97
Freeport, New York 11520
516-223-2522
Lila Diringer, Executive Director

founded: 1974
staff: 3 full-time, 3 part-time,
15 volunteer
major programs: school
programs, tours, lectures,
workshops, exhibits, periodical,
grants

Freeport Historical Society
P.O. Box 323
Freeport, New York 11520

Garden City

Garden City Historical Society
P.O. Box 179
Garden City, New York 11530
Jeanmarie DiNoto, President
members:950
founded: 1976
staff: all volunteer
major programs: library, school
programs, tours, lectures,
publications, historic
preservation

Glen Cove

Council for the Arts on the
North Shore
One Forest Avenue
Glen Cove, New York 11542
516-676-7474
Otto Erbar, Jr., Executive
Director

Glen Cove Historical Society
P.O. Box 248
Glen Cove, New York 11542

Great Neck

Great Neck Historical Society
122 Hampshire Road
Great Neck, New York 11023

Hempstead

Hempstead Village
Historical Society
115 Nichols Court
Hempstead, New York 11550
516-481-6990
James B. York, President
members: 200
founded: 1980
staff: 7 volunteer
major programs: library,
archives, photo collection, tours,
awards

Long Island Institute
Hofstra University
Hempstead, New York 11550
516-560-5974
Barbara M. Kelly, Curator

Kings Point

American Merchant Marine
Museum Foundation
Kings Point, New York 11024

Long Beach

Long Beach Council on the Arts
City Hall
One West Chester Street
Long Beach, New York 11561
516-431-1212
Mark Samuels, Executive
Director

Long Beach Historical and
Preservation Society
84 East Olive Street
Long Beach, New York 11561
516-431-3775

Lynbrook

Lynbrook Historical Society
56 Lenox Avenue
Lynbrook, New York 11563

Manhasset

Historical Society of the
Town of North Hempstead
220 Plandome Road
Manhasset, New York 11030

Massapequa

Town of Oyster Bay Arts Council
977 Hicksville Road
Massapequa, New York 11758
516-895-4707
Lois Manning, Executive
Director

Massapequa Park

Historical Society
of the Massapequas
115 Front Street
Massapequa Park, New York
11762

Merrick

Historical Society
of the Merricks
2279 South Merrick Avenue
Merrick, New York 11566
516-379-1887

Mildred M. Donnelly, President
members: 120
founded: 1975
staff: all volunteer
major programs: school
programs, tours, historic
preservation

Mill Neck

North Shore
Preservation Society
P.O. Box 367
Mill Neck, New York 11765

Mineola

Aviation Historical Society
4 Weybridge Road
Mineola, New York 11501

North Hempstead

Valley Road Restoration
Village of Manhasset
North Hempstead, New York
11550

North Merrick

North Merrick Public Library
1691 Meadowbrook Road
North Merrick, New York 11566
516-378-7474
Barbara Hopkins, Director

Oceanside

Historical Society of Oceanside
P.O. Box 294
Oceanside, New York 11572

Old Bethpage

Old Bethpage Village
Restoration
Round Swamp Road
Old Bethpage, New York 11804

Old Westbury

Association of Nassau County
Historical Organizations
Box 122, Pine Tree Lane
Old Westbury, New York 11568
Muriel Tatem, President

Old Westbury Gardens
Old Westbury Road,
P.O. Box 430
Old Westbury, New York 11568
516-333-0048
Jethro M. Hurt, III, Executive
Director

members: 2,000
founded: 1959
staff: 175 volunteer
major programs: archives,
museum, historic sites, photo
collection, research, tours,
lectures, workshops, exhibits,
publications, historic
preservation, periodical

Oyster Bay

Oyster Bay Historical Society
20 Summit Street, P.O. Box 297
Oyster Bay, New York 11771
516-922-5032
Charles D. Thompson,
President
members: 250
founded: 1960
staff: 2 part-time, 28 volunteer
major programs: library,
archives, museum, photo
collection, research, school
programs, tours, lectures,
exhibits, publications, surveys,
historic preservation, periodical,
revolving fund

Planting Fields Foundation
Planting Fields Road,
P.O. Box 58
Oyster Bay, New York 11771
516-922-0479
Lorraine Gilligan, Chief
Operating Officer
staff: 2 full-time, 1 part-time,
20 volunteer
major programs: archives,
museum, photo collection, tours,
historic preservation

Raynham Hall Museum
20 West Main Street
Oyster Bay, New York 11771
516-922-6808
Stuart A. Chase, Director
members: 280
founded: 1953
staff: 1 full-time, 1 part-time,
30 volunteer
major programs: archives,
museum, research, school
programs, tours, lectures,
workshops, exhibits, surveys,
historic preservation, periodical

Port Washington

Cow Neck Peninsula
Historical Society
336 Port Washington Boulevard
Port Washington, New York
11050

Residents for a More Beautiful
Port Washington
P.O. Box 864
Port Washington, New York
11050
516-883-3448
Myron Blumenfeld, Chair
members: 2,000
founded: 1968
staff: 1 full-time, 20 volunteer
major programs: historic
preservation, periodical

Roosevelt

Roosevelt Assistance
Corporation
455D Nassau Road
Roosevelt, New York 11575

Roslyn

Nassau County Office of
Cultural Affairs
Northern Boulevard, P.O. Box D
Roslyn, New York 11576
516-484-9333
Marcia O'Brien, Executive
Director

Roslyn Landmark Society
William M. Valentine House
Paper Mill Road
Roslyn, New York 11576
516-621-3040
Roger G. Gerry, President
members: 400
founded: 1961
staff: 85 volunteer
major programs: archives,
historic sites, photo collection,
research, tours, publications,
historic preservation, markers
program, technical preservation
services, periodical, grants,
revolving fund

Roslyn Harbor

Nassau County Museum
of Fine Art
One Museum Drive, P.O. Box D
Roslyn Harbor, New York 11576
516-484-9337

Thomas A. Saltzman, Director
members: 800
founded: 1975
staff: 6 full-time, 50 volunteer
major programs: museum, tours,
lectures, workshops, exhibits,
publications, historic
preservation, periodical

Sea Cliff

Sea Cliff Landmarks Association
P.O. Box 69
Sea Cliff, New York 11579
516-676-6146
Elizabeth O'Mara Klare,
President
members: 135
founded: 1972
staff: 5 volunteer
major programs: archives, photo
collection, research, tours,
lectures, exhibits, awards,
surveys, historic preservation,
periodical, matching grants

Seaford

Seaford Historical Society
34 Return Lane
Levittown, New York 11756
516-735-9119
mail to: 2234 Jackson Avenue,
Levittown, New York 11783
Joshua Soren, President
members: 250
founded: 1968
staff: 10 volunteer
major programs: museum, photo
collection, lectures, workshops,
exhibits, publications, historic
preservation, periodical

Syosset

Friends for
Long Island's Heritage
1864 Muttontown Road
Syosset, New York 11791
516-364-1050
Gerald S. Kessler, President
members: 2,800
founded: 1964
staff: 7 full-time, 3 part-time,
400 volunteer
major programs: museum,
historic sites, lectures, school
programs, exhibits, publications,
historic preservation, periodical,
grants

Nassau County Division of
Museum Services (Nassau
County Museum)
1864 Muttontown Road
Syosset, New York 11791
516-364-1050
Edward J. Smits, Director
founded: 1956
staff: 173 full-time, 110 part-
time, 400 volunteer
major programs: library,
archives, museum, historic sites,
photo collection, research,
school programs, exhibits,
publications, surveys, historic
preservation, archeology,
easements

Valley Stream

Valley Stream
Historical Society
123 South Central Avenue
Valley Stream, New York 11580

Wantagh

Wantagh Preservation Society
1700 Wantagh Avenue,
P.O. Box 132
Wantagh, New York 11793
516-826-8767
Joshua Soren, Corresponding
Secretary
founded: 1966
staff: 20 volunteer
major programs: museum, photo
collection, research, school
programs, tours, lectures,
exhibits, publications, historic
preservation, periodical

Westbury

Historical Society
of the Westburys
454 Rockland Street
Westbury, New York 11590
516-333-0176
Muriel Tatem, President
members: 130
founded: 1977
staff: 1 part-time, 1 volunteer
major programs: library,
archives, photo collection, school
programs, lectures, exhibits,
periodical

West Hempstead

West Hempstead Historical and
Preservation Society
460 Hempstead Avenue
West Hempstead, New York
11552

New York County

County Arts Council

see Alliance for the Arts; Lower
Manhattan Cultural Council;
New York Foundation for the
Arts

County Historian

Paul O'Dwyer
99 Wall Street
New York, New York 10005

County Historical Society

see Museum of the City of New
York; New-York Historical
Society

County Planning Office

Manhattan Office, Department
of City Planning
2 Lafayette Street
New York, New York
10007-1363
212-566-0522

New York

Abigail Adams Smith Museum
421 East 61st Street
New York, New York 10021
David L. Reese, Director

Adam Clayton Powell Jr.
Boulevard Corporation
2394 Adam Clayton Powell
Boulevard
New York, New York 10030

Alliance for the Arts
330 West 42nd Street
New York, New York 10036
212-947-6340
Patricia C. Jones, Executive Vice
President

Anonymous Arts Recovery
Society
380 West Broadway
New York, New York 10012
Ivan C. Karp, President

Architectural League
of New York
457 Madison Avenue
New York, New York 10022
212-753-1722
Rosalie Genevro, Executive
Director
members: 1,000
founded: 1881
staff: 3 full-time
major programs: lectures,
publications

Art Deco Society of New York
c/o Gibson Bauer Associates
90 West Street, 14th Floor
New York, New York 10006
major programs: lectures, tours,
historic preservation, periodical,
publications

Association Neighborhood
Housing Development
424 West 33rd Street
New York, New York 10001
Bonnie Brower, Executive
Director

Association of Village
Homeowners
P.O. Box 209, Village Station
New York, New York 10014
212-989-0003
Miriam Lee, President
members: 300
founded: 1960
major programs: publications,
historic preservation

Avery Architectural and
Fine Arts Library
Columbia University
Broadway at 115th Street
New York, New York 10027
212-280-3068
Angela Giral, Avery Librarian

Brownstone Revival Committee
200 Madison Avenue, 3rd Floor
New York, New York 10016
212-561-2154
Marvin Rock, Executive Director
members: 800
founded: 1960
staff: 1 full-time
major programs: tours, lectures,
workshops, publications,
periodical

Bryant Park Restoration
Corporation
6 East 43rd Street
New York, New York 10017
212-983-4142
Daniel A. Biederman, Executive
Director
founded: 1980
staff: 5 full-time, 3 part-time
major programs: tours, historic
preservation, park restoration

Carnegie Hill Neighbors
8 East 96th Street
New York, New York 10128

Cathedral Housing
Development Corporation
1047 Amsterdam Avenue
New York, New York 10025

Central Park Conservancy
The Arsenal
830 Fifth Avenue
New York, New York 10021
212-360-8239
Elizabeth Barlow Rogers,
Central Park Administration
founded: 1980
staff: 85 full-time, 25 part-time,
150 volunteer
major programs: historic sites,
photo collection, school
programs, exhibits, publications,
surveys, historic preservation,
periodical

Central Park West
Preservation Committee
36 West 76th Street
New York, New York 10023
212-249-6633
Lawrence J. Cohn, Chair
founded: 1984
staff: 5 volunteer
major programs: historic
preservation

Chelsea Historic District Council
425 West 21st Street
New York, New York 10011
212-243-0966

Chinese Historical Society
199 Lafayette Street
New York, New York 10012

Chinese-American Arts Council
45 Canal Street
New York, New York 10022

212-431-9740
Alan Chow, Executive Director

Civitas Citizens
177 East 87th Street
New York , New York 10128
212-996-0745
Genie Rice, President

Clinton Housing
Development Company
664 Tenth Avenue
New York, New York 10036
212-586-5444
Joe Restuccia, Executive Director
founded: 1973
staff: 17 full-time, 11 part-time
major programs: affordable
housing

Committee for the Washington
Market Historic District
90 West Broadway
New York, New York 10007
212-732-6196
Hal Bromm, Chair

Committee to Save the City
158 Waverly Place
New York, New York 10014
Margaret H. Moore, Chair

Community Board 1
49-51 Chambers Street
New York, New York 10007
212-374-1421
Hal Bromm, Chair, Landmarks
Preservation Commission

Community Board 6
330 East 26th Street
New York, New York 10010
212-679-0907
Gary Papush, Chair, Parks and
Cultural Affairs Landmarks
Commission

Cooper Square Community
Development Committee and
Business Association
61 West Fourth Street
New York, New York 10003

Cooper-Hewitt Museum
2 East 91st Street
New York, New York 10128
212-860-6868
Harold Pfister, Acting Director
members: 5,500
founded: 1976
staff: 35 full-time, 25 part-time,
75 volunteer

major programs: library,
archives, museum, research,
tours, lectures, workshops,
exhibits, publications, periodical

Council on the Environment of
New York City
51 Chambers Street, Room 228
New York, New York 10007
212-566-0990
Lys McLaughlin, Executive
Director
founded: 1970
staff: 23 full-time, 14 part-time
major programs: school
programs, workshops,
periodical, matching grants

Cultural Council Foundation
625 Broadway, 8th Floor
New York, New York 10012
212-473-5660

The Drive to Protect the
Ladies Mile District
P.O. Box 332, Cooper Station
New York, New York 10276
Jack Taylor, President

Dyckman House Museum
4881 Broadway
New York, New York 10034
212-304-9422

Eldridge Street Project
12 Eldridge Street
New York, New York 10002
212-219-0888
Roberta Brandes Gratz, Director
founded: 1983
staff: 1 full-time, 1 part-time
major programs: archives,
exhibits, surveys, historic
preservation, technical
preservation services

Emanuel Pieterson
Historical Society
35 West 125th Street
New York, New York 10027

Exploring the Metropolis
10 Gracie Square
New York, New York 10028
212-650-0211
Eugenie C. Cowan, Director
founded: 1982
staff: 1 full-time, 1 part-time
major programs: research,
workshops, urban issues

Federation to Preserve the
Greenwich Village Waterfront
and Great Port
81 Barrow Street
New York, New York 10014
212-675-4264

Fire Historical Society
of New York City
845 Third Avenue
New York, New York 10022

Forty-Second Street Development
Corporation
330 West 42nd Street
New York, New York 10036
212-695-4242
Frederic S. Papert, President

Fraunces Tavern Museum
54 Pearl Street
New York, New York 10004
212-425-1778
William Ayres, Director
members: 400
founded: 1907
staff: 6 full-time, 6 part-time,
30 volunteer
major programs: museum,
historic sites, research, tours,
lectures, exhibits, periodical,
publications, historic
preservation

Friends of Fort Tryon Park
100 Overlook Terrace, #33
New York, New York 10040
212-928-8144
Carol Weinstein, President
members: 450
founded: 1983
staff: 1 part-time, 100 volunteer
major programs: tours,
periodical

Friends of the Upper East Side
Historic Districts
140 East 63rd Street, Room 803
New York, New York 10021
212-644-2828
Halina Rosenthal, President
members: 700
founded: 1982
staff: 2 part-time, 120 volunteer
major programs: archives,
historic sites, photo collection,
research, tours, workshops,
periodical, publications, awards,
surveys, historic preservation,
technical preservation services,
urban planning

Fund for Architecture
and Environment
c/o Cultural Council Foundation
625 Broadway, 8th Floor
New York, New York 10012
212-473-5660

Gotham Walking Tour Group
7-13 Washington Square North
New York, New York 10003
212-777-4747
Gerard R. Wolfe, Director
founded: 1981
staff: 1 volunteer
major programs: historic sites,
tours, lectures, historic
preservation

Gracie Mansion Conservancy
88th Street and East End Avenue
New York, New York 10128
William Butler, Curator

Grand Central Partnership
6 East 43rd Street, Suite 2000
New York, New York 10017
212-818-1777
Daniel A. Biederman, President
staff: 2 full-time
major programs: historic sites,
historic preservation

Greenwich Village Society for
Historic Preservation
47 Fifth Avenue
New York, New York 10003
212-923-3895
Regina M. Kellerman, Executive
Director
members: 900
founded: 1980
staff: 3 part-time
major programs: research, tours,
lectures, exhibits, periodical,
publications, surveys, historic
preservation, technical
preservation services, archeology

Guggenheim Neighbors
c/o Michael Levy
4 East 89th Street
New York, New York 10128

Harlem Restoration Project
461 West 125th Street
New York, New York 10027

Heritage Preservation
P.O. Box 166, Bowling
Green Station
New York, New York 10004

Historic Districts Council
P.O. Box 2499
Times Square Station
New York, New York 10108
212-370-0903
Anthony C. Wood, President
major programs: historic
preservation, educational
programs

Historical Research Foundation
50 East 42nd Street
New York, New York 10017

Holland Society of New York
122 East 58th Street
New York, New York 10021

Hope Community
177 East 104th Street
New York, New York 10029
212-860-8821
George E. Calvert, Executive
Director
members: 200
founded: 1968
staff: 9 full-time, 3 volunteer
major programs: historic
preservation, affordable housing,
periodical, revolving fund

Horticultural Society
of New York
128 West 58th Street
New York, New York 10019
212-757-0915
Larry G. Pardue, Executive
Director

Institute for Architecture and
Urban Studies
8 West 40th Street
New York, New York 10018
212-947-0765

Institute for
Environmental Action
81 Leonard Street
New York, New York 10013
212-966-6390

Institute for Research in History
1133 Broadway, Suite 923
New York, New York 10010

Interfaith Adopt-A-Building
75 Avenue C
New York, New York 10009

International Center
of Photography
1130 Fifth Avenue

New York, New York 10128
212-860-1778
Cornell Capa, Executive Director
members: 3,000
founded: 1974
staff: 50 full-time, 15 part-time,
100 volunteer
major programs: archives,
museum, photo collection,
school programs, lectures,
workshops, exhibits, awards,
periodical

Inwood Preservation
Corporation
4844 Broadway
New York, New York 10034
212-569-5050
Katherine J. Stewart, Executive
Director
founded: 1978
staff: 1 full-time, 2 part-time
major programs: landlord/tenant
advocacy, housing rehabilitation,
periodical

Jewish Historical Society
of New York
8 West 70th Street
New York, New York 10023
212-873-0300

Junior League of the
City of New York
130 East 80th Street
New York, New York 10021
212-288-6220
Anne Covell, Co-chairman,
Historic Preservation Committee

Landmark West!
45 West 67th Street
New York, New York 10023
212-496-8110
Terri Rosen, Administrative
Director
members: 1,500
founded: 1985
staff: 1 full-time, 5 volunteer
major programs: workshops,
exhibits, historic preservation,
periodical

Lexington Planning Coalition
177 East 104th Street
New York, New York 10029

Lower East Side Coalition
Housing Development
Corporation
187-89 Avenue B
New York, New York 10009

Lower East Side
Historical Society
Peter Stuyvesant Station
New York, New York 10009

Lower East Side
Tenement Museum
97 Orchard Street
New York, New York 10002
212-431-0233

Lower Manhattan Cultural
Council
42 Broadway, Room 1749
New York, New York 10004
212-269-0320
Jenny Dixon, Executive Director

Lower Manhattan
Historical Society
60 Gramercy Park
New York, New York 10010

Manhattan Valley Housing
Clinic
18 West 103rd Street
New York, New York 10025
212-316-3091
Edward Fonte, Executive
Director
founded: 1981
staff: 1 full-time, 2 part-time,
15 volunteer
major programs: affordable
housing

Metropolitan Historic
Structures Association
4881 Broadway
New York, New York 10034
212-304-9422
members: 60
founded: 1976
staff: 1 part-time, 25 volunteer
major programs: museum,
historic sites, tours, lectures,
workshops, exhibits, awards,
historic preservation, periodical

Municipal Art Society
of New York
457 Madison Avenue
New York, New York 10022
212-935-3960
Kent Barwick, President
members: 2,500
founded: 1892

major programs: library, photo
collection, tours, lectures,
exhibits, periodical, publications,
awards, historic preservation,
markers program

The Murray Hill Committee
36 East 36th Street, Box Roof
New York, New York 10016
Stephen Weingrad, President

Museum of the American Indian
Broadway at 155th Street
New York, New York 10032

Museum of the City
of New York
1220 Fifth Avenue
New York, New York 10029
212-534-1672
Robert R. Macdonald, Director
members: 2,500
founded: 1923
staff: 59 full-time, 12 part-time,
12 volunteer
major programs: archives,
museum, photo collection,
school programs, tours, exhibits,
periodical

Native New Yorkers'
Historical Association
503 West 22nd Street
New York, New York 10011
212-847-9869

Neighborhood Open
Space Coalition
72 Reade Street
New York, New York 10007
212-513-7555
Tom Fox, Executive Director
founded: 1980
major programs: research,
workshops, open space policy
development for New York City

New York Chinatown
History Project
44 East Broadway, 2nd Floor
New York, New York 10002

New York City Department
of City Planning
22 Reade Street
New York, New York
10007-1216
212-720-3276

New York City Department of
Cultural Affairs
2 Columbus Circle
New York, New York 10019
212-974-1150

New York City Department of
Records and Information
Services
31 Chambers Street
New York, New York 10007
212-566-4292
Eugene Bockman, Commissioner

New York City Historic
Properties Fund
141 Fifth Avenue
New York, New York 10010
212-995-5260
Marcia Hochman, Manager
founded: 1983
staff: 1 full-time, 3 part-time,
1 volunteer
major programs: historic
preservation, technical
preservation services, revolving
fund, grants

New York City Landmarks
Preservation Commission
225 Broadway, 23rd Floor
New York, New York 10007
212-553-1100
Gene A. Norman, Chair
Joseph Bresnam, Executive
Director
staff: 60 full-time
major programs: photo
collection, research, surveys,
historic preservation, technical
preservation services, archeology,
grants

New York City Parks and
Recreation
Park Historian's Office
The Arsenal, Central Park
New York, New York 10021
212-360-3410
Ethan Carr, Park Historian
founded: 1983
staff: 3 full-time
major programs: library,
archives, photo collection,
research, exhibits, periodical,
publications

New York City Urban
Cultural Parks Program
New York City Parks and
Recreation

The Arsenal, Central Park
New York, New York 10021
212-360-1371
Karen Tsao, Urban Cultural
Park Liaison

New York Fire House Museum
278 Spring Street
New York, New York 10013

New York Foundation
for the Arts
5 Beekman Street, Room 600
New York, New York 10038
212-233-3900
Theodore S. Berger, Executive
Director

New York Landmarks
Conservancy
141 Fifth Avenue, 3rd Floor
New York, New York 10010
212-995-5260
Laurie Beckelman, Executive
Director
founded: 1973
staff: 14 full-time, 3 part-time
major programs: historic
preservation, technical
assistance, advocacy, easements,
grants, periodical, publications

The New-York Historical Society
170 Central Park West
New York, New York 10024
212-873-3400
James B. Bell, Director
members: 3,000
founded: 1804
staff: 90 full-time, 20 volunteer
major programs: library,
archives, museum, research,
tours, lectures, workshops,
exhibits, periodical

Northern Manhattan
Improvement
681 West 181st Street
New York, New York 10033

Old Merchant's House
of New York
29 East Fourth Street
New York, New York 10003
212-777-1089
Carolyn Roberto, Director
members: 500
founded: 1936
staff: 1 full-time, 10 volunteer
major programs: museum,
historic site, photo collection,
tours, historic preservation

Old York Foundation
12 East 61st Street
New York, New York 10021

Operation Open City
103 East 125th Street
New York, New York 10035

Park Terrace Block Association
77 Park Terrace East
New York, New York 10034

The Parks Council
457 Madison Avenue
New York, New York 10022
212-838-9410
Judith Spector, Executive
Director

Progress, Incorporated
2710 Broadway
New York, New York 10029

Pueblo Nuevo Housing
Development Association
125 Pitt Street
New York, New York 10002
212-673-3940
Roberto Caballero, Executive
Director
founded: 1970
staff: 10 full-time
major programs: surveys,
affordable housing, technical
preservation services, grants

Residents of Sylvan Terrace
8 Sylvan Terrace
New York, New York 10032
212-927-1793
Ruth E. Edwards, President
members: 20
founded: 1984
staff: 5 volunteer
major programs: historic
preservation

Riverside Park Fund
475 Riverside Drive
New York, New York 10115
212-870-3070
Susan Angevin, Executive
Director
members: 600
founded: 1986
major programs: historic
preservation, periodical, tours,
exhibits

Save the Theatres
165 West 46th Street
New York, New York 10036
212-869-8530
Curtis Hagedorn, Executive
Director

Society for the
Architecture of the City
45 Christopher Street, #2E
New York, New York 10014
212-741-2628

Storefront Art and Architecture
97 Kenmare Steet
New York, New York 10012

Synagogue Architectural
and Art Library
838 Fifth Avenue
New York, New York 10021

Tribeca Community Association
434 Greenwich Street
New York, New York 10013

Trinity Museum
Trinity Church, Room 408
74 Trinity Place
New York, New York 10006
212-602-0773
Julia Sefton, Museum Educator

Tudor City Historic
Preservation Committee
333 East 41st Street, #3C
New York, New York 10017
212-687-7849

Union Square Park
Community Coalition
P.O. Box 314, Cooper Station
New York, New York 10276
212-475-2850
Jack Taylor, Chair, Historic
Preservation Committee
members: 800
founded: 1980
staff: all volunteer
major programs: historic sites,
research, tours, lectures,
exhibits, periodical, publications,
surveys, historic preservation,
affordable housing

Urban Homesteading Assistance
Cathedral House
1047 Amsterdam Avenue
New York, New York 10025

Washington Headquarters
Association
Morris-Jumel Mansion
West 160th and
Edgecomb Avenue
New York, New York 10032
212-923-8008

Washington Heights-Inwood
Preservation / Restoration
Corporation
121 Bennett Avenue
New York, New York 10033

Washington Heights-Inwood
Historical Society
116 Pinehurst Avenue, Suite M2
New York, New York 10033
212-923-7800
Natalie Bunting, President
members: 130
founded: 1966
staff: 5 volunteer
major programs: historic sites,
photo collection, tours, lectures,
exhibits, historic preservation,
periodical

West Harlem Community
Organization
240-2 West 116th Street
New York, New York 10026
Leo Fitt, Chair

West Harlem
Group Assistance
140 Hamilton Place
New York, New York 10031
212-281-5552
Maurice Callender, Executive
Director
founded: 1971
staff: 18 full-time
major programs: workshops,
surveys, historic preservation,
affordable housing

West Village Committee Inc.
304 West 11th Street
New York, New York 10014
212-929-3169
William Bowser, President
members: 400
founded: 1962
staff: all volunteer
major programs: historic sites,
periodical, publications, historic
preservation

Wyckoff House Foundation
241 West 72nd Street
New York, New York 10023

14th Street Union Square Local
Development Corporation
124 East 15th Street, Room 708
New York, New York 10003

369th Historical Society
One 369th Plaza
2366 Fifth Avenue
New York, New York 10037
212-926-5800
Nathaniel James, President
members: 20
founded: 1981
staff: 20 volunteer
major programs: library,
archives, museum, historic sites,
photo collection, research,
school programs, tours, exhibits,
historic preservation

Roosevelt Island

Roosevelt Island
Historical Society
P.O. Box 5, Island Station
Roosevelt Island, New York
10044
Vera Hahn, President
members: 50
founded: 1977
staff: 10 volunteer
major programs: archives,
historic sites, tours, exhibits,
historic preservation, periodical

Niagara County

County Arts Council

Niagara Council of the Arts
P.O. Box 937, Falls Station
Niagara Falls, New York 14303
716-278-8149

County Historian

Dorothy Rolling
Civil Defense Building
Niagara and Hawley streets
Lockport, New York 14094

County Historical Society

Niagara County Historical
Society Museum Center
215 Niagara Street
Lockport, New York 14094
716-434-7433
James Swinnich, Curator

County Planning Office

Planning and Industrial
Development Department
County Office Building
59 Park Avenue
Lockport, New York 14094
716-439-6033

see also Erie and Niagara
Counties Regional Planning
Board, Amherst, Erie County;
Landmark Society of the Niagara
Frontier, Buffalo, Erie County;
Housing Assistance Center of the
Niagara Frontier, Buffalo, Erie
County; Housing Council of the
Niagara Frontier, Buffalo, Erie
County; Western New York
Association of Historical
Agencies, Avon, Livingston
County

Appleton

Niagara County
Genealogical Society
2650 Hess Road
Appleton, New York 14008
716-778-7555
Nancy B. Smith,
Secretary / Treasurer
members: 395
founded: 1979
staff: all volunteer
major programs: library,
archives, historic cemeteries,
research, periodical,
publications, historic
preservation

Barker

Town of Somerset
Historical Society
8700 Haight Road
Barker, New York 14012
716-795-3575
Wallace Coates, President
members: 160
founded: 1975

staff: 160 volunteer
major programs: museum,
school programs, exhibits,
publications, historic
preservation, markers program

Hartland

Town of Hartland
Historical Society
8942 Ridge Road
Gasport, New York 14067
716-735-7179
Florence Arnold, Town Historian
members: 77
founded: 1984
staff: 8 volunteer
major programs: photo
collection, exhibits, historic
preservation

Lewiston

Town of Lewiston Historic
Preservation Commission
Ridge Road
Lewiston, New York 14092
716-759-4170
founded: 1978
staff: all volunteer
major programs: historic sites,
awards, surveys, historic
preservation, rural preservation

Historical Association of
Lewiston
Plain Street at Niagara Street
P.O. Box 43
Lewiston, New York 14092
716-754-4214
Mrs. C.G. Chadwick, President
members: 130
founded: 1972
staff: 2 volunteer
major programs: museum, photo
collection, research, school
programs, lectures, exhibits,
periodical, publications

Lockport

City of Lockport, Department of
Community Development
One Locks Plaza
Lockport, New York 14094
716-439-6687
William J. Evert, Director of
Community Development
founded: 1974

staff: 4 full-time
major programs: historic
preservation, affordable housing,
revolving fund, grants

Historic Lockport
41 Main Street
Lockport, New York 14094
716-433-3828
members: 35
founded: 1973
staff: all volunteer
major programs: tours, exhibits,
historic preservation, periodical

Niagara County Federation of
Historical Agencies
3531 Ewings Road
Lockport, New York 14094
Rosemary Miller, Secretary

Middleport

Town of Royalton
Historical Society
5316 Royalton Center Road
Middleport, New York 14105
716-772-2974

Newfane

Town of Newfane
Historical Society
West Creek Road
P.O. Box 1824
Newfane, New York 14108
Charles R. Avery, President
members: 225
founded: 1975
staff: 15 volunteer
major programs: library,
museum, historic sites, tours,
lectures, workshops, exhibits,
periodical, publications, historic
preservation, rural preservation

Niagara Falls

Area 1 Community
Preservation Corporation
43F Southgate, Unity Park
P.O. Box 427, Bridge Station
Niagara Falls, New York 14305
716-285-1186
Arthur J. Brinson, Interim
Executive Director
founded: 1985
staff: 2 full-time, 1 part-time
major programs: workshops,
publications, surveys, periodical

Center City Neighborhood
Development Corporation
911 South Avenue
Niagara Falls, New York 14305
716-282-3738
Joanne L. Smith, Executive
Director
members: 300
founded: 1978
staff: 5 full-time, 1 part-time
major programs: affordable
housing, matching grants

Historical Society of the
North German Settlement
6697 Luther Street
Niagara Falls, New York 14304

ITC Rural
Preservation Company
MPO Box 2432
Niagara Falls, New York 14320

Niagara Falls
Historical Society
1425 Main Street
Niagara Falls, New York 14305
716-278-8229
Donald E. Loker, President
founded: 1897
major programs: library,
archives, photo collection,
periodical

Niagara Falls Neighborhood
Housing Services
419 24th Street
Niagara Falls, New York 14303
716-285-7778
John C. Merino, Executive
Director
founded: 1979
staff: 6 full-time
major programs: affordable
housing, periodical, revolving
fund, grants

Niagara Falls Public Library,
Local History Department
1425 Main Street
Niagara Falls, New York 14305
716-278-8229
Donald E. Loker, Local History
Specialist
founded: 1895
staff: 1 full-time, 1 part-time,
3 volunteer
major programs: library,
archives, photo collection

Town of Niagara
Historical Society
9670 Lockport Road
Niagara Falls, New York 14304
Gerald A. Hathaway, Chair
members: 50
founded: 1977
staff: 10 volunteer
major programs: museum,
historic sites, research, school
programs, exhibits, surveys,
historic preservation, periodical

North Tonawanda

Carousel Society of
the Niagara Frontier
180 Thompson Street
P.O. Box 672
North Tonawanda, New York
14120
716-694-2859
Raphaelle A. Proefrock, Chair
members: 350
founded: 1979
staff: 6 volunteer
major programs: museum,
historic sites, exhibits, historic
preservation, periodical

Pendleton

Pendleton Historical Society
5670 Campbell Boulevard
Lockport, New York 14094
Benjamin Sobczyk, President
members: 70
founded: 1981
staff: museum, rural
preservation, periodical

Sanborn

NiaCAP's Rural
Preservation Program
5839 Buffalo Street
P.O. Box 194
Sanborn, New York 14132
716-731-4133/4
A. Scott Field, Coordinator
founded: 1986
staff: 2 full-time, 1 part-time
major programs: rural
preservation, grants

Wilson

Wilson Historical Society
Lake Street
Wilson, New York 14172
716-751-9886
mail to: 4559 Chestnut Road
Wilson, New York 14172
Lois Jennings, Curator
members: 580
founded: 1972
staff: all volunteer
major programs: museum,
historic sites, periodical,
publications

Youngstown

Old Fort Niagara Association
Fort Niagara State Park
P.O. Box 169
Youngstown, New York 14174
716-745-7611
Brian Leigh Dunnigan, Executive
Director
members: 750
founded: 1927
staff: 7 full-time, 45 part-time,
65 volunteer
major programs: library,
archives, museum, historic sites,
photo collection, research,
school programs, tours, lectures,
periodical, publications, historic
preservation, archeology

Porter Historical Society
255 Lockport Street
Youngstown, New York 14174

Oneida County

County Arts Council

Central New York Community
Arts Council
261 Genesee Street
Utica, New York 13501
315-724-1113

County Historian

Virgina Kelly
Main Street
Holland Patent, New York
13354
315-865-8350

County Historical Society

Oneida County
Historical Society
318 Genesee Street
Utica, New York 13502
315-735-3642
Douglas M. Preston, Director
members: 592
founded: 1876
staff: 2 full-time, 1 part-time,
25 volunteer
major programs: library,
archives, museum, photo
collection, lectures, exhibits,
periodical

County Planning Office

Oneida County Planning Office
County Office Building
800 Park Avenue
Utica, New York 13501
315-798-5710

see also Regional Council of
Historical Agencies, Syracuse,
Onondaga County

Barneveld

Holland Patent Free Library
Powell Road South and Renton
Barneveld, New York 13304

Boonville

Boonville Historical Club
P.O. Box 220
Boonville, New York 13309

Camden

Queen Village Historical Society
P.O. Box 38
Camden, New York 13316

Clinton

Clinton Historical Society
P.O. Box 42
Clinton, New York 13323

Hamilton College
Department of Art
Clinton, New York 13323

Kirkland Art Center
East Park Row, P.O. Box 213
Clinton, New York 13323
Dare Thompson, Executive
Director

Old Burying Ground
Historical Society
Library College Street
Clinton, New York 13323

Deansboro

The Musical Museum
Deansboro, New York 13328
315-841-8774
Sharon Gibbons, Tour Director
founded: 1948
staff: 2 full-time, 3 part-time,
8 volunteer
major programs: library,
archives, museum, photo
collection, research, school
programs, tours, lectures,
workshops, exhibits,
publications, technical
preservation services

Deerfield

Deerfield Historical Society
6329 Walker Road
Utica, New York 13502
315-724-0605
Alice M. Folts, Town Historian
members: 18
founded: 1986
staff: 1 full-time
major programs: archives,
historic sites, photo collection,
historic preservation, periodical

Florence

Town of Florence
Historical Society
RD 3, Box 186
Camden, New York 13316

New Hartford

New Hartford Historical Society
P.O. Box 238
New Hartford, New York 13413

New York Mills

New York Mills
Historical Society
Main Street
New York Mills, New York
13417

Oriskany

Battle of Oriskany
Historical Society
806 Utica Street
Oriskany, New York 13424
315-736-2751
Robert H. Heeley, President
members: 40
founded: 1966
staff: 4 volunteer
major programs: library,
archives, museum, photo
collection, school programs,
publications

Oriskany Historical Society
Route 69
Whitestown, New York 13340

Oriskany Falls

Limestone Ridge
Historical Society
115 Madison Street
Oriskany Falls, New York 13425
315-821-7233 x3259
Gaylene Fairchild, President
members: 79
founded: 1975
staff: 6 volunteer
major programs: archives, photo
collection

Remsen

Adirondack Foothills
Historical Society
Remsen, New York 13438

Remsen Steuben
Historical Society
P.O. Box 116
Remsen, New York 13438

Rome

City of Rome Historic and
Scenic Preservation Commission
City Hall
Rome, New York 13440
315-336-6000 x243
Thomas H. Larrabee, City
Planner
founded: 1978
staff: 2 full-time, 7 volunteer
major programs: photo
collection, research, school
programs, tours, lectures,
workshops, exhibits, surveys,
historic preservation, technical
preservation services, grants

Historic Rome Development
Authority
5789 New London Road
Rome, New York 13440

New London Historical Society
RD 5
Rome, New York 13440

Oneida County Community
Action Agency
303 West Liberty Street
Rome, New York 13440

Rome Historical Society
200 Church Street
Rome, New York 13440
315-336-5870
Pamela Williams, Executive
Director
members: 760
founded: 1936
staff: 6 full-time, 12 volunteer
major programs: library,
museum, photo collection,
school programs, tours, exhibits,
periodical

Trenton

Kalonia Historical Society of the
Town of Trenton
Trenton, New York 13401

Utica

Children's Museum
311 Main Street
Utica, New York 13501
315-724-6128
members: 20
founded: 1978
staff: 25 volunteer
major programs: archives,
museum, historic sites, research,
tours, exhibits, publications,
technical preservation services,
periodical

Corn Hill People United
308 South Street
Utica, New York 13501

Landmarks Society
of Greater Utica
Union Station
Utica, New York 13501
315-732-7376
Barton R. Rasmus, President

members: 450
founded: 1974
staff: 10 volunteer
major programs: tours, lectures,
historic preservation, periodical

Mohawk Valley Museum
620 Memorial Parkway
Utica, New York 13501
315-724-2075

Munson-Williams-Proctor
Institute
310 Genesee Street
Utica, New York 13502
315-797-0000
Paul J. Farinella, President
members: 2,670
founded: 1919
staff: 75 full-time, 25 part-time,
85 volunteer
major programs: library,
museum, historic sites, school
programs, tours, lectures,
workshops, exhibits,
publications, periodical

Utica Neighborhood Housing
Services
322 South Street
Utica, New York 13501

Utica Public Library
303 Genesee Street
Utica, New York 13501
315-735-2279
Helen H. Dirtadian, Director

Vernon

Vernon Historical Society
5 Peterboro Street, P.O. Box 786
Vernon, New York 13476
315-829-2463
Jon Landers, President
members: 23
founded: 1972
staff: all volunteer
major programs: library, photo
collection, school programs

Waterville

Waterville Historical Society
P.O. Box 67
Waterville, New York 13480

Westmoreland

Westmoreland Historical Society
P.O. Box 200
Westmoreland, New York 13490

Onondaga County

County Arts Council

Cultural Resources Council of
Syracuse and Onondaga County
411 Montgomery Street
Syracuse, New York 13202
315-425-2155

County Historian

Richard Wright
311 Montgomery Street
Syracuse, New York 13202

County Historical Society

Onondaga Historical Association
311 Montgomery Street
Syracuse, New York 13202
315-428-1862
Tony King, Director
members: 200
founded: 1863
staff: 6 full-time, 1 part-time,
30 volunteer
major programs: library,
archives, museum, photo
collection, exhibits, periodical

County Planning Office

Syracuse-Onondaga County
Planning Agency
1100 Civic Center
421 Montgomery Street
Syracuse, New York 13202
315-425-2611

Baldwinsville

Beauchamp Historical Club
23 McHarrie Street
Baldwinsville, New York 13027

McHarrie's Legacy
P.O. Box 481
Baldwinsville, New York 13027
Nelson Butler, President
major programs: museum,
historic sites, photo collection,
tours, exhibits, awards, historic
preservation, markers program,
periodical

Northwest Neighbors
Preservation Corporation
23 Oswego Street
Baldwinsville, New York 13027
315-638-1051
Mike Reiley, Executive Director
founded: 1986
staff: 2 full-time
major programs: workshops,
surveys, rural preservation

Brewerton

Brerwerton Public Library
5437 Library Street
Brewerton, New York 13029

Fort Brewerton Historical Society
P.O. Box 392
Brewerton, New York 13029

Camillus

Camillus Historical Society
P.O. Box 57
Camillus, New York 13031

Town of Camillus
Erie Canal Project
109 East Way
Camillus, New York 13031
315-672-3079
David W. Beebe, Director

Cicero

Town of Cicero
Historical Society
P.O. Box 241
Cicero, New York 13039

Clay

Aviation Historical Society of
Central New York
7971 Vernon Road
Clay, New York 13041
315-458-4721
Kenneth W. Sweet, President
members: 14
founded: 1972
staff: 7 volunteer
major programs: photo
collection, research, exhibits,
historic preservation

Clay Historical Society
8030 Casilina Drive
Clay, New York 13041

East Syracuse

East Syracuse Free Library
122 Henrietta Street
East Syracuse, New York 13057
315-437-4841
Shirley M. Reichert, Director
founded: 1924
staff: 1 full-time, 14 part-time,
2 volunteer
major programs: library

Fayetteville

Grover Cleveland Yorkers
Wellwood Middle School
Fayetteville, New York 13066
315-682-9192
Lucinda Kiehl, Sponsor-Teacher

Jamesville

Jamesville Community Museum
6492 East Seneca Turnpike
P.O. Box 76
Jamesville, New York 13078
William J. Hopkins, President
members: 350
founded: 1977
staff: 10 volunteer
major programs: museum,
school programs, exhibits,
historic preservation

Liverpool

Friends of Historic
Onondaga Lake
P.O. Box 146
Liverpool, New York 13088

Historical Association of
Greater Liverpool
314 Second Street
Liverpool, New York 13088
Mary L. DeNeve, President
members: 52
founded: 1976
staff: all volunteer
major programs: publications,
surveys, markers program

Liverpool Public Library
Second and Tulip streets
Liverpool, New York 13088

Onondaga County Parks, Office
of Museums and Historic Sites
106 Lake Drive, P.O. Box 146
Liverpool, New York 13088
315-457-2990
Dennis J. Connors, Director

members: 150
founded: 1975
staff: 5 full-time, 10 part-time,
15 volunteer
major programs: library,
archives, museum, historic sites,
photo collection, research,
school programs, tours, lectures,
exhibits, publications,
archeology, periodical

Manlius

Manlius Historical Society
101 Scoville Avenue
P.O. Box 173
Manlius, New York 13104
315-682-6660
Carrie Gannett, Director
members: 300
founded: 1976
staff: 1 full-time, 60 volunteer
major programs: library,
archives, museum, photo
collection, school programs,
lectures, workshops, exhibits,
publications, periodical

Manlius Restoration and
Development Inc.
Manlius Village Centre
Elmbrook Drive
Manlius, New York 13104
Thirza B. Garwood, President
members: 100
founded: 1976
staff: all volunteer
major programs: workshops,
awards, surveys, historic
preservation

Marcellus

Marcellus Historical Society
40 South Street
Marcellus, New York 13108

North Syracuse

Plank Road Historical Society
P.O. Box 49
North Syracuse, New York
13212

Pompey

Town of Pompey
Historical Society
P.O. Box 82
Pompey, New York 13138

Skaneateles

Citizens to Preserve the
Character of Skaneateles
P.O. Box 12
Skaneateles, New York 13152
founded: 1987
major programs: historic
preservation

Skaneateles Historical
Society
P.O. Box 200
Skaneateles, New York 13152

Solvay

Solvay Public Library
615 Woods Road
Solvay, New York 13209

Syracuse

Central New York
Genealogical Society
P.O. Box 104, Colvin Station
Syracuse, New York 13202

Central New York Library
Resources Council
763 Butternut Street
Syracuse, New York 13208
315-478-6080
Keith E. Washburn, Executive
Director
members: 57
founded: 1968
staff: 1 volunteer
major programs: library,
research, workshops,
publications, periodical, grants

Central New York Regional
Planning and Development
Board
90 Presidential Plaza, Suite 122
Syracuse, New York 13202
315-422-8276
Gary G. Hayes, Executive
Director

Erie Canal Museum
318 Erie Boulevard East
Syracuse, New York 13202
315-471-0593
Vicki B. Quigley, Director
members: 500
founded: 1962

major programs: library,
archives, museum, historic sites,
photo collection, research,
school programs, tours, lectures,
workshops, exhibits, historic
preservation, periodical

Everson Museum of Art
401 Harrison Street
Syracuse, New York 13202
315-474-6064
Ronald A. Kuchta, Director
members: 2,350
founded: 1896
staff: 20 full-time, 20 part-time,
300 volunteer
major programs: library,
museum, school programs,
tours, lectures, exhibits,
publications, periodical

Institute for the Development of
Evolutive Architecture (IDEA)
329 Westcott Street
Syracuse, New York 13210
315-472-6492
Cleota Reed, Director
founded: 1977
staff: 4 volunteer
major programs: archives,
research, exhibits, publications

North East Hawley Development
101 Gertrude Street
Syracuse, New York 13203

Onondaga County Community
Development Division
1300 Civic Center
421 Montgomery Street
Syracuse, New York 13202
315-425-3558
Linda Richey, Administrator
founded: 1975
staff: 12 full-time
major programs: historic
preservation, rural preservation,
affordable housing, matching
grants

Onondaga County Public Library
327 Montgomery Street
Syracuse, New York 13202
315-473-2702
Helene Ballantyne, Public
Information Specialist

Onondaga Free Library
4840 West Seneca Turnpike
Syracuse, New York 13215

Preservation Association of
Central New York
1509 Park Street
Syracuse, New York 13208
315-475-0119
members: 400
founded: 1974
staff: 2 full-time, 15 volunteer
major programs: library, historic
site, photo collection, research,
tours, lectures, workshops,
awards, surveys, historic
preservation, technical
preservation services, periodical,
revolving fund, easements

Regional Council of
Historical Agencies
1400 North State Street
Syracuse, New York 13208
315-475-1525
Jackie Day, Executive Director
members: 525
founded: 1971
staff: 3 full-time, 1 part-time
major programs: workshops,
publications, technical
preservation services, periodical

Society for the Preservation and
Appreciation of Antique Motor
Fire Apparatus
P.O. Box 450, Eastwood Station
Syracuse, New York 13206
315-472-4293

Syracuse Model
Neighborhood Corporation
1721 South Salina Street
Syracuse, New York 13205

Syracuse Neighborhood
Housing Services
2331 South Salina Street
Syracuse, New York 13205

Syracuse University Bird Library
of Fine Arts
205 Bird Library
222 Waverly Avenue
Syracuse, New York 13244
315-423-2905
Barbara Opar, Architecture
Librarian

Syracuse Urban Cultural
Park Program
225 City Hall
Syracuse, New York 13202
315-473-5694

Tully

Southern Hills Preservation
Corporation
3 Elm Street, P.O. Box 661
Tully, New York 13159
315-696-5835
Julee Johnson, Executive
Director
founded: 1982
staff: 3 full-time
major programs: workshops,
surveys, rural preservation,
affordable housing, technical
preservation services, periodical

Tully Area Historical Society
22-24 State Street, P.O. Box 22
Tully, New York 13159
315-696-5219
Edwin Leonard, President
members: 300
founded: 1978
staff: 50 volunteer
major programs: library,
archives, historic preservation,
periodical

Ontario County

County Arts Council

Ontario County Arts Council
P.O. Box 25032
Farmington, New York 14425
716-394-3915

County Historian

Preston E. Pierce
120 North Main Street
Canandaigua, New York 14424
716-396-4034

County Historical Society

Ontario County
Historical Society
55 North Main Street
Canandaigua, New York 14424
716-394-4975
Christopher Clarke-Hazlett,
Director
members: 675
founded: 1902
staff: 4 full-time, 3 part-time,
20 volunteer

major programs: library,
archives, museum, photo
collection, school programs,
lectures, exhibits, publications,
awards, surveys, historic
preservation, rural preservation

County Planning Office

Ontario County Division of
Planning and Research
120 North Main Street
Canandaigua, New York 14424
716-396-4455

see also Genesee-Finger Lakes
Regional Planning Council,
Rochester, Monroe County;
Landmark Society of Western
New York, Rochester, Monroe
County; Regional Council of
Historical Agencies, Syracuse,
Onondaga County

Bristol

Historical Society of Bristol
RD 3
Canandaigua, New York 14424

Canandaigua

Granger Homestead Society
295 North Main Street
Canandaigua, New York 14424
716-394-7469
Christopher Clarke-Hazlett,
Director
members: 541
founded: 1946
staff: 2 full-time, 5 part-time,
50 volunteer
major programs: museum,
historic sites, research, school
programs, tours, workshops,
exhibits, periodical

Sonnenberg Gardens
151 Charlotte Street
P.O. Box 663
Canandaigua, New York 14424
716-394-6624
Mary Ann Bell, Director
members: 1,100
founded: 1973
staff: 8 full-time, 57 part-time,
223 volunteer

major programs: museum,
historic sites, tours, lectures,
workshops, exhibits, historic
preservation, periodical

Clifton Springs

Town of Manchester
Historical Society
County Road 7, Box 418
Clifton Springs, New York
14432

East Bloomfield

Town of East Bloomfield
Historical Society
8 South Avenue
East Bloomfield, New York
14443
Mrs. M. B. Herr-Gesell,
Executive Director

Farmington

Farmington
Historical Society
P.O. Box 176
Farmington, New York 14425
315-986-3170
Diana Van der Velder, President

Fishers

Victor Historical Society
Valentown Square
Fishers, New York 14453

Geneva

Ansley School
Preservation Society
4921 Preemption Road
Geneva, New York 14456

Community Unified Today
21 Milton Street
Geneva, New York 14456
315-789-2669
Patrisha Blue, Executive Director
members: 12
founded: 1974
staff: 4 full-time, 1 part-time,
20 volunteer
major programs: rural
preservation, affordable housing

Finger Lakes Regional Arts
Council Inc.
82 Seneca Street, P.O. Box 58
Geneva, New York 14456
315-789-2221
Richard Erwin, Executive
Director

members: 600
founded: 1980
staff: 2 full-time, 1 part-time,
60 volunteer
major programs: school
programs, tours, historic
preservation, periodical,
revolving fund

Geneva Historical Society
543 South Main Street
Geneva, New York 14456
315-789-5151
Michael F. Wajda, Executive
Director
members: 850
founded: 1883
staff: 5 full-time, 2 part-time,
26 volunteer
major programs: library,
archives, museum, historic sites,
photo collection, research,
school programs, tours, lectures,
workshops, exhibits,
publications, historic
preservation, markers program,
periodical, revolving fund, grants

Gorham

Marcus Whitman
Historical Society
P.O. Box 204
Gorham, New York 14461

Town of Gorham
Historical Society
Route 1
Stanley, New York 14561

Naples

Naples Historical Society
P.O. Box 115
Naples, New York 14512
William Vierhile, President
members: 105
founded: 1977
staff: 25 volunteer
major programs: historic sites,
photo collection, school
programs, tours, lectures,
exhibits, publications, historic
preservation, markers program

Phelps

Phelps Community
Historical Society
97 East Main Street
Phelps, New York 14532
315-548-4772
Richard Rathbun, Curator

Victor

Town of Victor
85 East Main Street
Victor, New York 14564
716-924-7141
Rose Marie Fagan, Historian
major programs: archives, photo
collection, research, school
programs, lectures, historic
preservation

West Bloomfield

West Bloomfield
Historical Society
P.O. Box 1776
West Bloomfield, New York
14585

Orange County

County Arts Council

Arts Council of Orange County
19 South Street
Middletown, New York 10940
914-342-2133

County Historian

Theodore Sly
County Government Center
Main Street
Goshen, New York 10924

County Historical Society

Orange County
Historical Society
Arden, New York 10910

County Planning Office

Orange County Planning
and Development
124 Main Street
Goshen, New York 10924
914-294-5151

Blooming Grove

Historic Blooming
Grove Association
P.O. Box 203
Blooming Grove, New York
10914
914-496-9205
Karin Lucas, President
members: 50
founded: 1986
staff: 12 volunteer
major programs: library, photo
collection, lectures, markers
program

Chester

Chester Historical Society
Meadow Avenue, P.O. Box 112
Chester, New York 10918

Cornwall-on-Hudson

Museum of the Hudson
Highlands
P.O. Box 181
Cornwall-on-Hudson, New York
12520

Cuddebackville

Neversink Valley Area Museum
Hoag Road, P.O. Box 263
Cuddebackville, New York
12729
914-754-8870
Charles R. Thomas,
Curator/Coordinator
members: 345
founded: 1967
staff: 1 full-time, 3 part-time,
22 volunteer
major programs: museum,
historic sites, photo collection,
research, school programs,
exhibits, surveys, historic
preservation, periodical

Fort Montgomery

Town of Highlands
Historical Society
P.O. Box 438
Fort Montgomery, New York
10922

Goshen

Goshen Historic Track
Main Street, P.O. Box 192
Goshen, New York 10924
914-294-5333
Pat Jessup, Administrator
members: 500
major programs: historic site,
periodical

Goshen Public Library/Historical
Society
203 Main Street
Goshen, New York 10924

Orange County Community of
Museums and Galleries
P.O. Box 527
Goshen, New York 10924
914-294-5657

Orange County Genealogical
Society
101 Main Street
Goshen, New York 10924

Orange County Rural
Development Advisory
Corporation
217 Greenwich Avenue
Goshen, New York 10924
914-294-8336
Alice Dickinson, Executive
Director
founded: 1983
staff: 4 full-time, 2 volunteer
major programs: affordable
housing

Highland Mills

Woodbury
Historical Society
Albany Turnpike (Route 32),
P.O. Box 30
Highland Mills, New York
10930
914-928-6770
Leslie Rose, Archivist
members: 126
founded: 1984
staff: 10 volunteer
major programs: library,
archives, historic sites, photo
collection, research, exhibits,
awards, historic preservation,
periodical

Middletown

Antique Clock Museum
4 South Street
Middletown, New York 10940

Middletown Preservation
League
P.O. Box 2082
Middletown, New York 10940
914-343-1281
Frederic C. Zanetti, Executive
Director
members: 100
founded: 1981
staff: 5 volunteer
major programs: historic sites,
photo collection, research,
publications, surveys, historic
preservation, markers program,
periodical

Ontario and Western Railway
Historical Society
P.O. Box 713
Middletown, New York 10940
Raymond A. Wood, President
members: 550
founded: 1963
staff: 24 volunteer
major programs: archives,
historic sites, photo collection,
tours, publications, markers
program, periodical

Monroe

Monroe Historical Society
c/o Town Hall, Stage Road
Monroe, New York 10950
914-783-7038
Paul M. Simon, President
members: 15
founded: 1973
staff: 10 volunteer
major programs: photo
collection, research, tours,
exhibits, historic preservation,
markers program

Museum Village in
Orange County
Museum Village Road
Monroe, New York 10950
Brooke Elkin, Director

Newburgh

Historical Society of Newburgh
Bay and the Highlands
189 Montgomery Street
Newburgh, New York 12550
914-561-2585
Thomas Kyle, Director
members: 250
founded: 1884
staff: 1 full-time
major programs: library,
museum, tours, exhibits,
periodical

Neighbors United for Justice
in Housing
177 Liberty Street
Newburgh, NY 12550
914-564-5496

Newburgh Preservation
Association
87 Liberty Street
Newburgh, New York 12550
914-565-6880
Theresa L. Farrell, Chair
members: 200
founded: 1973
staff: 3 part-time, 5 volunteer
major programs: tours, exhibits,
surveys, historic preservation,
technical preservation services,
periodical

Newburgh Revitalization
Corporation
89 North Street
Newburgh, New York 12550

Port Jervis

Depot Preservation Society
P.O. Box 1004
Port Jervis, New York 12771

Minisink Valley
Historical Society
138 Pike Street, P.O. Box 659
Port Jervis, New York 12771
914-856-2375
Peter Osborne, III, Executive
Director
members: 350
founded: 1889
staff: 1 full-time
major programs: museum,
historic sites, photo collection,
school programs, exhibits,
historic preservation, periodical

Slate Hill

Land of the Lenapes Society
Slate Hill, New York 10973

Tuxedo

Tuxedo Historical Society
P.O. Box 188
Tuxedo, New York 10987

Vails Gate

National Temple Hill Association
P.O. Box 315
Vails Gate, New York 12584
914-561-4590

Walden

Historical Society of Walden and
Walkill Valley
37 North Montgomery Street
P.O. Box 48
Walden, New York 12586
Anita Vandermark, President
members: 127
founded: 1958
major programs: historic site,
periodical

Warwick

Historical Society of the
Town of Warwick
P.O. Box 353
Warwick, New York 10990

West Point

Constitution Island Association
P.O. Box 41
West Point, New York 10996
914-446-8676
Mary K. McIntosh, Executive
Director
members: 386
founded: 1917
staff: 1 full-time, 1 part-time,
80 volunteer
major programs: museum,
school programs, tours,
publications, periodical

Orleans County

County Arts Council

Orleans County Arts Council
33 Meadowbrook Drive
Albion, New York 14411
716-589-6259

County Historian

C.W. Lattin
Court House
Albion, New York 14411

County Historical Society

Orleans County Historical
Association
16336 Church Street, RD 1
Holley, New York 14470
716-638-6994
Mary L. Isselhard, President
members: 80
founded: 1977
staff: all volunteer
major programs: lectures,
exhibits, publications, periodical

County Planning Office

Orleans County Planning and
Development Office
14016 Route 31W
Albion, New York 14411
716-589-7004/589-4831

see also Genesee-Finger Lakes
Regional Planning Council,
Rochester, Monroe County;
Landmark Society of Western
New York, Rochester, Monroe
County; Western New York
Association of Historical
Agencies, Leicester, Livingston
County

Albion

The Cobblestone Society
14407 Ridge Road East
Albion, New York 14411
716-589-4355
Delia Robinson, Research
Director

Housing Development Council of
Orleans County
53 North Main Street
Albion, New York 14411
716-589-7037
Chuck Wenzel, Executive
Director
founded: 1978
staff: 4 full-time, 2 part-time,
1 volunteer
major programs: rural
preservation, affordable housing,
revolving fund

Orleans County Planning Board
151 Platt Street
Albion, New York 14411
716-589-4491

Orleans/Genesee Rural
Preservation Corporation
409 East State Street
Albion, New York 14411

Swan Library
4 North Main Street
Albion, New York 14411
716-589-4246
C.W. Lattin, Museum Director
members: 435
founded: 1960
staff: 1 full-time, 12 volunteer
major programs: library,
museum, research, school
programs, tours, lectures,
workshops, exhibits,
publications, technical
preservation services, periodical

Clarendon

Clarendon Historical Society
P.O. Box 124
Clarendon, New York 14429
Lee Weaver, President
members: 20
major programs: publications

Holley

Murray-Holley
Historical Society
Wright Street, P.O. Box 346
Holley, New York 14470
716-638-8188
Marcia Defilipps, President
members: 35
founded: 1985
staff: 15 volunteer
major programs: archives,
museum, photo collection,
exhibits

Lyndonville

Yates Historical Society
76 West Avenue
Lyndonville, New York 14098

Medina

Medina Historical Society
406 West Avenue
Medina, New York 14103
716-798-3006
Marian E. Perry, President
members: 60
founded: 1971
staff: all volunteer
major programs: museum, photo
collection, tours, historic
preservation

Oswego County

County Arts Council

Oswego County Council
on the Arts
11 West Bridge Street
Oswego, New York 13126

County Historian

Anthony Slosek
41 Gerrit Street
Oswego, New York 13126

County Historical Society

Oswego County
Historical Society
135 East Third Street
Oswego, New York 13126
315-343-1342
Alice K. Askins, Director
members: 350
founded: 1896
staff: 3 full-time, 2 part-time
major programs: museum,
school programs, tours, exhibits

County Planning Office

Oswego County Planning Office
46 East Bridge Street
Oswego, New York 13126
315-349-8297

see also Central New York
Regional Planning and
Development Board, Syracuse,
Onondaga County; Regional
Council of Historical Agencies,
Syracuse, Onondaga County;
Preservation Association of
Central New York, Syracuse,
Onondaga County

Fulton

Friends of History in Fulton
177 South First Street
Fulton, New York 13069
315-598-4616
Michele Anne Bazley,
Coordinator
members: 300
founded: 1979
staff: 1 full-time, 2 volunteer
major programs: library,
museum, photo collection,
exhibits

Hannibal

Hannibal Historical Society
Oswego Street
Hannibal, New York 13074

Mexico

Mexico Historical Society
South Jefferson Street
Mexico, New York 13114
315-963-7882
Euloda Fetcha, Mexico Town
Historian
members: 58
founded: 1975
staff: 1 part-time, 12 volunteer
major programs: museum,
historic sites, photo collection,
school programs, tours, exhibits,
publications, historic
preservation, rural preservation,
periodical

Oswego

Heritage Foundation of Oswego
161 West First Street
P.O. Box 405
Oswego, New York 13126
315-342-3354
Sally A. Sappey, Coordinator
members: 250
founded: 1962
staff: 1 full-time, 1 part-time,
many volunteer
major programs: library,
research, school programs, tours,
workshops, publications,
awards, surveys, historic
preservation, markers program,
technical preservation,
periodical, revolving fund

Oswego Town Historical Society
RD 3
Oswego, New York 13126
Charles V. Groat, President
members: 65
founded: 1982
staff: all volunteer
major programs: library,
archives, historic sites, photo
collection, research, lectures,
exhibits

Parish

Oswego Housing
Development Council
7455 Main Street, P.O. Box 147
Parish, New York 13131
315-625-4520
Marilyn S. Loveless,
Administrator
founded: 1979
staff: 1 full-time, 1 part-time
major programs: rural
preservation, affordable housing

Pennellville

Pennellville Hotel Historical
Association
County Route 54 and Main
Street
Pennellville, New York 13132
315-695-2293
John R. Byard, Executive
Director

Phoenix

Greater Phoenix Improvement
Association
220 Church Street
Phoenix, New York 13135
315-695-6082
Janet D. Harder, President
members: 35
founded: 1974
staff: all volunteer
major programs: research, school
programs, tours, lectures,
workshops, exhibits, awards,
historic preservation

Schroeppel Historical Society
827 Main Street
Phoenix, New York 13135

Pulaski

Pulaski Historical Society
P.O. Box 302
Pulaski, New York 13142

Richland

Half-shire Historical Society
Main Street, P.O. Box 73
Richland, New York 13144
315-298-2986
George O. Widrig, President
founded: 1972
staff: 15 volunteer
major programs: library,
archives, museum, school
programs, workshops, exhibits

Scriba

Scriba Historical Society
RD 2
Scriba, New York 13126

Otsego County

County Arts Council

Upper Catskill Community
Council of the Arts
248 Main Street
Oneonta, New York 13820
607-432-2070
Victoria Faoro, Executive
Director

County Historian

County Office Building
197 Main Street
Cooperstown, New York 13326

County Historical Society

no listing

County Planning Office

Otsego County Planning
Department
County Office Building
197 Main Street
Cooperstown, New York 13326
607-547-4224

see also Southern Tier East
Regional Planning Development
Board, Binghamton, Broome
County; Regional Council of
Historical Agencies, Syracuse,
Onondaga County

Burlington Flats

Burlington Historical Society
RD 1
Burlington Flats, New York
13315
607-965-8306

Cherry Valley

Cherry Valley
Historical Association
RD 1, Box 9B
Cherry Valley, New York 13320
Marion J. Cornelia, Curator

Cooperstown

Cooperstown Indian Museum
Cooperstown, New York 13326

Otsego Rural Housing Assistance
27 Railroad Avenue
Cooperstown, New York 13326
607-547-9293
Anthony Scalici, Executive
Director
founded: 1984
staff: 5 full-time
major programs: research,
workshops, surveys, rural
preservation, affordable housing,
technical preservation services,
grants, matching grants

Town of Middlefield
Historical Association
P.O. Box 348
Cooperstown, New York 13326
Harriet R. Rogers, Town
Historian
members: 170
founded: 1987
staff: 12 volunteer
major programs: archives,
museum, photo collection,
research, school programs,
exhibits, periodical

Village of Cooperstown
Planning Board
22 Main Street, P.O. Box 346
Cooperstown, New York 13326
607-547-2411
Joe H. Cannon, Chair
staff: 1 part-time, 5 volunteer
major programs: historic
preservation

see also New York State
Historical Association (p.49)

Edmeston

Edmeston Museum
One North Street
Edmeston, New York 13335
607-965-8902
mail to: 59 South Street
Edmeston, New York 13335
Robert Nonenmacher, Director
founded: 1970
staff: 1 part-time
major programs: archives,
museum, photo collection,
school programs, exhibits

Gilbertsville

Historical Association of the
Town of Butternuts
P.O. Box 332
Gilbertsville, New York 13776

Historical Committee
Gilbertsville Free Library
Gilbertsville, New York 13776
607-783-2223

Major's Inn
P.O. Box 242
Gilbertsville, New York 13776
607-783-2427
Cecelia M. Rowe, Executive
Director
members: 100
founded: 1980
staff: 30 volunteer
major programs: museum,
historic preservation, periodical

Village Improvement Society
of Gilbertsville, NY
P.O. Box 121
Gilbertsville, New York 13776
607-783-2525
Douglas D. McKee, President
members: 55
founded: 1881
staff: 7 volunteer
major programs: museum,
historic sites, exhibits, historic
preservation

Hartwick

Town of Hartwick
Historical Society
Hartwick, New York 13348

Maryland

Town of Maryland
Historical Association
RD 1, Box 1038
Maryland, New York 12116
607-638-9362
Dorothy Scott Fielder, President
members: 40
founded: 1979
staff: 3 volunteer
major programs: exhibits,
periodical

Milford

Greater Milford
Historical Association
North Main Street
Milford, New York 13807
607-286-9948
Niles Eggleston, President
members: 50
founded: 1971
staff: all volunteer
major programs: museum, photo
collection, school programs,
workshops, exhibits, periodical

Morris

Morris Historical Society
Morris, New York 13808

Oneonta

Huntington Memorial Library
62 Chestnut Street
Oneonta, New York 13820
607-432-1980
Marie Bruni, Director

Museums at Hartwick College
Hartwick College
Oneonta, New York 13820
607-432-4200 x464
Jane desGrange, Director

Upper Susquehanna Historical
Society and Museum
203 River Street
Oneonta, New York 13820

Otego

Otego Historical Society
Main Street
Otego, New York 13825

Roland B. Hill Memorial
Museum of Archaeology
Main Street
Otego, New York 13825
607-988-2229
mail to: RD 3, Box 348
Oneonta, New York 13820
Calvin L. Behnke,
President
members: 22
founded: 1967
staff: 10 volunteer
major programs: library,
museum, photo collection,
school programs, lectures,
surveys, archeology

Richfield Springs

Richfield Historical Society
Richfield Springs, New York
13439

Roseboom

Town of Roseboom
Historical Association
RD 2
Cherry Valley, New York 13320

Schuyler Lake

Town of Exeter
Historical Society
Main Street
Schuyler Lake, New York 13457

Springfield

Friends of Hyde Hall
P.O. Box 721
Cooperstown, New York 13326
607-547-5098
Douglas R. Kent, Vice President
founded: 1964
staff: 1 full-time
major programs: museum,
historic site, historic preservation

Springfield Historical Society
Springfield Center, New York
13468

Worcester

Worcester Historical Society
Main Street
Worcester, New York 12197
Irene Smith, Curator

members: 150
founded: 1970
staff: 15 volunteer
major programs: library,
museum, photo collection,
research, historic preservation

Putnam County

County Arts Council

Putnam Arts Council
Kennicut Hill Road
P.O. Box 156
Mahopac, New York 10541
914-628-3664

County Historian

Isabel Walsh
Gipsy Trail Club
Carmel, New York 10512

County Historical Society

Putnam County Historical
Society Museum
63 Chestnut Street
Cold Spring, New York 10516
914-265-4010
Taylor Belcher, Chair
members: 500
founded: 1908
staff: 5 volunteer
major programs: library,
archives, museum, photo
collection, research, exhibits,
historic preservation

County Planning Office

Putnam County Planning
RR 9, Box 331
Fair Street
Carmel, New York 10512
914-878-3480

see also Lower Hudson
Conference, Elmsford,
Westchester County

Brewster

Landmarks Preservation Society
Starr Ridge Road
Brewster, New York 10509
914-279-6576
Eleanor B. Fitchen, President
members: 310
founded: 1969
staff: all volunteer

major programs: archives, historic sites, photo collection, research, school programs, tours, lectures, publications, awards, historic preservation, technical preservation services, periodical, easements

New Salem Historical Society
39 Seven Oaks Lane
Brewster, New York 10509

SAVE Open Spaces
Brewster, New York 10509
914-276-6576

Southeast Museum Association
Main Street, P.O. Box 88
Brewster, New York 10509
914-279-7500
Robin Imhoff, Director
members: 200
founded: 1963
staff: 3 part-time, 10 volunteer
major programs: museum, exhibits, periodical

Carmel

Putnam County Housing Corporation
110 Old Route 6, Building A
Carmel, New York 10512

Cold Spring

Foundry School Museum
63 Chestnut Street
Cold Spring, New York 10516

Historical Preservation Project
77 Main Street
Cold Spring, New York 10516

Hudson River Valley Association
(see also Troy, Rensselaer County)
72 Main Street
Cold Spring, New York 10516
914-265-3066
members: 175
founded: 1965
staff: 4 full-time
major programs: lectures, publications, periodical

Preservation, Revitalization of Cold Spring Area
258 Main Street, P.O. Box 15
Cold Spring, New York 10516
914-265-2111
Jack Kelly, Executive Director
founded: 1980
staff: 1 full-time, 1 part-time, 1 volunteer
major programs: research, workshops, surveys, rural preservation, affordable housing

Garrison

Manitoga
Old Manitou Road
Garrison, New York 10524
914-424-3812
Susan Eirich-Dehne, Executive Director
members: 250
founded: 1975
staff: 3 full-time, 1 part-time
major programs: historic sites, school programs, tours, lectures, workshops, publications, archeology, periodical

Kent

Kent Historical Society
P.O. Box 123
Carmel, New York 10512
Jean Murray, President
members: 100
founded: 1978
staff: 9 volunteer
major programs: library, historic sites, photo collection, research, school programs, tours, lectures, workshops, exhibits, publications, historic preservation, rural preservation, markers program, archeology, periodical

Patterson

Patterson Historical Society
South Street
Patterson, New York 12563

Putnam Preservation League
P.O. Box 534
Patterson, New York 12563
914-878-6169
Tom Keasbey, Treasurer
members: 65
founded: 1984

staff: all volunteer
major programs: historic sites, surveys, historic preservation, periodical

Putnam Valley

Putnam Valley Historical Society
Peekskill Hollow and Church roads, P.O. Box 297
Putnam Valley, New York 10579
914-526-3890
Barbara Doyle, President
members: 150
founded: 1968
staff: 10 volunteer
major programs: museum, photo collection, research, publications, periodical

Queens County

County Arts Council

Queens Council on the Arts
161-04 Jamaica Avenue
Jamaica, New York 11432
718-291-1100

County Historian

Harry Ludder
Queensboro Hall
120-55 Queens Boulevard
Kew Gardens, New York 11424

County Historical Society

Queens Historical Society
143-35 37th Avenue
Flushing, New York 11354
718-939-0647
Mary Anne Mrozinski, Executive Director
members: 500
founded: 1968
staff: 3 full-time, 1 part-time, 50 volunteer
major programs: library, archives, museum, historic sites, photo collection, research, school programs, tours, lectures, workshops, exhibits, publications, surveys, periodical

County Planning Office

Queens Office, Department of City Planning
29-27 41st Avenue
Long Island City, New York 11101
718-392-0565

see also New York County listings; Society for the Preservation of Long Island Antiquities, Setauket, Suffolk County

Arverne

Jamaica Bay Council
321 Beach 57 Street
Arverne, New York 11692
716-474-6507

Rockaway Cultural, Educational, Recreational and Historical Society
321 Beach 51 Street
Arverne, New York 11692

Astoria

Astoria Restoration Association
31-28 Ditmars Boulevard
Astoria, New York 11105
718-726-0034
Paul Sternberg, director
founded: 1977
staff: 4 full-time
major programs: lectures, workshops

Central Astoria Local Development Coalition
28-27 Steinway Street
Astoria, New York 11103

Greater Astoria Historical Society
34-31 35th Street
Astoria, New York 11106

Northwest Queens Housing Corporation
31-14 30th Avenue
Astoria, New York 11102

Bayside

Bayside Historical Society
P.O. Box 133
Bayside, New York 11361
718-224-5707
Mary Blake, President
members: 350
founded: 1964
staff: 25 volunteer
major programs: archives, historic sites, school programs, lectures, publications, historic preservation, periodical

College Point

College Point Historical Society
P.O. Box 182
College Point, New York 11356

Douglaston

Alley Pond Environmental Center
228-06 Northern Boulevard
Douglaston, New York 11363
718-229-4000
George O. Pratt, Executive Director
members: 890
founded: 1976
staff: 8 full-time, 5 part-time, 8 volunteer
major programs: school programs, tours, lectures, workshops, exhibits, historic preservation, nature center, periodical

East Elmhurst

Elmcor Youth and Adult Activities
98-04 Astoria Boulevard
East Elmhurst, New York 11369

Elmhurst

Newtown Historical Society
84-14 Grand Avenue
Elmhurst, New York 11373

Far Rockaway

Margert Community Corporation
1920 New Haven Avenue
Far Rockaway, New York 11691
718-471-3724
Ron Myers, Sr., Executive Director
founded: 1980
staff: 9 full-time, 1 part-time
major programs: school programs, surveys, affordable housing, technical preservation services

Flushing

Anthropology Museum of the People of New York
Department of Anthropology
Queens College
Flushing, New York 11367
718-428-5650
Margaret C.T. Kyrkostas, Director
members: 150
founded: 1977
staff: 10 volunteer
major programs: museum, school programs, tours, lectures, workshops, exhibits, awards, periodical

Bowne House Historical Society
37-01 Bowne Street
Flushing, New York 11354
718-359-0528
Audrey Braver, Director
members: 600
founded: 1945
staff: 1 full-time, 70 volunteer
major programs: museum, historic sites, school programs, tours, exhibits, historic preservation, periodical

Flushing Council on Culture and the Arts
136-73 41st Avenue
Flushing, New York 11355
718-463-7700
Jo-Ann Jones, Executive Director

Flushing. Historical Society
153-10 60th Avenue
Flushing, New York 11355

Friends Meeting House
136-16 Northern Boulevard
Flushing, New York 11354

Pomonok Neighborhood Center
67-09 Kissena Boulevard
Flushing, New York 11367
718-591-6060
Ruben Malave, Executive
Director
founded: 1976
staff: 3 full-time
major programs: affordable
housing, neighborhood
preservation

Queens Community
Civic Corporation
68-01A 136th Street
Flushing, New York 11367
718-261-8015
Carolyn Kagan, Executive
Director
staff: 2 full-time, 2 part-time
major programs: school
programs, surveys, affordable
housing, periodical

Queens Museum
New York City Building
Flushing Meadow Park
Flushing, New York 11368

Forest Hills

Forest Hills Community House
108-25 62nd Drive
Forest Hills, New York 11375

Hollis

Urban Renewal Committee of
South Jamaica
104-15 196th Street
Hollis, New York 11442

Jamaica

Allen A.M.E. Housing
Corporation
114-82 Guy R. Brewer
Boulevard
Jamaica, New York 11433

King Manor Association
of Long Island Inc.
150th Street and Jamaica Avenue
Jamaica, New York 11435
mail to: 87-77 146th Street,
Jamaica, New York 11435
Vera Rawlings, President
members: 85
founded: 1900
staff: 10 volunteer
major programs: historic
preservation

Neighborhood Housing
Services of Jamaica
160-16 121st Avenue
Jamaica, New York 11434

Ridgewood

Greater Ridgewood
Historical Society
1820 Flushing Avenue
Ridgewood, New York 11385

Greater Ridgewood Restoration
810 Fairview Avenue
Ridgewood, New York 11385

Rockaway Beach

Arverne Hammel Holland
Seaside Housing and
Neighborhood Preservation
Coalition
100-02 Rockaway Beach
Boulevard
Rockaway Beach, New York
11694
718-474-3232
David N. Weinraub, Executive
Director
founded: 1982
staff: 1 full-time, 1 part-time
major programs: lectures,
workshops, publications,
surveys, affordable housing,
technical preservation services,
periodical, revolving fund

Sunnyside

Gateway Community
Restoration
47-08 Greenpoint Avenue
Sunnyside, New York 11104
718-937-5000

Antonia A. Dosik, Executive
Director
founded: 1977
staff: 4 full-time, 3 part-time
major programs: affordable
housing, periodical, matching
grants

Queensborough Preservation
League
45-16 Skillman Avenue
Sunnyside, New York 11104
718-392-9139
Nina Rappaport, Coordinator
founded: 1985
staff: 10 volunteer
major programs: publications,
historic preservation

Sunnyside Foundation
45-16 Skillman Avenue
Sunnyside, New York 11104
718-392-9139
Nina Rappaport, Executive
Director
founded: 1981
staff: 3 full-time, 2 part-time
major programs: photo
collection, tours, workshops,
surveys, historic preservation,
affordable housing, technical
preservation services, periodical
easements, grants, matching
grants

Rensselaer County

County Arts Council

Rensselaer County
Council for the Arts
189 Second Street
Troy, New York 12180
518-273-0552
Raona M. Roy, Executive
Director
members: 500
founded: 1962
staff: 5 full-time, 1 part-time,
2 volunteer
major programs: school
programs, lectures, workshops,
exhibits

County Historian

City Hall
Rensselaer, New York 12144

County Historical Society

Rensselaer County
Historical Society
59 Second Street
Troy, New York 12180
518-272-7232
Breffny A. Walsh, Director
members: 575
founded: 1927
staff: 4 full-time, 3 part-time,
7 volunteer
major programs: library,
archives, museum, historic sites,
photo collection, school
programs, tours, lectures,
workshops, exhibits, historic
preservation, periodical

County Planning Office

Rensselaer County Bureau
of Planning
County Office Building
Troy, New York 12180
518-270-5275

see also Capital District Regional
Planning Commission,
Schenectady, Schenectady
County; Hudson-Mohawk
Urban Cultural Park
Commission, Cohoes, Albany
County

Berlin

Taconic Valley
Historical Society
P.O. Box 512
Berlin, New York 12022
Katherine G. Wells, President
members: 38
founded: 1973
staff: all volunteer
major programs: photo
collection, lectures, markers
program

Castleton

Casleton-on-Hudson
Neighborhood Association Inc.
Village Hall, 2nd Floor
85 South Main Street
Castleton, New York 12033
members: 80
founded: 1979
staff: volunteer

Historical Society of Esquatak
P.O. Box 151
Castleton, New York 12033
members: 138
founded: 1971
staff: all volunteer
major programs: archives, tours,
lectures, publications, awards,
genealogy, periodical

Cropseyville

Brunswick
Historical Society
P.O. Box 1776
Cropseyville, New York 12052
Clara H. Steiner, President
members: 150

East Greenbush

Greenbush
Historical Society
P.O. Box 66
East Greenbush, New York
12061

Hoosick Falls

Hoosick Township Historical
Society and Lewis Miller
Museum
166 Main Street, P.O. Box 336
Hoosick Falls, New York 12090
518-686-4682
Edith Beaumont, Director
members: 62
founded: 1974
staff: 8 volunteer
major programs: library,
museum, photo collection,
exhibits

Lansingburgh

Lansingburgh Historical Society
P.O. Box 219
Lansingburgh, New York 12182
Kathleen Tivnan, President

Poestenkill

Poestenkill Historical Society
P.O. Box 140
Poestenkill, New York 12140
518-283-5100
Marie H. Simm, President
members: 30
founded: 1977
major programs: publications

Rensselaer

City of Rensselaer
Historical Society
P.O. Box 161
Rensselaer, New York 12144

Schaghticoke

Hoosic Valley Yorkers
Pleasant Avenue
Schaghticoke, New York 12154
518-753-4491
Mark C. Van Sluyters, Advisor

Knickerbocker Historical Society
P.O. Box 90
Schaghticoke, New York 12154

South Schodack

Schodack Central Council
on the Arts
P.O. Box 3
South Schodack, New York
12162
518-732-2031

Stephentown

Stephentown Historical Society
Box 313, West Road
Stephentown, New York 12168
Sylvia Leibensperger, President

Tomhannock

Pittstown Historical Society
Pittstown Town Hall
Tomhannock, New York 12144

Troy

Federation of Historical Services
189 Second Street
Troy, New York 12180
518-273-3400
Cynthia Corbett, Director
members: 356
founded: 1977
staff: 2 full-time, 1 part-time,
2 volunteer
major programs: museum,
historic sites, workshops,
publications, awards, periodical

Hudson River Valley Association
(*see full listing under Cold
Spring, Putnam County*)
McCarthy Building
255 River Street
Troy, New York 12180
518-272-0707
David S. Sampson, Executive
Director

Hudson-Mohawk Industrial
Gateway
Burden Iron Works Building
Foot of Polk Street
Troy, New York 12180
518-274-5267
Theresa Lasher Winslow,
Executive Director
members: 300
founded: 1972
staff: 1 full-time, 2 part-time
major programs: library, photo
collection, school programs,
tours, lectures, publications,
historic preservation, periodical

Rensselaer County
Junior Museum
282 Fifth Avenue
Troy, New York 12182
518-235-2120
Ralph Pascale, Director
members: 350
founded: 1954
staff: 5 full-time, 8 part-time,
5 volunteer
major programs: museum,
school programs, tours, lectures,
workshops, exhibits

TAP, Inc.
406 Fulton Street
Troy, New York 12180
518-274-3050
Joe Fama, Executive Director
founded: 1969
staff: 6 full-time
major programs: affordable
housing

Troy Public Library
100 Second Street
Troy, New York 12180
518-274-7071

Troy Rehabilitation and
Improvement Program
415 River Street, P.O. Box 1249
Troy, New York 12181
518-272-8289
William Patrick Madden,
Executive Director
founded: 1968
staff: 13 full-time, 3 part-time,
1 volunteer
major programs: lectures,
affordable housing, periodical

West Sand Lake

Sand Lake Historical Society
P.O. Box 492
West Sand Lake, New York
12196
Katherine Mace, President
members: 150
founded: 1974
staff: 13 volunteer
major programs: tours, lectures,
periodical

Richmond County

County Arts Council

Staten Island Council on the Arts
c/o Pouch Terminal
One Edgewater Plaza, Room 311
Staten Island, New York 10305
718-447-4485

County Historian

Loring McMillen
3531 Richmond Road
Staten Island, New York 10306

County Historical Society

Staten Island
Historical Society
441 Clarke Avenue
Staten Island, New York 10306
718-351-1617
Barnett Shepherd, Executive
Director
members: 900
founded: 1856
staff: 35 full-time, 30 part-time,
200 volunteer
major programs: library,
archives, museum, historic sites,
photo collection, research,

school programs, tours, lectures,
workshops, exhibits,
publications, awards, surveys,
historic preservation, archeology,
periodical

County Planning Office

Staten Island Office, Department
of City Planning
56 Bay Street
St. George, Staten Island,
New York 10301
718-727-8453

see also New York County
listings

Staten Island

American Italian
Historical Association
209 Flagg Place
Staten Island, New York 10304

Friends of Alice Austen House
2 Hylan Boulevard
Staten Island, New York 10305
212-679-1940
Margaret R. Buckwalter,
Executive Director

Garibaldi and Meucci Museum,
Order Sons of Italy in America
420 Tompkins Avenue
Staten Island, New York 10305
718-442-1608
Joseph Sciame, Chair
members: 40
founded: 1907
staff: 1 full-time, 2 part-time,
2 volunteer
major programs: library,
archives, museum, historic sites,
exhibits

Jewish Historical Society of
Staten Island
475 Victory Boulevard
Staten Island, New York 10301

Neighborhood Housing Services
of West Brighton
1166 Castleton Avenue
Staten Island, New York 10310

Northfield Community Local
Development Corporation
1546 Castleton Avenue
Staten Island, New York 10302

Preservation League of
Staten Island
P.O. Box 32
Staten Island, New York 10301
Mitchell Allen Grubler, President
members: 200
founded: 1977
staff: 20 volunteer
major programs: research, tours,
lectures, workshops,
publications, awards, surveys,
historic preservation, markers
program, technical preservation
services, revolving fund

Snug Harbor Cultural Center
1000 Richmond Terrace
Staten Island, New York 10301
718-448-2500
Michael C. Hardy, President
members: 2,600
founded: 1976
staff: 43 full-time, 25 part-time,
50 volunteer
major programs: historic sites,
school programs, tours, lectures,
workshops, exhibits, publications, historic preservation,
markers program, periodical

Staten Island Children's Museum
940 Richmond Terrace
Staten Island, New York 10301
718-273-2060
Joanne Secor, Program Director

Rockland County

County Arts Council

Arts Council of Rockland
22 South Madison Avenue
Spring Valley, New York 10977
914-426-3660

County Historian

Thomas F.X. Casey
12 Ashwood Lane
Garnerville, New York 10923

County Historical Society

Historical Society of
Rockland County
20 Zukor Road
New City, New York 10956
Ralph D. Sessions, Director

County Planning Office

Rockland County Planning
Department
18 New Hempstead Road
New City, New York 10956
914-638-5480

see also Lower Hudson
Conference, Elmsford,
Westchester County

Garnerville

North Rockland Historical
Museum Foundation
20 Oak Street
Garnerville, New York 10923

Grand View

Tappan Zee Preservation
Coalition
204 River Road
Grand View, New York 10960
914-359-1222
S. Hazard Gillespie, President
major programs: scenic districts

Monsey

Rockland Community
Development Council
22 Main Street
Monsey, New York 10952
914-352-1400
Mendel Hoffman, Executive
Director
staff: 25 full-time
major programs: school
programs, rural preservation,
affordable housing, periodical,
grants

New City

West Branch Conservation
Association
443 Buena Vista Road
New City, New York 10956
914-634-9700
Martus Granirer, President
members: 100
founded: 1941
staff: 22 volunteer
major programs: photo
collection, rural preservation,
open space preservation,
easements

Nyack

Edward Hopper Landmark
Preservation Foundation
82 North Broadway
Nyack, New York 10960

Friends of the Nyacks
P.O. Box 384
Nyack, New York 10960
Pattie Murray-Smith, Chair
members: 275
founded: 1974
staff: 12 volunteer
major programs: photo
collection, research, tours,
surveys, historic preservation,
periodical

Nyack Library
59 South Broadway
Nyack, New York 10960
Joanne Mongelli, Program
Coordinator

Piermont

Piermont Historical Society
Piermont, New York 10968

Pomona

Village of Pomona
Old Route 202
Pomona, New York 10970
914-354-2746
mail to: Camp Hill Road,
Pomona, New York 10970
Mary Radzik, Historian
staff: 5 volunteer
major programs: library, historic
sites, photo collection, research,
tours, lectures, exhibits,
publications, historic
preservation, rural preservation

Sloatsburg

Sloatsburg Historical Society
Orange Turnpike
Sloatsburg, New York 10974

South Nyack

Tappan Zee Historical Society
South Nyack, New York 10960

Tappan

Tappantown Historical Society
P.O. Box 71
Tappan, New York 10983
Leonora LoMedico, President
members: 500
founded: 1965
staff: 30 volunteer
major programs: library, historic
sites, photo collection, research,
school programs, tours, lectures,
exhibits, publications, awards,
historic preservation, periodical,
grants

St. Lawrence County

County Arts Council

see North Country Library
System, Watertown, Jefferson
County, for decentralization
information

County Historian

Garrett Cook
3 East Main Street, P.O. Box 8
Canton, New York 13617

County Historical Society

St. Lawrence County
Historical Association
3 East Main Street, P.O. Box 8
Canton, New York 13617
315-386-8133
Garret Cook, Director
members: 1,180
founded: 1948
staff: 2 full-time, 3 part-time
major programs: archives,
museum, school programs,
tours, exhibits, publications,
periodical, easements

County Planning Office

St. Lawrence County
Planning Office
Courthouse
Canton, New York 13616
315-379-2292

see also Regional Council of
Historical Agencies, Syracuse,
Onondaga County; St.
Lawrence-Eastern Ontario
Commission (p.68)

Canton

St. Lawrence County
Housing Council
13 Main Street
Canton, New York 13617
315-386-8576
Frederick J. Hanss, Executive
Director
founded: 1981
staff: 2 full-time, 1 part-time
major programs: rural
preservation, affordable housing,
revolving fund, grants, matching
grants

Chase Mills

Chase Mills Historical Society
Chase Mills Inn
Chase Mills, New York 13621

Colton

Colton Historical Society
Main Street, P.O. Box 20
Colton, New York 13625
Cynthia S. Hennessy, Director
members: 109
founded: 1979
staff: 7 volunteer
major programs: museum,
historic sites, photo collection,
research, school programs, tours,
exhibits, publications, periodical

Gouverneur

Gouverneur Historical Society
Johnston, RD 2
Gouverneur, New York 13642

Marble City Housing
Corporation
68 East Main Street
Gouverneur, New York 13642
315-287-0143
Ernest J. Deuval, Executive
Director
founded: 1 full-time, 1 part-time
major programs: rural
preservation, affordable housing,
revolving fund, grants

Macomb

Macomb Historical Association
Route 1
Rossie, New York 13646

Massena

Massena Historical Center
and Museum
200 East Orvis Street
Massena, New York 13662

Norfolk

Town of Norfolk
Historical Museum
39 Main Street, P.O. Box 645
Norfolk, New York 13667
315-384-4575
Jean A. Young, Curator
founded: 1985
staff: 1 part-time
major programs: museum,
exhibits

Norwood

Norwood Museum and
Historical Association
Main Street, P.O. Box 163
Norwood, New York 13668
Jean Cotey, Director
members: 130
founded: 1956
staff: all volunteer

Ogdensburg

Association for Neighborhood
Rehabilitation
201 State Street
Ogdensburg, New York 13669

Ogdensburg Public Library
312 Washington Street
Ogdensburg, New York 13669
315-393-4325

Parishville

Friends of Brainard Art Gallery
Mill Street, P.O. Box 298
Parishville, New York 13672

Parishville Museum
Main Street, P.O. Box 534
Parishville, New York 13672
315-265-7617
Emma Remington,
Curator / Historian
members: 36
staff: 1 part-time
major programs: archives,
museum, photo collection,
school programs, historic
preservation

Pierrepont

Pierrepont Museum and
Historical Society
Route 4
Potsdam, New York 13676
315-265-7459
Carl Newton, Curator/President
members: 10
founded: 1978
staff: 10 volunteer
major programs: museum,
school programs, exhibits,
historic preservation

Potsdam

Potsdam Public Museum
Civic Center, P.O. Box 191
Potsdam, New York 13676
315-365-6910
Betsy Travis, Director

Rensselaer Falls

Oswegatchie River House
Museum and Art School
Front Street
Rensselaer Falls, New York
13680
315-344-7247
Kyle David Hartman, President
members: 10
founded: 1977
staff: 3 volunteer
major programs: library,
museum, photo collection,
workshops, exhibits, historic
preservation

Rooseveltown

Mohawk Indian Housing
Corporation
P.O. Box 402
Rooseveltown, New York 13683

Winthrop

Stockholm Historical
Organization
Box 206, Municipal Building
Winthrop, New York 13697
315-389-5171
Patricia Furgison, President
members: 100
founded: 1979
staff: 12 volunteer
major programs: photo
collection, exhibits, historic
preservation

Saratoga County

County Arts Council

Saratoga County Arts Council
494 Broadway
Saratoga Springs, New York
12866
518-584-3255
Linda Toohey, Executive
Director

County Historian

Dorothy Alsdorf
Saratoga County Administration
Building
31 Woodlawn Avenue
Saratoga Springs, New York
12866

County Historical Society

Saratoga County
Historical Society
Brookside
Ballston Spa, New York 12020
518-885-4000

County Planning Office

Saratoga County
Planning Office
County Municipal Center
40 McMaster Street
Ballston Spa, New York 12020
518-885-5381

see also Capital District Regional
Planning Commission,
Schenectady, Schenectady
County; Hudson-Mohawk
Urban Cultural Park
Commission, Cohoes, Albany
County; Federation of Historical
Services, Troy, Rensselaer
County

Ballston Spa

National Bottle Museum
P.O. Box 621
Ballston Spa, New York 12020
518-885-7589

Charlton

Charlton Historical Society
Maple Avenue, RD 3
Charlton, New York 12019
mail to: RD 2 Sweetman Road
Ballston Spa, New York 12020
Torben Aabo, President

members: 140
founded: 1972
staff: 35 volunteer
major programs: museum,
school programs, tours, lectures,
exhibits, awards, historic
preservation, rural preservation,
markers program

Corinth

Corinth Area
Historical Society
Palmer Avenue
Corinth, New York 12822

Galway

Galway Preservation Society
RD, Box 145
Galway, New York 12074
Patricia Sanders, President

Gansevoort

Upper Hudson
Historical Federation
10 Waller Road
Gansevoort, New York 12831
Lorraine Westcott, President
members: 100
founded: 1970
major programs: workshops,
publications, periodical

Greenfield Center

Town of Greenfield
Historical Society
Town Hall, P.O. Box 154
Greenfield Center, New York
12833
518-893-7432
Jayne E. Lynch, Town Historian
members: 60
founded: 1983
staff: 1 full-time, 60 volunteer
major programs: library,
archives, photo collection,
research, school programs, tours,
lectures, workshops, exhibits,
publications, awards, historic
preservation, rural preservation,
periodical

Mechanicville

Mechanicville
Historical Society
South Main Street
Mechanicville, New York 12118

Round Lake

Round Lake
Historical Society
P.O. Box 25
Round Lake, New York 12151
518-457-2239

Saratoga Springs

City of Saratoga Springs
138 Nelson Avenue
Saratoga Springs, New York
12866
518-587-2358
Martha Stonequist, City
Historian
staff: 1 part-time
major programs: archives

Historical Society
of Saratoga Springs
The Casino, Congress Park
P.O. Box 216
Saratoga Springs, New York
12866
518-584-6920
Heidi A. Fuge, Museum Director
members: 525
founded: 1883
staff: 2 full-time, 2 part-time,
25 volunteer
major programs: archives,
museum, school programs,
lectures, exhibits, periodical

Saratoga County Rural
Preservation
510 North Broadway
Saratoga Springs, New York
12866

Saratoga Springs Preservation
Foundation
6 Lake Avenue, P.O. Box 442
Saratoga Springs, New York
12866
518-587-5030/0474
Theodore Corbett, Executive
Director
members: 350
founded: 1977
staff: 6 full-time, 1 part-time,
120 volunteer
major programs: library,
archives, historic sites, research,
school programs, tours, lectures,

workshops, exhibits, publications, awards, surveys, historic
preservation, affordable housing,
markers program, technical
preservation services, periodical,
revolving fund, easements,
grants, matching grants

Saratoga Springs Urban Cultural
Park Program
City Hall
Saratoga Springs, New York
12866
518-587-3555

Schuylerville

Old Saratoga Historical
Association of Schuylerville
RD 1, Box 168
Schuylerville, New York 12871

South Glens Falls

Historical Society of Moreau and
South Glens Falls
144 Main Street
South Glens Falls, New York
12803

Stillwater

Stillwater Historical
Society
Box 161, Route 423
Mechanicville, New York 12188
Mrs. David Ferris, President
members: 47
founded: 1971
major programs: awards

Waterford

Waterford Historical Museum
and Cultural Center
2 Museum Lane
Waterford, New York 12188
Paul E. Grattan, President
members: 110
founded: 1964
staff: 18 volunteer
major programs: library,
museum, historic sites,
publications, periodical

Waterford Village Foundation
53 Broad Street
Waterford, New York 12188
Garry F. Douglas, President
founded: 1986
staff: 9 volunteer

major programs: tours, historic
preservation, affordable housing,
markers programs, annual
community festival, farmers
market, summer concert series

Schenectady County

County Arts Council

Schenectady Arts Council
432 State Street
Schenectady, New York 12305
518-374-3321
Carole Civale, Administrator
members: 200
founded: 1977
staff: 1 part-time
major programs: school
programs, workshops, exhibits,
surveys

County Historian

Larry Hart
195 Droms Road
Scotia, New York 12302

County Historical Society

Schenectady County
Historical Society
32 Washington Avenue
Schenectady, New York 12305
518-374-0263
Wayne H. Harvey, Program
Chair

County Planning Office

Schenectady County Planning
County Office Building,
6th Floor
620 State Street
Schenectady, New York 12307
518-382-3286

see also Albany-Schenectady-
Greene Counties Agricultural
and Historical Societies,
Altamont, Albany County;
Federation of Historical Services,
Troy, Rensselaer County

Delanson

Duanesburg
Historical Society
Route 2
Delanson, New York 12053

Niskayuna

Niskayuna Historical Society
1335 Balltown Road
Niskayuna, New York 12309

Princetown

Princetown Historical Society
369 North Kelly Road
Schenectady, New York 12306

Schenectady

Capital District Regional
Planning Commission
214 Canal Square
Schenectady, New York 12305
Chungchin Chen, Executive
Director
518-393-1715

City of Schenectady
Department of Development
Jay Street
Schenectady, New York 12305
518-382-5147
Greg Semos, Director
major programs: museum,
surveys, historic preservation,
affordable housing, grants

Junior League of Schenectady
1555 Dean Street
Schenectady, New York 12309
518-346-6681
Kathy Miller, Project Co-Chair

Schenectady County Public
Library
Liberty and Clinton Streets
Schenectady, New York 12305
518-382-3543
Ronald L. Lagasse, Director

Schenectady Museum
Nott Terrace Heights
Schenectady, New York 12308

Schenectady Urban
Cultural Park Program
City of Schenectady
City Hall, Room 7
Schenectady, New York 12305
518-382-5055

Stockade Association
P.O. Box 1661
Schenectady, New York 12301

Schoharie County

County Arts Council

Schoharie County Arts Council
P.O. Box 730
Cobleskill, New York 12043
518-234-7380

County Historian

Mildred R. Bailey
RFD 1
Stamford, New York 12167

County Historical Society

Schoharie County
Historical Society
North Main Street, P.O. Box 69
Schoharie, New York 12157
518-295-7192
Helene S. Farrell, Director
members: 900
founded: 1888
staff: 3 full-time, 8 part-time
major programs: library,
archives, museum, historic sites,
photo collection, school
programs, publications,
periodical

County Planning Office

Schoharie County Planning and
Development Agency
P.O. Box 429
Schoharie, New York 12157
518-295-8522

see also Southern Tier East
Regional Planning Development
Board, Binghamton, Broome
County; Federation of Historical
Services, Troy, Rensselaer
County; Mohawk Valley
Museums Consortium,
Amsterdam, Montgomery
County; Catskill Center for
Conservation and Development,
Arkville, Delaware County

Charlotteville

Anonymous Arts
Recovery Society
(*see also* New York City)
Star Route
Charlotteville, New York 12036
Ivan C. Karp, President
founded: 1958

staff: 2 full-time, 10 volunteer
major programs: library,
archives, museum, historic sites,
photo collection, research,
historic preservation, rural
preservation

Charlotteville Museum
Charlotteville, New York 12036

Cobleskill

Cobleskill Restoration and
Development
P.O. Box 773
Cobleskill, New York 12043
Jack E. Ingels, Chair

Town of Cobleskill
Historical Society
Cobleskill, New York 12043

Esperance

Esperance Historical
Society and Museum
Church Street
Esperance, New York 12066
518-875-6417
Kenneth M. Jones, President
members: 75
founded: 1970
staff: 35 volunteer
major programs: museum, photo
collection, exhibits/
demonstrations, historic
preservation, rural preservation

North Blenheim

Blenheim Historical Society
North Blenheim, New York
12131

Lansing Manor House
Lansing Manor Visitors Center
Route 30
North Blenheim, New York
12131
518-627-6121

Richmondville

Old Plank Road
Historical Society
3 West Main Street
Richmondville, New York 12149
518-294-7751

Schoharie

Schoharie Colonial Heritage
Association
351 Main Street
Schoharie, New York 12157
518-295-8513
Gail Breed, Historical Awareness
Committee

Schohaire County Rural
Preservation Corporation
Route 30, Box 489
Schoharie, New York 12157
518-295-8185
Ronald S. Filmer, Jr., Executive
Director
founded: 1984
staff: 4 full-time, 1 part-time
major programs: rural
preservation, affordable housing

Schoharie Museum of the
Iroquois Indian
North Main Street, P.O. Box 58
Schoharie, New York 12157
518-295-8553
Christina B. Johannsen,
Director
members: 500
founded: 1980
staff: 1 full-time, 2 part-time,
30 volunteer
major programs: library,
archives, museum, photo
collection, research, school
programs, lectures, exhibits,
archeology, periodical

Sharon Springs

Providence Preservation Society
RR 2, Box 538
Sharon Springs, New York
13459

Sharon Historical Society
Main Street, P.O. Box 176
Sharon Springs, New York
13459
518-284-2327
Edith M. Bell, President
members: 35
founded: 1971
staff: 35 volunteer
major programs: museum,
publications, historic
preservation, technical
preservation services

Schuyler County

County Arts Council

see Chemung Valley Arts
Council, Corning, Steuben
County for decentralization
information

County Historian

Barbara Bell
RD 1, Box 192
Watkins Glen, New York 14891

County Historical Society

Schuyler County
Historical Society
South Catherine Street
Montour Falls, New York 14865
607-535-9741
Belva Dickenson, Director of
Museum
members: 400
staff: 1 full-time, 2 part-time,
1 volunteer
major programs: library,
museum, historic sites, research,
tours, lectures, workshops,
exhibits, publications, historic
preservation, periodical

County Planning Office

Schuyler County Planning and
Industrial Development
Rural Urban Center
208 Broadway
Montour Falls, New York 14865
607-535-7391

see also Regional Housing
Council of Southern Tier,
Elmira, Chemung County;
Southern Tier Central Regional
Planning and Development
Board, Corning, Steuben
County; Regional Council of
Historical Agencies, Syracuse,
Onondaga County

Tyrone

Dundee Area
Historical Society
P.O. Box 96
Tyrone, New York 14487

Watkins Glen

Watkins Glen Historical Society
Watkins Glen, New York 14891

Seneca County

County Arts Council

see Cayuga County Arts Council,
Auburn, Cayuga County for
decentralization information

County Historian

Betty Auten
20 Clark Street
Waterloo, New York 12165

County Historical Society

no listing

County Planning Office

Seneca County Department of
Planning and Development
31 Thurber Drive
Waterloo, New York 13165
315-539-5004

see also Genesee-Finger Lakes
Regional Planning Council,
Rochester, Monroe County;
Landmarks Society of Western
New York, Rochester, Monroe
County; Regional Council of
Historical Agencies, Syracuse,
Onondaga County

Interlaken

Interlaken Historical Society
P.O. Box 323
Interlaken, New York 14847
607-532-4430
Maurice L. Patterson, President
members: 150
founded: 1952
staff: 10 volunteer
major programs: library,
archives, museum, photo
collection, school programs,
lectures, publications, periodical

Lodi

Lodi Historical Society
2 Main Street
Lodi, New York 14860
Noel Clawson, President
members: 75
founded: 1973
major programs: historic sites,
tours, lectures, exhibits, historic
preservation, grants

Seneca Falls

Seneca Falls
Historical Society
55 Cayuga Street
Seneca Falls, New York 13148
315-568-8412
Ed Polk Douglas, Executive
Director
members: 300
founded: 1895
staff: 1 full-time, 3 part-time,
many volunteer
major programs: library,
archives, museum, photo
collection, research, school
programs, tours, lectures,
workshops, exhibits,
publications, periodical,
easements

Seneca Falls Urban Cultural
Park Commission
Village of Seneca Falls
60 State Street
Seneca Falls, New York 13148
315-568-6894

Waterloo

Waterloo Historical Society
31 East Williams Street
Waterloo, New York 13165

Steuben County

County Arts Council

Chemung Valley Arts Council
Baron Steuben Place
Market Street
Corning, New York 14830
607-962-5871
Kevin Geoghan, Executive
Director
members: 70
founded: 1972
staff: 3 full-time, 1 part-time
major programs: research, school
programs, workshops, surveys,
periodical, revolving fund, grants

County Historian

Mrs. James Hope
88 Geneva Street
Bath, New York 14810

County Historical Society

Steuben County
Historical Society
P.O. Box 39
Bath, New York 14810

County Planning Office

Steuben County Planning
Department
21 East Morris Street
Bath, New York 14810
607-776-2151

see also Regional Housing
Council of Southern Tier,
Elmira, Chemung County;
Western New York Association
of Historical Agencies, Avon,
Livingston County

Arkport

Canisteo Valley
Historical Society
4 Park Street
Arkport, New York 14807
607-324-2800
Mary Ann Ordway Rutski,
Town Historian
members: 64
founded: 1875
staff: all volunteer
major programs: library,
archives, historic sites, photo
collection, research, school
programs, tours, lectures,
publications, surveys, periodical

Bath

Bath Historic Committee
Cameron Street
Bath, New York 14810

Canisteo

Towelsville Community Society
RD 2, Box 133
Canisteo, New York 14823
607-776-2454

Cohocton

Cohocton Historical Society
14 Maple Avenue, P.O. Box 177
Cohocton, New York 14826
Ruth Sprague, President
members: 300
founded: 1962
staff: 8 volunteer

major programs: archives, photo
collection, research, publications,
periodical

Steuben-Livingston
Agricultural Project
One North Main Street
Cohocton, New York 14826
716-384-5239
Thomas M. Carey, Director
founded: 1980
staff: 5 full-time, 4 volunteer
major programs: rural
preservation, affordable housing,
revolving fund, grants, matching
grants

Corning

Corning-Painted Post
Historical Society
59 West Pulteney Street
Corning, New York 14830
607-937-5281
Phyllis Martin, Director
members: 300
founded: 1948
staff: 1 full-time, 1 part-time,
10 volunteer
major programs: archives,
museum, photo collection,
school programs, periodical

Market Street
Restoration Agency
5 East Market Street
Corning, New York 14830
607-937-5427
Douglas A. Loescher, Executive
Director
founded: 1974
staff: 3 full-time
major programs: historic
preservation, technical
preservation services, periodical

The Rockwell Museum
Cedar Street at Denison Parkway
Corning, New York 14830
607-937-5386
Dwight P. Lanmon, Acting
Director
members: 650
founded: 1976
staff: 14 full-time, 2 part-time
major programs: library,
museum, research, school
programs, tours, lectures,
workshops, exhibits, publications,
periodical

Southern Tier Central
Regional Planning and
Development Board
53½ Bridge Street
Corning, New York 14830
607-962-5092
William D. Hess, Executive
Director

Three Rivers Development
Foundation
37 East Market Street
Corning, New York 14830
607-962-4693

Hammondsport

Glenn H. Curtiss Museum of
Local History
P.O. Box 585
Hammondsport, New York
14840
607-569-2160
Lindsley A. Dunn, Assistant
Director
members: 343
founded: 1961
staff: 1 full-time, 6 volunteer
major programs: library,
archives, museum, photo
collection, tours, periodical

Hornby

Hornby Historical Society
Route 41
Town of Hornby, New York
14812
mail to: RFD 3, Corning
New York 14830
John Carlineo, President
founded: 1958
major programs: museum

Hornell

Hornell Area Arts Council
P.O. Box 298
Hornell, New York 14843

Hornell Area Historical Society
Hornell, New York 14843
607-324-7524

Howard

Town of Howard
RD 2
Canisteo, New York 14823
Marry Kenny, Historian
founded: 1976
staff: all volunteer

major programs: library,
museum, photo collection,
research, exhibits, publications

Painted Post

Erwin-Painted Post Museum
Town Hall
Water Street
Painted Post, New York 14870
607-962-1382
Joseph J. Kane,
Historian/Curator
founded: 1935
staff: 2 part-time
major programs: library,
archives, museum, photo
collection, school programs,
tours, lectures

Prattsburg

Prattsburg Museum
South Main Street
Prattsburg, New York 14873
607-522-4537
mail to: 21 North Main Street
Prattsburg, New York 14873
Gloriette Kingsley, Town
Historian
founded: 1986
staff: 1 part-time, 20 volunteer
major programs: library,
archives, museum, historic sites,
photo collection, research,
school programs, exhibits,
historic preservation, periodical

Suffolk County

County Arts Council

Suffolk County Office of
Cultural Affairs
Montauk Highway
P.O. Box 144
West Sayville, New York 11796
516-567-7775

County Historian

J. Lance Mallamo
Montauk Highway
P.O. Box 144
West Sayville, New York 11796

County Historical Society

Suffolk County Historical Society
300 West Main Street
Riverhead, New York 11901
Wallace W. Broege, Director

County Planning Office

Suffolk County Planning
Department
Veterans Memorial Highway
Happauge, New York 11788
516-360-5189

Amagansett

Amagansett Historical
Association
Main Street
P.O. Drawer AS
Amagansett, New York 11930

Amityville

Amityville Historical Society
P.O. Box 764
Amityville, New York 11701
516-598-1486
Elodie Dibbins, Assistant
Director
members: 520
founded: 1969
staff: 1 part-time, 45 volunteer
major programs: library,
archives, museum, photo
collection, research, school
programs, lectures, exhibits,
publications, awards, historic
preservation, markers program,
periodical

Babylon

Ocean Beach
Historical Society
300 John Street, P.O. Box 490
Babylon, New York 11702

Village of Babylon Historical and
Preservation Society
117 West Main Street
P.O. Box 484
Babylon, New York 11702
William E. Holmes, President
members: 200
founded: 1977
staff: 1 part-time, 20 volunteer
major programs: museum, photo
collection, school programs,
exhibits, historic preservation,
markers program, periodical

Bayport

Bayport Heritage Association
P.O. Box 4
Bayport, New York 11705

Sachem Historical Society
288 Gillette Avenue
Bayport, New York 11705
516-472-1559
Helen C. Reuter, President
members: 27
founded: 1953

Bay Shore

Bay Shore Historical Society
66 Ridgeway Boulevard
Bayshore, New York 11706

Fire Island Lighthouse
Preservation Society
99 Maple Avenue, P.O. Box 373
Bayshore, New York 11706
516-968-8899
Suzanne R. Schaper,
Administrator
members: 4,000
founded: 1982
staff: 2 full-time, 1 part-time,
10 volunteer
major programs: library,
archives, museum, historic sites,
photo collection, research,
school programs, tours, lectures,
workshops, exhibits,
publications, historic
preservation, periodical

Bellport

Bellport-Brookhaven
Historical Society
31 Bellport Lane
Bellport, New York 11713
516-286-9064
Ethel Koennecke, Chair,
Curatorial Committee
members: 450
founded: 1958
staff: 30 volunteer
major programs: museum, photo
collection, school programs,
tours, lectures, workshops,
exhibits, periodical

Bohemia

Bohemia Historical Society
P.O. Box 454
Bohemia, New York 11716
516-589-5718
Fay L. Pagels, President
members: 190
founded: 1985
staff: all volunteer
major programs: photo
collection, school programs,
lectures, exhibits, historic
preservation, periodical

Bridgehampton

Bridgehampton Historical Society
Corwith Homestead
Montauk Highway, P.O. Box R
Bridgehampton, New York
11932

Center Moriches

Moriches Bay Historical Society
P.O. Box 31
Center Moriches, New York
11934

Centerport

Vanderbilt Museum
180 Little Neck Road
Centerport, New York 11721

Coram

Brookhaven Town
Historical Society
P.O. Box Box 225
Coram, New York 11727

Suffolk Community Development
625 Middle Country Road
Coram, New York 11727
516-698-8201
Elaine L. Weiss, Executive
Director
founded: 1969
staff: 19 full-time, 3 part-time,
25 volunteer
major programs: workshops,
rural preservation, affordable
housing, grants

Cutchogue

Cutchogue-New Suffolk
Historical Council
Main Road, P.O. Box 714
Cutchogue, New York 11935
516-734-6532
Mrs. W. Preston Tuthill,
President
members: 125
founded: 1960
staff: 21 volunteer
major programs: museum,
historic sites, school programs,
tours, lectures, exhibits,
publications, historic
preservation, markers program

East Hampton

East Hampton Historical Society
101 Main Street
East Hampton, New York 11937
516-324-6850
Ellen Freedman, Director of
Public Programs

Guild Hall of East Hampton
158 Main Street
East Hampton, New York 11937
Judith B. Sneddon, Director

Ladies Village
Improvement Society
9 Barnes Lane
East Hampton, New York 11937
516-324-1220

Springs Historical Society
807 Fireplace Road
East Hampton, New York 11937

Village Preservation Society
P.O. Box 2015
East Hampton, New York 11937
516-324-5617
John G. Cartier, President
members: 150
founded: 1982
major programs: historic
preservation, rural preservation

East Islip

Islip Arts Council
50 Irish Lane
East Islip, New York 11730
516-224-5420
Lillian Barbash, Executive
Director
founded: 1976
staff: 1 full-time, 2 part-time,
35 volunteer
major programs: school
programs, workshops, periodical

East Setauket

Three Village Historical Society
P.O. Box 1776
East Setauket, New York 11733
516-928-9534
Mr. Beverly C. Tyler, President
members: 375
founded: 1964
staff: 3 part-time, 110 volunteer
major programs: archives, photo
collection, school programs,
lectures, publications, markers
program, archeology, periodical

Greenlawn

Greenlawn-Centerport Historical
Association
P.O. Box 354
Greenlawn, New York 11740

Greenport

North Fork Housing
Alliance Inc.
18 South Street
Greenport, New York 11944
516-477-1070 / 0557
Bessie E. Swann, Executive
Director
founded: 1980
staff: 3 full-time, 4 part-time
major programs: affordable
housing, periodical, revolving
fund, grants, matching grants

North Fork Museum and
Historical Society
530 Main Street
Greenport, New York 11944

Stirling Historical Society
P.O. Box 500
Greenport, New York 11944

Hauppague

Long Island Regional
Planning Board
Dennison Building, 12th Floor
Veterans Memorial Highway
Hauppague, New York 11788
516-360-5189
Lee E. Koppelman, Executive
Director

Suffolk County Council on
Environmental Quality
Dennison Building, 12th Floor
Veterans Memorial Highway
Hauppague, New York 11788
516-360-5202
James J. Bagg, Jr., Principal
Planner
founded: 1971
staff: 3 full-time, 9 volunteer
major programs: historic sites,
historic preservation, archeology

Huntington

Association of Suffolk County
Historical Societies
99 Crescent Beach Drive
Huntington, New York 11743

Conklin House
2 High Street
Huntington, New York 11743

Heckscher Museum
Prime Avenue
Huntington, New York 11743
516-351-3250
Christopher Crosman, Director
members: 600
founded: 1920
staff: 8 full-time, 6 part-time,
30 volunteer
major programs: museum,
research, school programs, tours,
lectures, workshops, exhibits,
publications, periodical

Huntington Arts Council
213 Main Street
Huntington, New York 11743
516-271-8423
Ashley Kiebitz, Executive
Director

Huntington Historical Society
209 Main Street
Huntington, New York 11743
516-427-7045
members: 1,400
founded: 1903
staff: 6 full-time, 6 part-time,
200 volunteer
major programs: library,
archives, museum, historic sites,
photo collection, research,
school programs, workshops,
exhibits, publications, awards,
historic preservation, technical
preservation services, periodical

Huntington Preservation Society
2 High Street
Huntington, New York 11743

Lloyd Harbor Historical Society
P.O. Box 582
Huntington, New York 11743

Huntington Station

Housing Help
165 Beverly Road
Huntington Station, New York
11746

Walt Whitman Birthplace
Associates
246 Old Walt Whitman Road
Huntington Station, New York
11746
516-427-5240
Barbara Mazor Bart, Director
members: 250
founded: 1949
staff: 4 part-time, 12 volunteer
major programs: museum,
historic sites, research, exhibits,
publications, historic
preservation, periodical, grants,
matching grants

Islip

Historical Society of Fire Island
Fire Island
Islip, New York 11706

Suburban Housing Development
and Research
P.O. Box 12P
Islip, New York 11786

Lake Ronkonkoma

Lake Ronkonkoma Historical
Society
328 Hawkins Avenue
Lake Ronkonkoma, New York
11779

Lindenhurst

Babylon Citizens Council
on the Arts
200 East Sunrise Highway
Lindenhurst, New York 11757
516-226-4130
Michael Kenny, Executive
Director

Lindenhurst Historical Society
P.O. Box 296
Lindenhurst, New York 11757

Mattituck

Mattituck Historical Society
Main Road
Mattituck, New York 11952

Miller Place

Miller Place-Mount Sinai
Historical Society
P.O. Box 651
Miller Place, New York 11764

Montauk

Montauk Historical Society
P.O. Box 943
Montauk, New York 11954
516-668-5652
Peg Joyce, President
members: 250
founded: 1962
major programs: museum,
research, school programs, tours,
exhibits, publications, historic
preservation, periodical

North Great River

North Great River Historical
Society
327 East Manhasset Street
North Great River, New York
11752
516-581-3344
Lois J. Raffone, President

Northport

Northport Historical
Society/Museum
215 Main Street, P.O. Box 545
Northport, New York 11768
516-757-9859
Marguerite Mudge, Director
members: 450
founded: 1962
staff: 4 part-time
major programs: archives,
museum, photo collection,
school programs, exhibits,
periodical, grants

Oakdale

W. K. Vanderbilt Historical
Society of Dowling College
P.O. Box 433
Oakdale, New York 11769
516-537-3908

Orient

Oysterponds Historical Society
Village Lane, P.O. Box 844
Orient, New York 11957
516-323-2480
Stephen S. Hadley, Director
founded: 1944
staff: 1 full-time, 1 part-time,
125 volunteer
major programs: library,
archives, museum, photo
collection, school programs,
periodical

Patchogue

Greater Patchogue
Historical Society
P.O. Box 102
Patchogue, New York 11772

Port Jefferson

Historical Society of Greater
Port Jefferson
P.O. Box 586
Port Jefferson, New York 11777

Quogue

Quogue Historical Society
Quogue Street East
P.O. Box 1207
Quogue, New York 11959
516-653-4111

Mrs. Edwin Shuttleworth,
Co-chair
members: 130
founded: 1975
staff: 8 volunteer
major programs: archives,
museum, photo collection,
research

Riverhead

East End Arts Council
133 East Main Street
Riverhead, New York 11901
516-727-0900
Judith Kaufman Weiner,
Executive Director
members: 900
founded: 1971
staff: 2 full-time, 3 part-time,
25 volunteer
major programs: presentor
(dance, music, children's
theater), workshops, exhibits,
publications, services to artists
and arts organizations, periodical

Hallockville Museum Farm
Sound Avenue, P.O. Box 765
Riverhead, New York 11901
516-298-5292
Andrew F. Shick, Site
Administrator
members: 560
founded: 1975
staff: 1 full-time, 3 part-time,
20 volunteer
major programs: archives,
museum, historic sites, research,
school programs, tours, exhibits,
periodical

Riverhead Preservation and
Landmarks Society
P.O. Box 495
Riverhead, New York 11901

Sag Harbor

Eastville Community
Historical Society
P.O. Box 2036
Sag Harbor, New York 11963
516-725-4270

Sag Harbor Historical Society
P.O. Box 870
Sag Harbor, New York 11963

Village of Sag Harbor
Main Street, P.O. Box 660
Sag Harbor, New York 11963
516-725-0222
Joan E. Feehan, Clerk-Treasurer
founded: 1985
staff: 1 part-time, 5 volunteer
major programs: historic sites,
historic preservation

Sayville

Sayville Historical Society
P.O. Box 658
Sayville, New York 11782

Selden

Suffolk County
Community College
533 College Road
Selden, New York 11784
516-451-4352/3
Barbara Karyo, Professor of Fine
Arts/Gallery Director

Setauket

Society for the Preservation of
Long Island Antiquities
93 North Country Road
Setauket, New York 11733
516-941-9444
Robert B. MacKay, Director
members: 1,436
founded: 1946
staff: 12 full-time, 13 part-time,
75 volunteers
major programs: historic sites,
photo collection, research,
school programs, periodical,
publications, surveys, historic
preservation, technical
preservation services, revolving
fund, easements

Shelter Island

Shelter Island Historical Society
16 South Ferry Road
Shelter Island, New York 11964

Smithtown

Smithtown Historical Society
North Country Road (Route
25A), P.O. Box 69
Smithtown, New York 11787
516-265-6768
Louise P. Hall, Director
members: 450
founded: 1955
staff: 1 full-time, 8 part-time
major programs: archives,
museum, historic sites, school
programs, historic preservation

Southampton

Town of Southampton
116 Hampton Road
Southampton, New York 11968
516-283-6000
Robert Keene, Town Historian
founded: 1983
staff: 5 volunteer
major programs: archives,
historic sites, photo collection,
research, school programs,
exhibits, historic preservation

Southold

Southold Historical
Society Museums
Main Road and Maple Lane
P.O. Box 1
Southold, New York 11971
516-765-5500
George D. Wagoner, Director
members: 500
founded: 1960
staff: 1 full-time, 1 part-time,
50 volunteer
major programs: library,
archives, museums, photo
collection, research, school
programs, tours, lectures,
exhibits, publications, historic
preservation, markers program,
periodical

Town of Southold Landmarks
Preservation Commission
Town Hall
Main Road
Southold, New York 11971
516-765-1800

Frank Murphy, Supervisor
founded: 1983
staff: 5 volunteer
major programs: historic sites,
research, lectures, surveys,
historic preservation

St. James

Smithtown Township
Arts Council
660 Route 25A
St. James, New York 11787
516-862-6572
Norma Cohen, Executive
Director

Stony Brook

Long Island Archives Conference
Department of Special
Collections, SUNY Library
Stony Brook, New York 11794
516-632-7119
Arthur F. Sniffin, President
members: 100
founded: 1974
staff: 12 volunteer
major programs: library,
archives, photo collection,
lectures, workshops, periodical

The Museums at Stony Brook
Route 25A
Stony Brook, New York 11790
516-751-0066

Suffolk County
Archeological Association
P.O. Drawer AR
Stony Brook, New York 11790
516-929-8725
Donna Ottusch-Kianka,
President
members: 100
founded: 1975
staff: 6 part-time
major programs: archives,
museum, photo collection,
research, school programs,
lectures, workshops, exhibits,
publications, archeology,
periodical

Terryville

Terryville Historical Society
P.O. Box 371
Port Jefferson, New York 11776

Water Mill

Water Mill Museum
Old Mill Road
Water Mill, New York 11976

West Bay Shore

Sagtikos Manor
Historical Society
Montauk Highway
P.O. Box 344
West Bay Shore, New York
11706
516-669-6956
Robert Mills Smith, President
members: 150
founded: 1962
staff: 30 volunteer
major programs: library,
museum, historic sites, research,
school programs, tours, lectures,
awards, historic preservation

West Sayville

Suffolk County Division of
Historic Services
Suffolk County Department
of Parks
P.O. Box 144
West Sayville, New York 11796
516-567-1487
J. Lance Mallamo, Director of
Historic Services

Suffolk Marine Museum
Montauk Highway
West Sayville, New York 11796
516-567-1733

Westhampton Beach

Long Island Early Flyers Club
Suffolk County Airport
Westhampton Beach, New York
11978

Wyandach

Wyandach Community
Development Corporation
1527-B Straight Path
Wyandach, New York 11798
516-643-4786
James Wallace, Executive
Director

members: 23
founded: 1971
staff: 3 full-time
major programs: research,
surveys, rural preservation,
affordable housing

Yaphank

Yaphank Historical Society
P.O. Box 111
Yaphank, New York 11980
Kathy Schmidt, President
members: 100
founded: 1974
staff: 11 volunteer
major programs: historic sites,
tours, historic preservation,
periodical

Sullivan County

County Arts Council

Sullivan County Arts Council
Loch Sheldrake, New York
12759
Allan W. Dampman, President
914-434-5750

see Delaware Valley Arts
Alliance, Narrowsburg, for
decentralization information

County Historian

William Smith
2 Ann Street
Monticello, New York 12701

County Historical Society

Sullivan County Historical
Society
P.O. Box 247
Hurleyville, New York 12747

County Planning Office

Sullivan County Planning
Department
County Government Center
100 North Street
Monticello, New York 12701
914-794-3000

see also Catskill Center for
Conservation and Development,
Arkville, Delaware County

Hurleyville

Catskill Arts Society
P.O. Box N
Hurleyville, New York 12747
Dorothy Langseder, Director

Long Eddy

Basket Historical Society of the
Upper Delaware Valley
Long Eddy, New York 12769

Mongaup Valley

Upper Delaware Heritage
Alliance
P.O. Box 209
Mongaup Valley, New York
12762
914-583-6174
Bert Feldman, President

Monticello

Rural Sullivan County
Housing Opportunities
375 Broadway
Monticello, New York 12701
914-794-0348
Ellen Baier, Executive Director
founded: 1981
staff: 6 full-time, 5 part-time,
14 volunteer
major programs: photo
collection, research, workshops,
surveys, rural preservation,
affordable housing, technical
preservation services, grants,
matching grants

Narrowsburg

Delaware Valley Arts Alliance
Main Street, P.O. Box 170
Narrowsburg, New York 12764
914-252-7576
Elaine Giguere, Executive
Director
members: 215
founded: 1976
staff: 1 full-time, 2 part-time,
5 volunteer
major programs: exhibits,
periodical

Tioga County

County Arts Council

Tioga County
Council on the Arts
72 North Avenue
Owego, New York 13827
607-687-0785
Margaret Crocker, Executive
Director

see Chemung Valley Arts
Council, Corning, Steuben
County, for decentralization
information

County Historian

Ileen Weaver
Box 124, Pennsylvania Avenue
Apalachin, New York 13732

County Historical Society

Tioga County
Historical Society
110 Front Street
Owego, New York 13827
607-687-2460
Jean W. Neff, Director
members: 600
founded: 1914
staff: 1 full-time, 1 part-time,
25 volunteer
major programs: library,
archives, museum, research,
school programs, lectures,
exhibits, periodical

County Planning Office

Tioga County Planning Board
Tioga County Office Building
56 Main Street
Owego, New York 13827
607-687-1240

see also Preservation Association
of the Southern Tier,
Binghamton, Broome County;
Southern Tier East Regional
Planning Development Board,
Binghamton, Broome County;
Regional Council of Historical
Agencies, Syracuse, Onondaga
County

Newark Valley

Newark Valley
Historical Society
P.O. Box 222
Newark Valley, New York 13811
607-642-8075
Ed Nizalowski,
Secretary/Treasurer
members: 176
founded: 1976
staff: 4 part-time, 50 volunteer
major programs: school
programs, tours, historic
preservation, periodical, grants

Owego

Tioga Historical
Transportation Society
RD 4, Box 4240, Route 38
Owego, New York 13827
607-642-5511
Cornelia Dana Mead, Secretary
members: 140
founded: 1981
staff: 4 volunteer
major programs: museum,
historic sites, school programs,
periodical

Tioga Opportunities Program
P.O. Box 600
Owego, New York 13827

Spencer

Spencer Historical Society
P.O. Box 71
Spencer, New York 14883

Tompkins County

County Arts Council

Arts Council of
Tompkins County
DeWitt Building
215 North Cayuga Street
Ithaca, New York 14850
607-277-4906
John R. Goss, III, Executive
Director
members: 500
founded: 1976
staff: 2 full-time, 3 volunteer
major programs: historic sites,
school programs, workshops,
awards, historic preservation,
rural preservation, periodical,
grants

County Historian

Margaret Hobbie
116 North Cayuga Street
Ithaca, New York 14850

County Historical Society

DeWitt Historical Society of
Tompkins County
116 North Cayuga Street
Ithaca, New York 14850
607-273-8284
Margaret Hobbie, Director
members: 800
founded: 1935
staff: 1 full-time, 7 part-time,
60 volunteer
major programs: library,
archives, museum, photo
collection, research, school
programs, exhibits, publications,
periodical

County Planning Office

Tompkins County
Planning Office
Biggs Building A
Dates Drive
Ithaca, New York 14850
607-274-5360

see also Southern Tier East
Regional Planning Development
Board, Binghamton, Broome
County; Regional Council of
Historical Agencies, Syracuse,
Onondaga County

Brooktondale

Historical Association of
Caroline Township
14 Whipporwill Lane
Brooktondale, New York 14817

Dryden

Dryden Historical Society
P.O. Box 283
Dryden, New York 13053
607-844-4691
Gina P. Prentiss, President

Groton

Town of Groton
Historical Society
168 Main Street, P.O. Box 142
Groton, New York 13073

Ithaca

City of Ithaca Planning and
Development Department
108 East Green Street
Ithaca, New York 14850
607-272-1713 x222
Jonathan C. Meigs, Principal
Planner
Leslie A. Chatterton,
Preservation/Neighborhood
Planner

Hinkley Museum
410 East Seneca Street
Ithaca, New York 14850
607-273-7053
Kelly Grant-Horrocks, Director
members: 152
founded: 1972
staff: 2 part-time, 10 volunteer
major programs: library,
museum, workshops, exhibits,
periodical

Historic Ithaca and
Tompkins County
120 North Cayuga Street
Ithaca, New York 14850
607-273-6633
Barbara E. Ebert, Executive
Director
members: 600
founded: 1966
staff: 4 full-time, 1 part-time
major programs: library, photo
collection, research, school
programs, tours, lectures,
workshops, exhibits,
publications, awards, surveys,
historic preservation, rural
preservation, affordable housing,
technical preservation services,
periodical, revolving fund

Ithaca Neighborhood
Housing Services
520 West Green Street
Ithaca, New York 14850
607-277-4500
Doug Dylla, Executive Director
members: 250
founded: 1977
staff: 10 full-time, 4 part-time,
75 volunteer
major programs: workshops,
affordable housing, periodical,
revolving fund, grants

South Central Research
Library Council
215 North Cayuga Street
Ithaca, New York 14850
607-273-9106
Janet Steiner, Executive Director
members: 77
founded: 1920
staff: 9 full-time
major programs: library,
workshops, periodical, grants

Newfield

Newfield Historical Society
P.O. Box 183
Newfield, New York 14867

Trumansburg

Ulysses Historical Society
Main Street
Trumansburg, New York 14886
607-387-5659
mail to: Elm Street,
Trumansburg, New York 14886
Ruth Wolverton, President
members: 220
founded: 1975
staff: 50 volunteer
major programs: museum, photo
collection, school programs,
exhibits, periodical

Ulster County

County Arts Council

Ulster Arts Alliance
P.O. Box 1280
Kingston, New York 12401
914-255-8222

County Historian

Kenneth Hasbrouck
401 Route 208
New Paltz, New York 12561

County Historical Society

Ulster County Historical Society
Route 209, RD 3
P.O. Box 3752
Kingston, New York 12401

County Planning Office

Ulster County Planning Board
244 Fair Street, P.O. Box 1800
Kingston, New York 12401
914-331-9300

see also Catskill Center for
Conservation and Development,
Arkville, Delaware County

Greenfield Park

Greenfield Park Historical
Association
Greenfield Park, New York
12435

High Falls

D&H Museum
Mohonk Road
High Falls, New York 12440
mail to: P.O. Box 23
High Falls, New York 12440
914-687-9311
Linda Loomis, Museum Director
members: 370
founded: 1966
staff: 1 full-time, 2 volunteer
major programs: library,
archives, museum, photo
collection, research, school
programs, tours, lectures,
publications, historic
preservation, periodical

Marbletown Historic
Preservation Commission
Route 213, Box 96
High Falls, New York 12440
914-687-7700
John Novi, Chair
founded: 1969

Kingston

Friends of Historic Kingston
UPO Box 3763
Kingston, New York 12401
Robert A. Slater, President
members: 400
founded: 1952
staff: 15 volunteer
major programs: tours, awards,
historic preservation

Hudson River Maritime Center
One Rondout Landing
Kingston, New York 12401

Junior League of Kingston
UPO Box 464
Kingston, New York 12401
914-658-3101

Kingston Urban Cultural
Park Program
225 Albany Street
Kingston, New York 12401
914-331-9506
Sara Wilde, UCP Coordinator

Rural Ulster Preservation
Company
14 Pearl Street
Kingston, New York 12401
914-331-2140
Kathleen Burton Maxwell,
Executive Director
founded: 1981
staff: 3 full-time, 1 part-time
major programs: historic
preservation, rural preservation,
affordable housing, revolving
fund

Strand Community Organization
to Rehabilitate the Environment
21-27 West Strand Avenue
Kingston, New York 12401
914-339-3934
Lance A. Seunarine, Executive
Director
founded: 1977
staff: 3 full-time, 2 part-time
major programs: lectures,
workshops, affordable housing,
revolving fund

Marlboro

Marlboro Free Library
Route 9W and Bloom Street
P.O. Box 780
Marlboro, New York 12542
914-236-7272
Elizabeth S. Manion, Director
founded: 1912
staff: 4 full-time, 1 part-time
major programs: library,
lectures, workshops, exhibits,
publications, periodical

New Paltz

Heritage Task Force
21 South Putt Corners
New Paltz, New York 12561

Huguenot Historical Society
of New Paltz
18 Broadhead Avenue
New Paltz, New York 12561
914-255-1660
Kenneth E. Hasbrouck, President

members: 4,500
founded: 1894
staff: 8 full-time, 23 part-time
major programs: library,
archives, museum, historic sites,
photo collection, tours, exhibits,
publications

Phoenicia

Sharp Committee
Main Street, P.O. Box 362
Phoenicia, New York 12464
914-688-5777
Elies A. Miller, Executive
Director
members: 475
founded: 1981
staff: 3 full-time
major programs: surveys, rural
preservation, revolving fund

Shokan

Historical Society of the
Town of Olive
Shokan Post Office
Shokan, New York 12481

Ulster Park

Klyne-Esopus Historical
Society Museum
Route 9W
Ulster Park, New York 12487
914-338-8109
mail to: P.O. Box 598
Port Ewen, New York 12466
Marjorie Lomoriello, Executive
Secretary
members: 375
founded: 1969
staff: 1 part-time, 200 volunteer
major programs: library,
museum, research, school
programs, lectures, exhibits,
periodical

Wallkill

Historical Society of
Shawangunk and Gardiner
Box 141, Plains Road
Wallkill, New York 12589

Shawangunk Valley Conservancy
1165 Fifth Avenue
New York, New York 10129
212-534-5501
Peter Bienstock, Chair
founded: 1976
staff: 5 volunteer
major programs: library, historic

sites, surveys, historic
preservation, rural preservation,
markers program, revolving
fund, grants

Woodstock

Historical Society of Woodstock
P.O. Box 841
Woodstock, New York 12498

Warren County

County Arts Council

see Lower Adirondack Regional
Arts Council, Glens Falls
see Warren County Board of
Supervisors, Selection
Committee, c/o Lake George
Regional Arts Project, Lake
George 12845 for
decentralization information

County Historian

Pamela Vogel
Warren County Municipal
Center
Lake George, New York 12845

County Historical Society

no listing

County Planning Office

Warren County Planning
Department
Municipal Center
Lake George, New York 12845
518-761-6410

see also Federation of Historical
Services, Troy, Rensselaer
County; Warren-Hamilton
Housing Corporation, Indian
Lake, Hamilton County

Athol

John Thurman Historical Society
Athol, New York 12810

Bolton Landing

Historical Society
of the Town of Bolton
Route 9N
Bolton Landing, New York
12814

Brant Lake

Horicon Historical Society
P.O. Box 51
Brant Lake, New York 12815

Chestertown

Historical Society of
the Town of Chester
Chestertown, New York 12817

Glens Falls

The Chapman
Historical Museum
Glens Falls/Queensbury
Historical Association
348 Glen Street
Glens Falls, New York 12801
518-793-2826
Gayle A. Rettew, Executive
Director
members: 1,300
founded: 1967
staff: 3 full-time, 2 part-time,
40 volunteer
major programs: library,
archives, museum, historic sites,
photo collection, research,
school programs, tours, lectures,
exhibits, publications, historic
preservation, periodical

Crandall Library
City Park
Glens Falls, New York 12801
518-792-6508
Christine McDonald, Director

The Hyde Collection Trust
161 Warren Street
Glens Falls, New York 12801
518-792-1761
Frederick J. Fisher, Director
members: 1,000
founded: 1962
staff: 11 full-time, 6 part-time,
200 volunteer
major programs: museum,
historic sites, school programs,
tours, lectures, workshops,
exhibits, historic preservation

Lower Adirondack
Regional Arts Council
10 Ridge Street, #C
P.O. Box 659
Glens Falls, New York 12801
Patricia Joyce, Executive
Director

Hague

Hague Historical Society
Hague, New York 12836

Lake George

Lake Champlain-Lake George
Regional Planning Board
Lake George Institute
Lake George, New York 12845
518-668-5773
William F. Davidson, Director

Lake George Arts Project
Canada Street
Lake George, New York 12845
John Strong, Program Director

Lake George Historical
Association
P.O. Box 472
Lake George, New York 12845
518-668-5044
Donald P. Fangboner,
Director/Curator

Lake Luzerne

Hadley-Lake Luzerne
Historical Society
2144 Main Street, P.O. Box 275
Lake Luzerne, New York 12846
518-696-2645
John Bennett, President
members: 69
founded: 1973
major programs: museum, photo
collection, school programs,
exhibits, awards, periodical

North Creek

North Creek Chamber of
Commerce
North Creek, New York 12853
518-251-2500
Barbara Delczeg, Secretary

Stony Creek

Stony Creek Historical
Association
Stony Creek, New York 12878

Warrensburg

Warrensburg Historical Society
100 Main Street
Warrensburg, New York 12885

Washington County

County Arts Council

see Hubbard Hall Projects,
Cambridge, for decentralization
information

County Historian

Mildred Southard
County Clerk's Office
Fort Edward, New York 12828

County Historical Society

Washington County
Historical Society
167 Broadway
Fort Edward, New York 12828
518-747-9108

County Planning Office

Washington County Department
of Planning and Community
Development
Upper Broadway
Fort Edward, New York 12828
518-747-4687

see also Federation of Historical
Services, Troy, Rensselaer
County

Argyle

Argyle Historical Society
Main Street
Argyle, New York 12809

Cambridge

Cambridge Historical Society
112 East Main Street
Cambridge, New York 12816
Dorothy Hesse, Curator

Hubbard Hall Projects
25 East Main Street
Cambridge, New York 12816

Fort Edward

Fort Edward Historical
Association
22 and 29 Broadway
Fort Edward, New York 12828
518-747-9600
R. Paul McCarty,
President / Director
members: 377
founded: 1925
staff: 6 part-time, 30 volunteer
major programs: library,
archives, museum, historic sites,
photo collection, research,
school programs, tours, exhibits,
archeology, periodical

Washington County Advisory
Council on Historic Preservation
Washington County
Municipal Building
Upper Broadway
Fort Edward, New York 12828
518-747-4687
Sally Brillon, Chair
founded: 1977
staff: 21 volunteer
major programs: photo
collection, research, publications,
awards, surveys

Granville

Granville Slate Museum
9 Church Street
Granville, New York 12832
518-642-2640
Angelo J. Scott, Jr., Village
Justice
founded: 1975
staff: all volunteer
major programs: museum, tours

Pember Museum of
Natural History
33 West Main Street
Granville, New York 12832
518-642-1515
Delight Gartelin, Museum
Director
members: 175
founded: 1909
staff: 1 full-time, 25 volunteer
major programs: museum,
school programs, lectures,
periodical

Town of Granville
Heritage Society
Granville, New York 12832

Greenwich

Greenwich Historical Association
Academy Street
Greenwich, New York 12834

Hartford

Hartford Historical Group
Main Street
Hartford, New York 12838

Hebron

Hebron Preservation Society
RD 2
Salem, New York 12865

Putnam

Putnam Historical Society
P.O. Box 24
Putnam, New York 12861

Shushan

Shushan Covered Bridge
Association
P.O. Box B
Shushan, New York 12873

Whitehall

Historical Society of Whitehall
P.O. Box 238
Whitehall, New York 12887
518-499-0754
Carol B. Greenough, President
members: 200
founded: 1951
staff: 5 part-time, 10 volunteer
major programs: library,
museum, historic sites, photo
collection, research, exhibits,
surveys, historic preservation,
rural preservation

Skenesborough Museum of the
Historical Society of Whitehall
Whitehall, New York 12887
518-499-0754

Whitehall Urban Cultural
Park Program
Village of Whitehall
Whitehall, New York 12887
518-499-0871

Wayne County

County Arts Council

Wayne County Council
for the Arts
205 Church Street
P.O. Box 28
Newark, New York 14513
315-331-3242
Carol Countryman, Executive
Director

County Historian

Marjory Allen Perez
21 Butternut Street
Lyons, New York 14489

County Historical Society

Wayne County Historical Society
21 Butternut Street
Lyons, New York 14489

County Planning Office

Wayne County Planning
Department
9 Pearl Street
Lyons, New York 14489
315-946-4721

see also Genesee-Finger Lakes
Regional Planning Council,
Rochester, Monroe County;
Landmark Society of Western
New York, Rochester, Monroe
County; Regional Council of
Historical Agencies, Syracuse,
Onondaga County

Clyde

Galen Historical Society
South Sodus Street, P.O. Box 43
Clyde, New York 14433
315-923-4501
James Earley, President

Macedon

Macedon Historical Society
1185 Macedon Center Road
Macedon, New York 14502

Marion

Marion Historical Society
Marion, New York 14505

Newark

Arcadia Historical Association
Newark, New York 14513

Ontario

Town of Ontario Historical
Preservation Society
Ontario Center Road
P.O. Box 462
Ontario, New York 14519

Palmyra

Historic Palmyra
132 Market Street, P.O. Box 96
Palmyra, New York 14522
315-597-6981
Richard V. Palmer, Executive
Director
members: 210
founded: 1967
staff: 1 full-time, 57 volunteer
major programs: museum,
lectures, exhibits, historic
preservation, periodical

Pultneyville

Pultneyville Historical Society
P.O. Box 92
Pultneyville, New York 14538
Irene D. Mullie, President
members: 100
founded: 1964
major programs: archives,
school programs, awards,
periodical

Sodus

Sodus Bay Historical Society
5519 Allen Road
Sodus, New York 14551
315-483-4013
Marjorie McCleery, Program
Director
members: 300
founded: 1972
staff: 25 volunteer
major programs: museum,
school programs, tours, historic
preservation

Walworth

Walworth Historical Society
P.O. Box 142
Walworth, New York 14568
Kay Scott, President
members: 75
founded: 1976
staff: all volunteer
major programs: museum,
lectures, periodical

Westchester County

County Arts Council

Council for the Arts
in Westchester
One East Pond Road
White Plains, New York 10601
914-428-4220
Christopher Bruhl, Executive
Director

County Historian

Susan C. Swanson
Michaelian Building, Room 618
White Plains, New York 10601

County Historical Society

Westchester County
Historical Society
75 Grasslands Road
Valhalla, New York 10595
914-592-4323
Karolyn Wrightson, Executive
Director
members: 620
founded: 1874
staff: 1 full-time, 1 part-time,
12 volunteer
major programs: library,
archives, museum, historic sites,
photo collection, research,
school programs, tours, lectures,
workshops, publications,
awards, surveys, periodical

County Planning Office

Westchester County Planning
County Office Buidling
148 Martine Avenue, Room 418
White Plains, New York 10601
914-285-2412

Ardsley

Ardsley Historical Society
547 Almena Avenue
Ardsley, New York 10502

Armonk

North Castle
Historical Society
440 Bedford Road
Armonk, New York 10504
914-273-9773
Susan R. Shimer, President
members: 350
founded: 1971
staff: 40 volunteer

major programs: library,
museum, photo collection,
exhibits, historic preservation,
periodical

Bedford

Bedford Historical Society
Bedford, New York 10506
914-234-9328
Susan Jessup, Director of
Development
members: 417
founded: 1916
staff: 2 full-time, 1 part-time
major programs: library,
archives, museum, historic sites,
photo collection, research,
school programs, tours, lectures,
exhibits, historic preservation,
matching grants

Briarcliff Manor

Briarcliff Manor-Scarborough
Historical Society
P.O. Box 11
Briarcliff Manor, New York
10510
Rosemary B. Cook, President
members: 165
founded: 1974
major programs: archives, photo
collection, school programs,
tours, publications

Bronxville

Eastchester Historical Society
396 California Road
P.O. Box 37
Bronxville, New York 10708
914-793-1900
Madeline Schaeffer, President
members: 450
founded: 1958
staff: 10 volunteer
major programs: library,
archives, historic sites, photo
collection, school programs,
tours

Village of Bronxville
Village Hall
200 Pondfield Road
Bronxville, New York 10708
914-337-6500
Mary Huber, Village Historian
founded: 1967
major programs: library,
archives, museum, historic sites,

photo collection, research,
school programs, tours, lectures,
workshops, exhibits,
publications, awards, surveys,
historic preservation, markers
program, technical preservation
services

Chappaqua

Chappaqua Historical Society
P.O. Box 55
Chappaqua, New York 10514
914-238-3074

New Castle Historical Society
185 South Greeley Avenue
P.O. Box 55
Chappaqua, New York 10514
914-238-4666
Susan Dichter, Museum
Administrator
members: 400
founded: 1966
staff: 1 part-time, 20 volunteer
major programs: archives,
research, exhibits, publications,
periodical

Cortlandt

Cortlandt Historical Society
P.O. Box 493
Peekskill, New York 10566

Croton-on-Hudson

Croton Council on the Arts
P.O. Box 277
Croton-on-Hudson, New York
10520
914-271-9243
Ruth Smath, President
members: 200
founded: 1977
staff: 20 volunteer
major programs: lectures,
exhibits, publications, awards,
periodical

Croton Historical Society
171 Cleveland Drive
Croton-on-Hudson, New York
10520
914-271-3536
Marion Dymes, Secretary-
Treasurer
members: 150
founded: 1972
staff: all volunteer

major programs: archives, photo
collection, research, school
programs, tours, lectures,
exhibits, periodical

Van Cortlandt Manor
(*see* Historic Hudson Valley,
Tarrytown
South Riverside Avenue
Croton-on-Hudson, New York
10520
914-631-8200

Village of Croton-on-Hudson
231 Mount Airy Road
Croton-on-Hudson, New York
10520
Jane Northshield, Historian

Village of Croton-on-Hudson
Advisory Board on Visual
Environment
P.O. Box 249
Croton-on-Hudson, New York
10520
Don A. Wallance, Chair
founded: 1979
staff: 5 volunteer
major programs: architectural
review

Dobbs Ferry

Dobbs Ferry Historical Society
153 Main Street
Dobbs Ferry, New York 10522
914-693-7766
Frances Neill, Director
members: 300
founded: 1978
staff: 1 part-time
major programs: archives, photo
collection, school programs,
tours, workshops, publications,
periodical, grants

Elmsford

Elmsford Historical Society
P.O. Box 1776
Elmsford, New York 10523

Greenburgh Public Library
300 Tarrytown Road
Elmsford, New York 10523
914-993-1602
Robert Trudell, Director
founded: 1967
staff: 29 full-time, 7 part-time
major programs: library,
archives, historic sites, photo

collection, research, school
programs, lectures, exhibits,
publications, awards, periodical

Lower Hudson Conference
2199 Saw Mill River Road
Elmsford, New York 10523
914-592-6726
Ann Kiewel, Executive Director
members: 325
founded: 1979
staff: 1 full-time, 1 part-time
major programs: library,
workshops, publications,
awards, periodical

Town of Greenburgh Arts and
Culture Committees
P.O. Box 205
Elmsford, New York 10523
914-993-1540
Madeleine Gutman, Executive
Director
founded: 1965
staff: 1 full-time, 8 volunteer
major programs: lectures,
exhibits, awards, periodical

Hartsdale

Odell-Rochambeau
Historical Society
425 Ridge Road
Hartsdale, New York 10530

Hastings-on-Hudson

Hastings Historical Society
41 Washington Avenue
Hastings-on-Hudson, New York
10706
914-478-2249
Marion Martin, President
members: 886
founded: 1971
staff: all volunteer
major programs: library,
archives, museum, photo
collection, research, tours,
lectures, exhibits, historic
preservation, archeology,
periodical

Irvington

Irvington Historical Society
P.O. Box 1
Irvington, New York 10533

Katonah

Caramoor Center for Music
and the Arts
Girdle Ridge Drive, P.O. Box R
Katonah, New York 10536
914-232-5035
Michael Sweeley, Executive
Director
members: 1,200
founded: 1946
staff: 5 full-time, 35 volunteer
major programs: archives,
museum, photo collection,
research, school programs, tours,
lectures, workshops, exhibits,
periodical

Katonah Historical Museum
Bedford Road
Katonah, New York 10536
914-232-3508
Jewell Stuckert, Treasurer
members: 145
founded: 1984
staff: 10 volunteer
major programs: museum,
periodical

Larchmont

Larchmont Historical Society
P.O. Box 742
Larchmont, New York 10538
914-834-5712
Eleanor H. Lucas, President
members: 200
founded: 1980
staff: all volunteer
major programs: archives,
research, school programs, tours,
exhibits, publications, technical
preservation services

Mahopac

Town of Carmel
Historical Society
Town Hall
McAlpin Avenue
Mahopac, New York 10541
914-628-1500/0500
Dorothy G. Jewell,
Coordinator/Director
members: 106
founded: 1979
staff: 1 part-time, 5 volunteer
major programs: library,
museum, historic sites, photo

collection, research, school
programs, tours, workshops,
exhibits, publications, awards,
historic preservation, periodical

Mamaroneck

Mamaroneck Historical Society
Mamaroneck, New York 10543

Mohegan Lake

Association for Improvement
in Mohegan
P.O. Box 103
Mohegan Lake, New York
10547
914-528-3300
Judith A. Shephard, Executive
Director
members: 200
founded: 1980
staff: 1 full-time, 2 part-time
major programs: historic
preservation, rural preservation,
affordable housing, technical
preservation services, periodical

Mount Kisco

Mount Kisco Historical
Committee
104 Main Street
Mount Kisco, New York 10549

Mount Vernon

Housing and Neighborhood
Development Institute
250 South Sixth Avenue
Room 4
Mount Vernon, New York 10550
914-668-9126
William Jones, Executive
Director
staff: 4 full-time, 5 part-time,
4 volunteer
major programs: research,
workshops, publications,
surveys, affordable housing,
technical preservation services

Mount Vernon Landmark and
Historical Society
Mount Vernon Public Library
28 South First Avenue
Mount Vernon, New York 10550
914-668-1840 x315
Marry Morra, President

Society of the National Shrine
of the Bill of Rights
897 South Columbus Avenue
Mount Vernon, New York 10550
914-667-4116
Connie M. Cullen,
Administrator
founded: 1945
staff: 4 full-time, 30 volunteer
major programs: archives,
museum, historic sites, photo
collection, research, school
programs, tours, lectures,
workshops, exhibits, periodical

New Rochelle

Huguenot-Thomas Paine
Historical Association
983 North Avenue
New Rochelle, New York 10804

North Salem

North Salem
Historical Society
Keeler Lane, P.O. Box 1731
North Salem, New York 10560
Diane D. Damerau, President
members: 200
founded: 1969
staff: 15 volunteer
major programs: archives,
historic sites, photo collection,
school programs, lectures,
publications, periodical

North Tarrytown

Philipsburg Manor
(see Historic Hudson Valley,
Tarrytown)
Route 9
North Tarrytown, New York
10591
914-631-8200

Ossining

Ossining Historical Society
196 Croton Avenue
Ossining, New York 10562
914-941-0001
Roberta Y. Arminio, Director
members: 375
founded: 1939
staff: 1 full-time, 2 part-time,
7 volunteer

major programs: library,
archives, museum, historic sites,
photo collection, research,
school programs, tours, lectures,
workshops, exhibits, publications, awards, historic
preservation, markers program,
periodical

Ossining Urban Cultural Park
Community Development Office
2 Church Street
Ossining, New York 10562
914-941-0751
Natalie Mackintosh, Assistant to
the Village Manager

Society for the Preservation of
Historic Ossining
P.O. Box 1976
Ossining, New York 10562

Westchester Preservation League
36 South Highland Avenue
Ossining, New York 10562
914-941-2750
Nancy Coe Wixom, President
members: 185
founded: 1979
staff: 1 part-time, 10 volunteer
major programs: historic sites,
tours, lectures, workshops,
historic preservation, technical
preservation services, periodical

Peekskill

Peekskill Area Health Center
Preservation Company
1037 Main Street
Peekskill, New York 10566
914-739-8147
Anne Kaufmann Nolon,
Executive Director
founded: 1986
staff: 2 full-time
major programs: rural
preservation, affordable housing,
periodical

Peekskill Museum
P.O. Box 84
Peekskill, New York 10566

Van Cortlandville
Historical Society
297 Locust Avenue
Peekskill, New York 10566

Pelham

Pelham Historical Society
314 Pelham Avenue
Pelham, New York 10566

Pocantico Hills

Union Church of Pocantico Hills
(see Historic Hudson Valley,
Tarrytown)
Route 448
Pocantico Hills, New York
10591
914-631-8200

Port Chester

Port Chester
Historical Society
Bush Homestead
479 King Street, P.O. Box 1511
Port Chester, New York 10573
914-939-6040
Goldie Solomon, President
members: 115
founded: 1971
staff: 9 volunteer
major programs: archives,
lectures, historic preservation,
periodical

Pound Ridge

Pound Ridge
Historical Society
Salem Road, P.O. Box 1718
Pound Ridge, New York 10576

Pound Ridge Museum
The Hamlet
P.O. Box 1718
Pound Ridge, New York 10576
914-763-5137
Ethel M. Scofield, Museum
Director
members: 250
founded: 1973
staff: 1 part-time
major programs: library,
archives, museum, photo
collection, school programs,
tours, lectures, exhibits,
publications, awards, periodical

Rye

The Jay Coalition
P.O. Box 661
Rye, New York 10580
914-937-2350
major programs: preservation of
Jay property in Rye

Rye Historical Society
One Purchase Street
Rye, New York 10580
914-967-7588
Susan Morison, Director
members: 800
founded: 1964
staff: 4 full-time, 1 part-time,
75 volunteer
major programs: library,
archives, museum, historic sites,
photo collection, research,
school programs, tours, exhibits,
publications, surveys, periodical

Scarsdale

Scarsdale Historical Society
937 Post Road, P.O. Box 431
Scarsdale, New York 10583
914-723-1744
Eda L. Newhouse, President
members: 1,362
founded: 1973
staff: 2 full-time, 3 part-time,
10 volunteer
major programs: library,
museum, research, school
programs, lectures, exhibits,
historic preservation, periodical

Somers

Somers Historical Society
Elephant Hotel, P.O. Box 336
Somers, New York 10589

South Salem

Lewisboro Historical Society
South Salem, New York 10590

Tarrytown

Four Centuries Incorporated
P.O. Box 245
Tarrytown, New York 10591

Friends of Lyndhurst
635 South Broadway
Tarrytown, New York 10591
914-631-0046

Susanne Brendel-Pandich,
Director
members: 500
founded: 1982
staff: 9 full-time, 25 part-time,
10 volunteer
major programs: historic sites,
school programs, tours, lectures,
exhibits, publications, historic
preservation, technical
preservation services, periodical

Historic Hudson Valley
150 White Plains Road
Tarrytown, New York 10591
914-631-8200
members: 1,000
founded: 1951
staff: 75 full-time, 125 part-time,
50 volunteers
major programs: historic sites,
museums, research, school
programs, lectures, exhibits,
tours, periodical, publications,
special events, workshops,
historic preservation

Historical Society of The
Tarrytowns
One Grove Street
Tarrytown, New York 10591
914-631-8374
Adelaide Smith, Curator
members: 334
founded: 1889
staff: 1 full-time, 1 part-time,
20 volunteer
major programs: library,
archives, museum, photo
collection, research, tours,
lectures, exhibits, publications,
historic preservation, archeology,
periodical

History Research Society of the
Tappan Zee
Tarrytown, New York 10591

Sunnyside
(*see* Historic Hudson Valley,
Tarrytown)
West Sunnyside Lane
Tarrytown, New York 10591
914-631-8200

Valhalla

Hammond House
Route 100C
Valhalla, New York 10595

Mount Pleasant
Historical Society
2 Maple Street
Valhalla, New York 10595

Verplanck

Historic Verplanck
Lafayette Street
Verplanck, New York 10596

White Plains

Charles Dawson History Center
2 East Madison Street
White Plains, New York 10604
914-948-2550
Michael R. Casarella, Town
Historian
members: 75
founded: 1981
staff: 2 part-time, 20 volunteer
major programs: archives,
historic sites, photo collection,
research, school programs, tours,
lectures, exhibits, surveys,
historic preservation, markers
program

City of White Plains
5 Belmont Street
White Plains, New York 10605
Renoda Hoffman, Historian

Heritage 300
225 Fisher Avenue
White Plains, New York 10606

White Plains
Historical Society
Jacob Purdy House
60 Park Avenue
White Plains, New York 10603
914-328-1776
Irving Natter, President
members: 100
founded: 1983
major programs: historic sites,
historic preservation, periodical

White Plains Housing
Information Service
228 Fisher Avenue
White Plains, New York 10606
Kathleen E. Walsh, Executive
Director

Yonkers

Hudson River Museum
511 Warburton Avenue
Yonkers, New York 10701
Laura Byers, Public Relations
Director

North Yonkers Preservation and
Development Corporation
219 Ridge Avenue
Yonkers, New York 10703
914-423-9754
Charles A. Cola, Executive
Director
founded: 3 full-time, 6 part-time,
15 volunteer
major programs: affordable
housing, technical preservation
services

Sherwood House
340 Tuckahoe Road
Yonkers, New York 10710

United States Catholic
History Society
P.O. Box 498
Yonkers, New York 10702

Yonkers Historical Society
Hudson River Museum
511 Warburton Avenue
Yonkers, New York 10701
914-963-4550
Tristam Metcalfe, President
members: 225
founded: 1952
staff: 35 volunteer
major programs: archives,
museum, lectures, publications,
awards, markers program,
periodical

Yonkers Planning Bureau
87 Nepperhan Avenue
Room 311
Yonkers, New York 10701
914-964-3386
Dean J. Grandin, Director
founded: 1929
staff: 5 full-time, 1 part-time
major programs: research,
publications, surveys, historic
preservation

Yorktown Heights

Friends of Yorktown Museum
1886 Hanover Street
Yorktown Heights, New York
10598

Town of Yorktown Museum
1974 Commerce Street
Yorktown Heights, New York
10598
914-962-2970
Doris E. Auser, Director

Yorktown Historical Society
P.O. Box 355
Yorktown Heights, New York
10598
914-245-6348
Robert L. Lockhart, President

Wyoming County

County Arts Council

Arts Council for
Wyoming County
63 South Main Street
P.O. Box 249
Perry, New York 14530
716-237-3015
Anne C. Humphrey, Executive
Director
members: 652
founded: 1976
staff: 2 full-time, 4 part-time,
60 volunteer
major programs: archives, photo
collection, school programs,
workshops, exhibits,
publications, surveys, rural
preservation, periodical, grants

County Historian

John Gilbert Wilson
26 Linwood Avenue
Warsaw, New York 14569

County Historical Society

no listing

County Planning Office

Wyoming County
Planning Office
P.O. Box 232
Warsaw, New York 14569
716-786-2334

see also Landmark Society of
Western New York, Rochester,
Monroe County; Western New
York Association of Historical
Agencies, Avon, Livingston
County

Arcade

Arcade Historical Society
331 West Main Street
P.O. Box 237
Arcade, New York 14009
716-492-4466
Shirley J. Yansick, President
members: 15
founded: 1956
major programs: photo
collection, research, lectures,
publications

Wyoming Historical Pioneer
Association
18 East Main Street
Arcade, New York 14009

Attica

Attica Historical Society
130 Main Street
Attica, New York 14011
716-591-2161
Mrs. Robert Bathrick, President
members: 175
founded: 1937
staff: 35 volunteer
major programs: museum, photo
collection, school programs

Castile

Castile Historical Society
17 Park Road East
P.O. Box 256
Castile, New York 14427
716-493-5370
Elsie Buttles, Curator
major programs: museum, photo
collection, research, school
programs, lectures, workshops,
exhibits

Cowlesville

Town of Bennington
Historical Society
211 Clinton Street
Cowlesville, New York 14037

Strykersville

Sheldon Historical Society
Main Street
Strykersville, New York 14145
716-535-7250
mail to: 2760 Maxon Road
Varysburgh, New York 14167
Raymond L. Caryl, President
members: 15
founded: 1979
staff: 6 volunteer
major programs: museum, rural
preservation

Warsaw

Warsaw Historical Society
4870 Wilder Road, RD 2
Warsaw, New York 14569
716-786-3111 x49
John S. Bracken, President

Wyoming

Middlebury Historical Society
Academy Street
Wyoming, New York 14591
716-495-6556
mail to: 1061 Tower Road
Wyoming, New York 14591
Willa T. Bishop, President
members: 105
founded: 1918
staff: 48 volunteer
major programs: museum,
historic sites, school programs,
tours, workshops, historic
preservation, periodical

Yates County

County Arts Council

Yates County Arts Council
119 East Elm Street
Penn Yan, New York 14527
315-536-8226
Linda M. Canham, Executive
Director
members: 375
founded: 1975
staff: 1 full-time, 1 part-time,
20 volunteer
major programs: periodical

County Historian

Virgina Gibbs
RD 2
Penn Yan, New York 14527

County Historical Society

Yates County Genealogical and
Historical Society
200 Main Street
Penn Yan, New York 14527
315-536-7318
members: 350
founded: 1860
staff: 2 full-time
major programs: archives,
museum, photo collection,
research, school programs,
exhibits, historic preservation,
rural preservation, periodical

County Planning Office

Yates County Planning Office
431 Liberty Street
Penn Yan, New York 14527
315-536-7328

see also Genesee-Finger Lakes
Regional Planning Council,
Rochester, Monroe County;
Landmark Society of Western
New York, Rochester, Monroe
County; Western New York
Association of Historical
Agencies, Avon, Livingston
County

Italy

Nundawaga Society for History
and Folklore
518 Liberty Street
Italy, New York 14527

Middlesex

Middlesex Heritage Association
Middlesex, New York 14507

Preservation League of New York State

Preservation League of New York State

The Preservation League of New York State was founded in 1974 by a group of concerned citizens to provide a statewide voice, united and powerful, in support of preservation activities. The League, a not-for-profit, membership organization, is dedicated to the principle that the best way to protect our architectural heritage is to make valuable older buildings an integral part of everyday life, not by creating museum pieces, but by meeting the needs of the present through reinvesting in the past and preserving for the future.

Serving a statewide constituency, the Preservation League coordinates the preservation activities of a host of organizations and individuals. It acts as a clearinghouse for technical information and provides a timely overview of legislative activity. By publicizing preservation issues, not only to its members but to all New Yorkers, the League stimulates public participation in the protection of the Empire State's built environment. Where isolated organizations or a few citizens might struggle to make an impact, the League provides a united front which has scored significant victories in defending the historic structures and landscapes which make our cities, towns, and rural areas unique and beautiful.

Education

The Preservation League works in many ways to enhance public understanding of the aesthetic and economic benefits of historic preservation, and to promote the wise stewardship of our architectural heritage. Through its enthusiastically attended annual conference, held in a different New York community each year, the League provides a forum at which preservationists gather to discuss their common goals and problems, and to share ideas and information. The League recognizes and celebrates exemplary preservation projects and programs through its coveted annual awards. Frequent workshops on specific topics are conducted across the state throughout the year to provide guidance and specialized technical advice to property owners, local groups, and government agencies.

In 1986 the League conceived and produced "Architectural Heritage Year," a multi-dimensional celebration of three centuries of building in New York State, involving more than 350 organizations and thousands of individuals. The League's film, *A Fair Land to Build In: The Architecture of the Empire State*, identifying some of the state's worthiest historic structures, has been broadcast on every public television station in New York.

Publications

The Preservation League's handbooks and technical leaflets teach both professional and novice preservationists everything from how to care for stone buildings to how to create a local revolving fund for financing restoration. A quarterly newsletter features a unique series on architects and landscape architects who have worked in New York State, timely articles on preservation issues and legislative activity, a calendar of events, and reviews of new publications. The League's *Preservation Directory* is a comprehensive statewide guide to legislation, educational programs, funding sources, and local organizations. Our handbook, *How to Care for Religious Properties,* has contributed to the revitalization of hundreds of churches and synagogues throughout the nation. And the League's library of printed materials, films, and slides is one of the largest information resources of its kind.

Advocacy

The Preservation League represents the statewide preservation community on state and federal legislative issues; creating a partnership between government and the private sector. From its headquarters in Albany, the League monitors federal, state, and local legislation that has an impact on historic resources, land use, landmark designation, and funding for preservation activities.

Recognizing the necessity for an informed and organized electorate, the League keeps issues before New Yorkers by participating in public forums, issuing legislative alerts, organizing coalitions, and mounting educational voter campaigns. These efforts successfully influenced passage of the State Historic Preservation Act of 1980; the Camp Sagamore ballot proposal in 1983, which effectively saved this Adirondack Great Camp; and the Environmental Quality Bond Act of 1986, which provided, for the first time, funding for restoration of buildings owned by municipalities and not-for-profit organizations, including religious congregations and libraries.

Advisory Services

To encourage sound preservation techniques, planning, and policy, the League offers professional legal and technical assistance to individuals and to private and public organizations. Field visits, correspondence, and telephone advice complement the League's publications as a means of providing guidance in identifying and protecting architecturally, culturally, and historically significant properties. Preservation specialists are available on-site or in Albany for consultation on the planning and implementation of specific aspects of preservation projects.

The Preservation League's legal staff advises on the drafting of preservation legislation, counsels on the interpretation of preservation law, and participates in litigation. Through its Coalition of Local Landmark and Historic District Commissions, the League provides assistance in dealing with the complexities of protective regulation.

For more information on League membership, publications, programs, and film rental, contact the Preservation League of New York State, 307 Hamilton Street, Albany, New York 12210, telephone 518-462-5658.

Preservation League Publications

A Fair Land to Build In: The Architecture of the Empire State. Brendan Gill. The historically and visually rich architectural legacy of New York has been dramatized in this book written by Brendan Gill, architecture critic of *The New Yorker* and Chairman Emeritus of the Preservation League. Based on the League's acclaimed film of the same name, *A Fair Land to Build In* is a Baedeker to the state's vast architectural heritage. The book illustrates, in 440 duotone photographs, some of the state's most outstanding structures and identifies them by date, location, and architect. The accompanying text traces the architectural evolution of New York State from wilderness to high civilization. Publication was made possible through the generous assistance of The J.M. Kaplan Fund, the American Express Foundation, Mohawk Paper Mills, the New York State Council on the Arts, and anonymous donors. 1984. 60 pp., illus. $5.50.

Good Buildings, Good Times: A Manual of Program Ideas for Promoting Local Architecture. Kathlyn Hatch. This handbook is a resource for all kinds of organizations and institutions—civic groups, local governments, arts councils, museums, schools and colleges, historical societies, preservation organizations, land- mark commissions, and profes- sional associations—which are concerned with promoting public understanding of local architec- ture and buildings. In the first section, expert organizers of ten prototypical programs reveal in- sider's tips on how to execute successful educational projects and celebrations that will focus public attention on local buildings. The second section is a catalogue of 111 ideas for ac- tivities related to buildings found in both large and small com- munities. Many of these ac- tivities can be implemented at low cost and many are ap- propriate for involving large au- diences of all ages. Publication was made possible by The Bowers Foundation, Inc., AT&T, and The J.M. Kaplan Fund. 1985. 56 pp. $4.00.

How to Care for Religious Properties. Michael F. Lynch. An illustrated, step-by-step guide to architectural stewardship of religious buildings, with guidelines on how to establish a maintenance program, how to conduct a building inspection, and chapters on caring for building materials, decorative features and stained glass, and many other topics. 1982. 40 pp., illus. $2.00.

Preservation for Profit: Ten Case Studies in Commercial Rehabilitaiton. Cornelia Brooke Gilder. Each illustrated case study includes a history of the project, a description of the rehabilitation work, and finan- cial information. 1980. 28 pp., illus. $3.00.

In addition to these handbooks, the Preservation League publishes technical leaflets and circulates a film and slide/tape library. Complete lists of publications and films are available free. To order publica- tions, send check or money order (less 10 percent discount for Preservation League members) to Preservation League, 307 Hamilton Street, Albany, N.Y. 12210. A discount of 30 percent applies to orders of 10 or more copies of one title, 40 percent to orders of 25 or more copies of one title. New York residents should include local sales tax.

Index